MW00352490

THE ART OF THE

CONFECTIONER

THE ART OF THE
CONFECTIONER
SUGARWORK AND PASTILLAGE

EWALD NOTTER

PHOTOGRAPHY BY JOE BROOKS AND LUCY SCHAEFFER

WILEY

JOHN WILEY & SONS, INC.

This book is printed on acid-free paper. ∞

Copyright © 2012 by John Wiley & Sons, Inc. All rights reserved

Step-by-step technique photographs on marble copyright © 2012 by Joe Brooks Photography.

All other color photographs copyright © 2012 by Lucy Schaeffer.

Published by John Wiley & Sons, Inc., Hoboken, New Jersey

Published simultaneously in Canada

No part of this publication may be reproduced, stored in a retrieval system, or transmitted in any form or by any means, electronic, mechanical, photocopying, recording, scanning, or otherwise, except as permitted under Section 107 or 108 of the 1976 United States Copyright Act, without either the prior written permission of the Publisher, or authorization through payment of the appropriate per-copy fee to the Copyright Clearance Center, Inc., 222 Rosewood Drive, Danvers, MA 01923, (978) 750-8400, fax (978) 646-8600, or on the web at www.copyright.com. Requests to the Publisher for permission should be addressed to the Permissions Department, John Wiley & Sons, Inc., 111 River Street, Hoboken, NJ 07030, (201) 748-6011, fax (201) 748-6008, or online at http://www.wiley.com/go/permissions.

Limit of Liability/Disclaimer of Warranty: While the publisher and author have used their best efforts in preparing this book, they make no representations or warranties with respect to the accuracy or completeness of the contents of this book and specifically disclaim any implied warranties of merchantability or fitness for a particular purpose. No warranty may be created or extended by sales representatives or written sales materials. The advice and strategies contained herein may not be suitable for your situation. You should consult with a professional where appropriate. Neither the publisher nor author shall be liable for any loss of profit or any other commercial damages, including but not limited to special, incidental, consequential, or other damages.

For general information on our other products and services or for technical support, please contact our Customer Care Department within the United States at (800) 762-2974, outside the United States at (317) 572-3993 or fax (317) 572-4002.

Wiley also publishes its books in a variety of electronic formats. Some content that appears in print may not be available in electronic books. For more information about Wiley products, visit our web site at www.wiley.com.

Library of Congress Cataloging-in-Publication Data
Notter, Ewald, 1955-
  The art of the confectioner : sugarwork and pastillage / Ewald Notter ; photography by Joe Brooks and Lucy Schaeffer.
    p. cm.
  Includes bibliographical references and index.
  ISBN 978-0-470-39892-0 (cloth); ISBN 978-0-470-40268-9 (ebk);
  ISBN 978-1-118-28068-3 (ebk); ISBN 978-1-118-28069-0 (ebk)
1. Sugar art. 2. Confectionery. I. Title.
  TX799.N68 2012
  641.86--dc23
                              2011035307

Printed in U.S.A.

10 9 8 7 6 5 4

Designed by Memo Productions, NY

Acknowledgments

My sincere thanks to Christine McKnight for her advice and patience with me through the process of creating this book.

My warmest thanks to Lucy Schaeffer and Joe Brooks for their artful and creative pictures that grace each page.

My deepest thanks to Kimberly Voelker and Laurie Merz for being so generous with their time in assisting me with writing this book.

My gratitude to my business partner Beverly Karshner for her continuing support.

Contents

Preface

I was very excited to be asked to write this book. Sugar décor has been around for more than one hundred years, but during this time there have been periods in which it almost became a lost art. During World War II and the decade following the war, in particular, sugar décor was almost completely forgotten. Today, there has been a resurgence in the popularity of sugarwork. Sugar is very trendy right now, but as new techniques emerge, it is important that the older, classic techniques, such as weaving a basket or blowing a figurine, not be lost. In this book, you will find instructions for all the traditional techniques as well as new trends in sugarwork.

Without a doubt, sugar is the most fascinating décor material to work with. Sugar can be pulled, blown, cast, and modeled. Each of these techniques requires different hand skills and can be used by itself or in combination with the other techniques. It may take a while to understand and master the techniques—even boiling sugar to the right consistency takes some experience—but the beautiful shine, color, cleanliness, and lightness of the art will make you forget all the challenges.

I have learned the most about sugarwork through traveling, teaching, and competing in other countries, which has given me the opportunity to share with and learn from friends and colleagues around the world. These experiences have given me a broader understanding of not only how to master the techniques, but also how to understand style, color, and culture. Simply put, the more I have shared, the more I have gained. I encourage you to go beyond this book by traveling and competing in order to gain a true understanding of all that the world of sugarwork has to offer.

Sugar has been a part of my life for more than three decades, and has brought me joy, hope, and success. With sugarwork, I have made more people happy and put more smiles on people's faces than with anything else. I hope that this book will provide you with the tools and skills you need to enter this exciting and enriching field.

1

Introduction

Pastillage and sugarwork are two ways in which we can use sugar to create sculptures and elegant artistry. They are similar in that the main ingredient is sugar, but are different in how the mediums are worked and the results that can be achieved. Pastillage is made with confectioners' sugar and is similar to a sugar dough. It is opaque and white by nature, but it can be rolled out, textured, and bent into a variety of shapes. It is often painted or airbrushed with color, making it a great medium for showing detailed designs. Sugarwork, on the other hand, is made primarily of granulated sugar or Isomalt that is cooked into a very hot syrup. This medium has incomparable shine and is translucent, giving it the elegance of glasswork.

While both sugar mediums are worked differently and render diverse results, they are very complementary to one another and work well when used together. The shine of the sugarwork is heightened by the opaqueness of the pastillage, and the varying textures possible in both mediums allow for a more interesting and eye-pleasing balance of techniques.

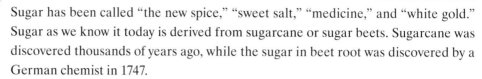

History of Sugar

Sugar has been called "the new spice," "sweet salt," "medicine," and "white gold." Sugar as we know it today is derived from sugarcane or sugar beets. Sugarcane was discovered thousands of years ago, while the sugar in beet root was discovered by a German chemist in 1747.

The cultivation of sugar is thought to have originated in New Guinea, and later spread to Southeast Asia and India. It was in India that the technique was first used of pressing out the juice of sugarcane by grinding and pounding it, boiling it down, and then drying it in the sun to yield sugary solids that looked like gravel.

In 510 BC, when the Persians invaded India, they found "the reed which gives honey without bees." Like many other discoveries, the secret of cane sugar was kept closely guarded while the finished product was exported for a rich profit. The secret was revealed when Arabs invaded Persia in the seventh century AD. They found sugarcane being grown and learned how cane sugar was made. As the Arab conquests continued, sugar production was established in other lands that they conquered, including North Africa and Spain. The Arabs and Berbers were the first to set up sugar mills, refineries, factories, and plantations. They spread the cultivation of sugar throughout the Arab Empire across much of the Old World.

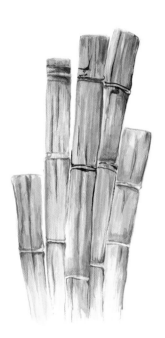

On the other side of India, traveling Buddhist monks brought sugar crystallization methods to China. They taught sugarcane cultivating methods in China, and built so much interest in sugar that the Chinese traveled back to India between AD 630 and 650 to obtain more technology for sugar refining. In South Asia, the Middle East, and China, sugar became a key ingredient in cooking and dessert making.

By the seventh and eighth centuries, sugar bakers already existed under the rule of the Caliphs, the Muslim heads of state. On the Oriental market, you could find fruit loaves and a rich assortment of different nougats made out of white sugar and natural honey mixed with pistachio nuts, almonds, and candied fruit. The words rock candy, nougat, citron, and sugar have their origins in the Arabic language.

Sugar was discovered by Western Europeans during the Crusades in the eleventh century AD. The first records of sugar appeared in England in 1099. The Turks brought a lot of Asian culture to Europe, and helped to introduce sugar with its many possibilities, including sugar showpieces for banquets. By 1319, sugar was available in London at two shillings a pound, which was equal to several months of wages for an average laborer. It was a luxury, and huge quantities of sugar were used in noble circles. The rich enjoyed decorating their tables with sculptures made out of sugar. When Henry III of France visited Venice in 1574, a party was given in his honor featuring plates, silverware, and linens all made of spun sugar. At this time sugar was mainly refined in Venice, and the showpieces were made out of finely ground candy sugar moistened and pressed into forms and molds.

The name "sugar baker" came from the process of binding sugar crystals. In the middle of the sixteenth century, many sugar refineries opened where sugar was clarified and filled into pointed receptacles. The mixture was then left to sit until it

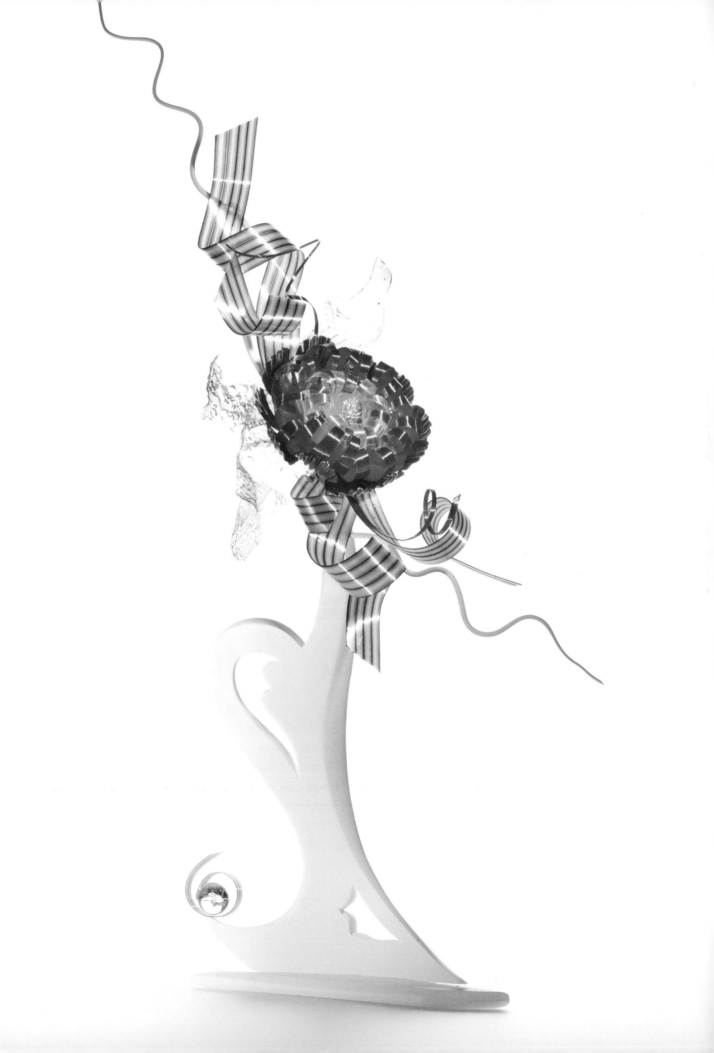

became hard and was ready to unmold. Decorations could be chiseled out of these pointed receptacles. Because sugar was still very expensive, only wood and stone chiselers (artists) were allowed to do so for fear of wasting this precious substance.

At this time, sugar boiling was still a secret of the pharmacist, who used sugar as a way to create a sweet coating around bitter medicines. Because sugar was a luxury item, it was often assumed to be medicinal. Many of the medicinal guides of the thirteenth through fifteenth centuries recommended giving sugar to invalids to bolster their strength.

In August 1492, shortly before his historic voyage to the New World, Christopher Columbus came in touch with sugarcane at Comera in the Canary Islands. The purpose of his visit was to pick up some wine and water for the trip. He became romantically involved with the convener of the island, Beatriz de Bobadilla y Ossorio, and stayed for a month. When he finally left, she gave him cuttings of sugarcane, which became the first to reach the New World. The Portuguese took sugar to Brazil, and the Dutch took it from South America to the Caribbean. With the European colonization of South America, the Caribbean became the world's largest source of sugar.

During the eighteenth century, sugar became very popular. By 1750, sugar surpassed grain as the most valuable commodity in European trade. It made up a fifth of all European imports. In the last decade of the century, four-fifths of the sugar came from British and French colonies in the West Indies. Sugar marketing went through a series of booms as eating habits included consuming jams, candy, and processed food and drinking tea and coffee.

Beet sugar was first identified in Germany in 1747 by Andreas Marggraf. The discovery remained a mere curiosity for some time. Marggraf's student built a sugar beet processing factory, but it was never profitable. It was not until after the Napoleonic Wars, when England blocked sugar imports and cut off the supply of cane sugar, that beet sugar became profitable in Europe. Sugar beet production increased in the United Kingdom at the time of the First World War, when Britain's sugar import was threatened.

Today the annual consumption of sugar is about 120 million tons worldwide and is expanding at a rate of 2 million tons a year. The amount of sugar produced from sugarcane is about six times higher than that produced from beets.

Only the best-quality refined, pure crystal sugar should be used for the decorations in this book. Sugar blowing and pulling are not new techniques—you may find books published as early as 1890 that explain very similar techniques. Most show pieces made at that time were for banquets celebrating holidays or festivals such as Christmas, New Year's, Mother's Day, Easter, Thanksgiving, and of course weddings.

The use of Isomalt has changed the style of sugar pieces drastically over the last fifteen years. Isomalt provides the capability of casting sugar that is as clear as glass, so the showpieces become more transparent, resulting in lighter, more contemporary-shaped pieces. Cast pieces are also widely used today due to the time and cost factors associated with creating figurines and natural-looking pieces. There have been times throughout history when the art of sugar showpieces has almost disappeared, such as during the decade after the Second World War. Now, I am very happy to say, sugar showpieces are again popular in pastry competitions, in the finest of hotels, country clubs, and restaurants, on luxury cruise lines, and in upscale pastry shops. A sugar showpiece is the one piece that truly reflects the unique skills of the pastry chef–artist.

Pastillage

Pastillage is sugar dough used to create showpieces and small, personalized sculptures to display pralines and sweet confections, which can be used to decorate a table or room. It is made of confectioners' sugar, cornstarch, gelatin, and water. Acid is sometimes added to decrease drying time. Pastillage is more resistant to humidity and has a longer shelf life than other sugarwork.

Pastillage is a perfect complement to sugar showpieces. Its dull, white surface contrasts vividly with the shiny colorfulness of sugar. This also works in reverse when a pastillage showpiece is enhanced with jewel-toned sugar accents.

The fast pace demanded by pastillage is exciting. Before the sugar dough is made, there must be a solid plan for its use and all tools must be in place. The plan must be executed rapidly and accurately. Pastillage is rolled out in small pieces that are then immediately cut and shaped. If too large a piece of pastillage is rolled out, the surface will dry and crack, becoming unusable before you have finished cutting and shaping it. Roll, cut, form, and dry—the quick pace and immediate results motivate and inspire.

Sugar and Isomalt

When using sugar to produce amenities and showpieces, the purity of the sugar is the most important factor to be considered. Commercially processed cane sugar and beet sugar are available in the United States in various forms. In Europe, double refined sugar is available. Double refined sugar is sugar that has been melted after crystallization and all impurities have been removed. For sugar decoration, only the best-quality, refined white cane sugar should be used: single or double refined. Natural or brown sugars are unsuitable for this type of work as they contain high levels of impurities.

Isomalt, a.k.a. hydrogenated isomaltulose, is a sugar replacer made from beets. Isomalt is manufactured in a two-stage process in which sucrose is transformed into isomaltulose, which is then hydrogenated using a metal catalyst. It is available in a wide range of particle sizes, from granules to powder. This is a good alternative to sugar for the production of amenities and showpieces. The density and viscosity of boiled Isomalt solutions are similar to that of sugar; however, Isomalt has low hygroscopicity, even lower than sugar.

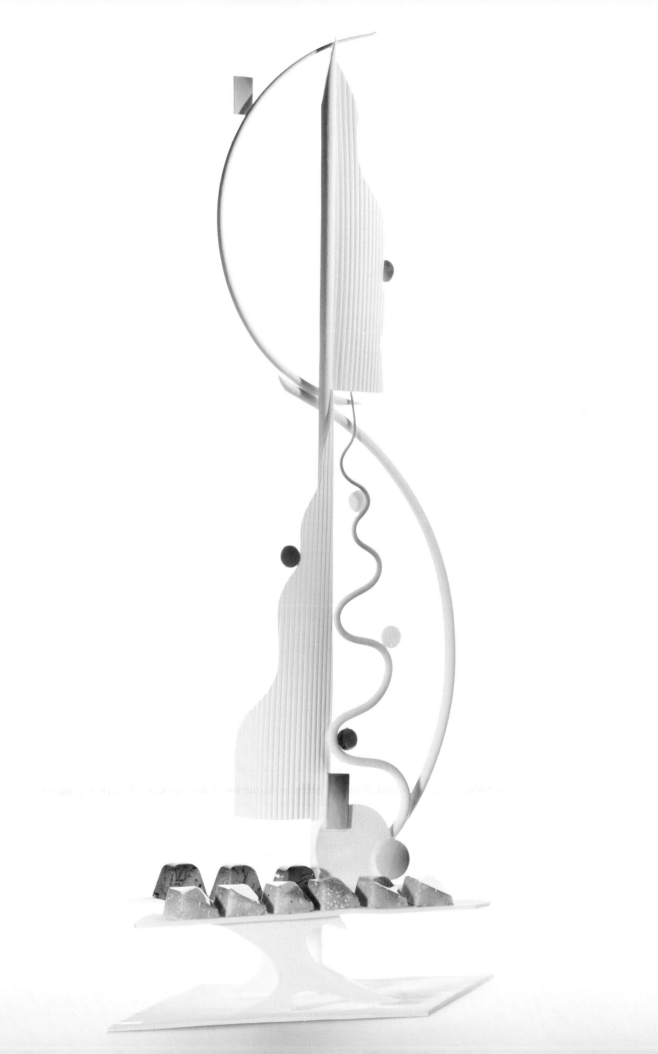

When choosing between sugar and Isomalt, keep in mind the information given in the table below. Cost, climate, and the desired end product are factors to consider. In a dry area during winter, when humidity is not a factor, I recommend the use of sugar, or a sugar and Isomalt combination, as it is less costly.

	SUGAR	**ISOMALT**
Cost	Less costly	More costly
Hygroscopic	High hygroscopic—the surface becomes sticky when exposed to humid conditions.	Low hygroscopic—the surface is less sticky in humid conditions, which makes it easier to work with. Mold, yeast, and fungus resistant.
Shine	Sugar cools faster than Isomalt. It is easier to achieve shine when pulling. The sugar can be worked at warmer temperatures yet retain shine.	Retains heat longer than sugar. Isomalt must be worked at a cooler temperature to attain the same shine as sugar. This leaves less time to form the Isomalt into the desired shape. Loses shine immediately in humid conditions.
Color	Always has an ivory or yellowish appearance from the caramelization that occurs during long boiling times.	Does not caramelize. It stays clear.
Crystallization	Sugar is easier to overwork when it is reused, which causes crystallization. Sugar that is rewarmed too often, or to too high a temperature, will crystallize.	Does not crystallize as easily as sugar. It can be rewarmed and reused over a longer period of time.
Recipes	A large amount of water is required to dissolve sugar when boiling. Acid and glucose are required for pulling/ blowing recipes.	Water is not required to dissolve it.
Impurities	Contains impurities that must be removed during the boiling process.	Does not contain impurities.

The pane on the left is Isomalt.
The pane on the right is sugar.

Equipment

Some basic equipment is needed to facilitate working with sugar and pastillage. The items listed below are available from online specialty vendors, restaurant supply outlets, and home improvement stores. Using the right equipment and tools for specific tasks will enhance your final results.

Basic Kitchen Tools

Small Appliances

COOKING STOVE OR INDUCTION PLATE Sugar or Isomalt solutions are boiled over the strong flame of a gas stove or on an induction plate. The heat provided by induction is different from the heat provided by a gas burner. I use an induction burner when preparing sugar and Isomalt solutions.

GAS BURNER A gas burner heats the sides of the pan as well as the bottom. When cooking sugar, the solution bubbles up onto the inside of the pan. The heat on the sides causes the water to evaporate, leaving the sugar stuck to the inside wall. The heat crystallizes this sugar and it begins to turn yellow. This affects the rest of the solution, causing it to develop a yellowish color. To prevent the crystals from forming, it is important to wash down the sides of the pan with a brush dipped in water, and to prevent the gas flame from coming up around the outside of the pan.

Basic hand equipment used when working with pastillage includes, clockwise from bottom left: scissors, exacto knife, scale, scrapers, mixing spoon, bowl, plastic storage bags, rolling pins, templates, air compressor, cutters, foam board form, Styrofoam, metal bars, airbrush, paintbrushes, liquid food coloring, piping bag, sandpaper, cell pad, ball modeling tool, ruler, chef's knife, molds, cornstarch pouch, cake board.

Basic hand equipment used for working with sugar includes, clockwise from top left: foam board with Teflon sheet, induction stove top, heat-resistant spatula, pan, food warmer, Silpat mat, hair dryer, cooling rack, round aluminum plate, blowtorch, parchment paper, rolling pin, vinyl, airbrush, airbrush compressor, spun sugar tool, gloves, scale, metal half spheres, vinyl tube, noodles, silicone inserts, round cutters, skimmer, scrapers, basket weaving stand, spoon, scissors, exacto knife, pencil, alcohol burner, silicone molds, neoprene cutout, sugar pump, metal bars, whisk, bench scraper, brush, paring knife, clamps.

INDUCTION An induction plate provides heat only to the bottom of the pan. When the boiling sugar solution bubbles onto the sides of the pan, the water does not evaporate. Crystals will not form on the inside wall of the pan so there is no need to wash it down. Because the sides of the pan stay cool, the sugar solution will not develop as yellow a color. However, crystals are more likely to form in the final product.

MICROWAVE OVEN A microwave uses microwave radiation for heating and cooking. It is used in sugarwork to heat the gelatin and water mixture for pastillage without losing water due to evaporation.

Hand Equipment

ALCOHOL BURNER This burns alcohol cleanly so that it will not leave soot on your sugar pieces.

ALUMINUM FOIL Aluminum prepared in very thin metal sheets. It comes in rolls and is crumbled to give the cast sugar an interesting appearance.

ALUMINUM PLATE Fine strings of sugar can be piped onto a vegetable oil–coated aluminum plate to create a fan.

BALL MODELING TOOL This tool is used to thin the edges of pastillage leaves and flowers.

BASKET WEAVING STAND In sugarwork, this stand, designed for weaving baskets, is used to hold small spheres while they are drying.

BLOWTORCH Blowtorches are used to apply direct heat to a piece of sugar or Isomalt, for example, to clear small surface bubbles from cast sugar or Isomalt.

BOTTLE WITH DROPPER Bottles with droppers are used to add tartaric acid by drops into a boiling sugar solution.

BOWLS A variety of stainless steel bowls are used when mixing pastillage, and to hold water for washing down the sides of the pan when boiling a sugar solution.

BRUSHES Fine paint brushes are used to apply paint to dry pastillage and cooled sugar or Isomalt pieces. Wider pastry brushes, 2 to 4 in/5 to 10 cm wide, are dampened with water to wash down the inside wall of the pan when boiling a sugar solution.

CAKE BOARD An 8-in/20-cm round cake board can be used to roll vines out of pastillage.

FOAM CELL PAD When thinning the edges of pastillage leaves and flowers with a ball modeling tool, a foam cell pad provides a soft work surface.

CLAMPS Clamps are used in sugarwork to hold vinyl tubing to secure an object when a hot solution is poured into it, and to firmly close the ends of the vinyl tubing when it contains a hot solution.

COLD SPRAY This is an aerosol spray used to cool or freeze parts of cast sugar immediately to enforce and design cracks. Cold spray may also be used when assembling pastillage pieces to form an immediate attachment.

COLOR, FOOD-GRADE
- **FOOD-GRADE POWDER COLOR** Food-grade powder color is recommended for addition to sugar and Isomalt solutions. Mix the powder color with a small amount of water to dissolve the powder before adding it to the solution. Many liquid colors contain acid and are not recommended for use with sugar solutions. This additional acid in the color will soften the sugar solution; in the worst case it will invert the sugar. Regular acid-based airbrush color is recommended for airbrushing color onto finished pieces. Alcohol-based airbrush color may turn Isomalt dull.
- **LIQUID FOOD COLORING** Food coloring in liquid form adds color to finished pieces when applied with an airbrush or handheld paintbrush.

CORNSTARCH POUCH When working with pastillage, a beggar's purse can be made out of nylon stockings. Cut the stockings into 4-in/10-cm pieces, fill with cornstarch, and tie a knot in each end. This is used during rolling to dust the work surface and the surface of the pastillage.

CUTTING TOOLS

- **STENCILS AND CUTTERS** Stencils can be used as patterns to paint on pastillage or to cut out shapes. Cutters also facilitate cutting out specific shapes, such as with round cutters. Cutters made of metal are best suited for sugarwork.
- **EXACTO KNIFE** A small craft knife with changeable blades allows for cleaner cuts when cutting out patterns on pastillage.
- **FRENCH OR CHEF'S KNIFE** A 10-in/25-cm chef's knife is used to make long, straight cuts through pastillage as well as sugar when it is still pliable.
- **PARING KNIFE** A paring knife is used to make small cuts and to score lines into pastillage.
- **SMALL KNIFE** A small knife can be used for all cutting jobs in pastillage and for creating colored designs on cast sugar.
- **HEAVY-DUTY, SHARP SCISSORS** These should be kept cool, and are needed for cutting through cooked sugar to portion it before it has cooled completely, as well as for cutting and shaping modeled pieces of sugar.
- **PUTTY KNIFE** A putty knife can be heated with a blowtorch to cut through pulled sugar ribbons.

DENATURED ALCOHOL Used to fuel the flame on an alcohol burner to melt and attach small pieces of blown and pulled sugar and to create color rings on pastillage stones.

DRYING SURFACES

- **STYROFOAM AND PLYWOOD** Most effective for drying flat pieces of pastillage, both Styrofoam and plywood allow airflow underneath the pieces.
- **FOAM BOARD AND POSTER BOARD** Can be used to create bent and shaped drying surfaces for pastillage and sugar pieces.
- **PVC PIPE** Cut in half lengthwise, PVC pipe is used for drying cutout pastillage pieces in curved shapes.
- **CARDBOARD MAILING TUBES** Cut in half lengthwise, these can be used for the same purposes as the PVC pipe but may be more readily accessible and cost-effective.
- **TEFLON AND SILPAT** Teflon sheets and Silpat mats are coated with Teflon or silicone to create a nonstick surface. They can withstand high temperatures and are microwave-, freezer-, and refrigerator-safe. In sugarwork, they are particularly useful as a nonstick surface to cool and reheat sugar and isomalt.

GLOVES Latex or vinyl gloves protect your hands when working with hot sugar or Isomalt.

HAIR DRYER A hair dryer with a cool or cold setting and a stand for hands-free use assists in cooling sugar quickly.

METAL BARS Pastillage Recipe II is rolled between two metal bars to keep the thickness of the pastillage even. Metal bars are also used in casting sugar and Isomalt.

METAL HALF SPHERES Can be used as a mold to press in a mixture of granulated sugar and water.

MOLDS AND TEXTURED SURFACES Molds and textured surfaces can be hard or soft. They are used with Pastillage Recipe I to achieve different shapes and textured finishes, and to create textures in sugar and Isomalt pieces. The molds used in chapters 3 and 7 are made using clay, neoprene, metal bars, noodles, plaster of Paris, and silicone.

NEOPRENE A flat mat, used to cut out designs for casting sugar and Isomalt.

NOODLES Noodles are strips made out of silicone, used to frame simple curvy shapes for casting sugar or Isomalt.

PANS Saucepans are used for boiling sugar. On a gas stove, a copper pan is best at conducting heat. The pan should be large enough to cover the flame of the gas stove. A flame that comes up the sides of the pan will cause the sugar to crystallize and will turn the sugar solution a yellowish color. Induction burners require specific pans and will not conduct heat to aluminum or copper.

PARCHMENT PAPER Indispensable in the pastry kitchen, parchment paper can be used as a nonstick surface on which to cast sugar and Isomalt, can be folded and rolled to form piping bags, and can be crumbled to create bubble sugar.

PENCIL, GRAPHITE Used to draw designs on paper, which can then be transferred onto clay for an outline to be cut out.

PIPING BAGS/CORNETS Piping bags, often called cornets, are hand-shaped bags made of parchment paper cut into triangles and rolled into a cone shape. These are used to pipe sugar ornaments onto oiled marble and to glue pastillage pieces together.

PLASTIC WRAP/BAGS Pastillage dries quickly when exposed to air. Unused pastillage must be wrapped tightly with plastic wrap or kept in a plastic bag with the air expelled. Sugar and Isomalt pieces must be kept in bags or containers with a hygroscopic drying agent such as crushed limestone or blue silica gel.

ROLLING PINS Different types of pins are used for rolling out pastillage prior to cutting it. Rolling pastillage with acrylic and PVC tubes will give a smooth finish, or textured rolling pins can be purchased in preset designs such as basket weave. Pressed sugar can be rolled with a smooth rolling pin.

RULER Rulers are used in sugarwork to make precise measurements. Metal rulers that have both metric and American measurements are the most desirable.

SANDPAPER Fine-grit sandpaper is used to shape the pieces cut from Pastillage Recipe II sugar dough.

SCALE Digital scales are necessary for accurately weighing ingredients. Purchase one that can convert from ounces to grams. Pocket scales are helpful for scaling in 1-gram increments.

SCRAPERS Two kinds of scrapers are used in sugarwork to clean surfaces and bowls, and to cut pastillage dough. Scrapers are straight for flat surfaces or are shaped to fit contours of bowls.
- **METAL** Rectangular, stainless steel bench scraper.
- **PLASTIC** Contoured edges for use with round bowls.

SILICONE INSERTS Used to lay on a surface such as vinyl or parchment paper in order to create impressions into cast sugar pieces.

SPATULA, HEAT-RESISTANT Heat-resistant spatulas can withstand temperatures of up to 400°F/204°C and are used for stirring boiling sugar or Isomalt to maintain an even and consistent temperature.

SPUN SUGAR TOOL A handheld tool consisting of a flat plate with a handle on top and many spikes underneath. The tool can be dipped into a hot sugar solution and used to pull strings of sugar. Useful for making items such as a bird's nest.

STRAINER, FINE-MESH OR SKIMMER These items are used to remove the impurities as they rise to the surface of boiling sugar.

SUGAR PUMP A rubber pump with a wooden, aluminum, or copper tube at the end, this is used to incorporate air into pieces of sugar or Isomalt that are attached to the tube.

TEMPLATES Templates are cutouts of cardboard or plastic sheets used as guides to cut out pastillage pieces.

THERMOMETERS
- **BAUMÉ HYDROMETER SCALE** Used to measure the density of sugar.
- **CANDY THERMOMETER** Required to accurately measure the temperature of a boiling sugar solution. Look for the type of candy thermometer that has a clip that attaches it to the pan for hands-free use. Be sure the tip is fully immersed and not touching the bottom of the pan. As the temperature rises, the mercury or other liquid in this type of thermometer moves upward, making it easy to see when the sugar is at the correct temperature.

TITANIUM DIOXIDE This compound is used to create white sugar pieces. For opaque white, add 2 drops of titanium dioxide for every 35.25 oz/1000 g of sugar or Isomalt.

WARMING CASE OR FOOD WARMER A warming case is used to keep pulling and blowing sugar pieces warm as you work with them. The warming case shown in this book (see page 118) is composed of three sides of Plexiglas hinged together, with a top and bottom of wood, a cable with a socket to hold the infrared lamp, and a clip on the cable to control the height of the lamp. The frame inside the case is wooden and is covered with a soft PVC sheet. The food warmer shown in this book (see page 21) has heat and light control settings separate for the top and for the bottom.

WHISK OR SPOON Whisks or spoons are used to stir the sugar and water together at the beginning of sugar recipes, which helps the sugar crystals dissolve more easily.

WORK SURFACE A clean, smooth, flat work surface is needed to roll out pastillage. Marble, granite, glass, and Plexiglas surfaces that are not marred work well. A nonstick silicone mat placed on a marble or granite work surface is the best surface upon which to pour hot syrup for sugar or Isomalt pieces.

Professional Tools

AIR COMPRESSOR
- **COMPRESSOR** A machine used to provide power to a variety of tools by compressing and blowing pressurized air through a hose attached to the tool. Select a compressor with a high CFM rating, not by the horsepower.
- **AIRBRUSH HEAD** A small handheld tool that is attached to a compressor for airbrushing items. The air is pushed through a chamber that has liquid coloring in it. The forced air disperses the color into the air in minute droplets. Airbrushes are available in single- and dual-action triggers. Single-action triggers disperse the compressed air and color together. Dual-action triggers allow the user control over how much air and how much color is released. Dual-action airbrushes are more expensive than single action.
- **GLASS JARS** Liquid coloring for the air gun is kept in glass jars. Some compressors have attachments that allow the small jar to screw onto it with a tube that rests inside the jar. The color is sucked into the tube and out through the nozzle of the air gun.

MIXER A professional-grade stand mixer is required for Pastillage Recipe II. The mixer must have sufficient power to handle the demands of the 30-to-40 minute mix time.

Ingredients

Listed below are some of the more common ingredients needed when working with pastillage and sugar solutions. Most are available commercially at grocery or pastry supply stores, but a few like tartaric acid may need to be purchased from an online specialty vendor.

ACID Acid increases drying time in pastillage. Types of acids include:

- **WHITE VINEGAR** Other types of vinegar may tint the pastillage. Vinegar is produced from many products such as fruits, berries, potatoes, beets, malt, grains, and even coconuts. Vinegar occurs when the natural sugars of the product ferment to alcohol and then continue on to a secondary fermentation that changes them into vinegar.
- **LEMON JUICE** Freshly squeezed and strained juice is best. Prebottled juice is not always 100 percent natural, and may contain ingredients that can affect the sugar adversely.
- **CREAM OF TARTAR** This is the common name for potassium bitartrate, also known as potassium hydrogen tartrate, which is an acid salt. Cream of tartar can be found in most grocery stores alongside spices and baking ingredients.
- **TARTARIC ACID** This white crystalline organic acid occurs naturally in many plants, particularly in bananas and grapes. Tartaric acid is one of the main acids found in wine. It is available from online specialty vendors.
- **CITRIC ACID** Citric acid is sold in a white crystalline powder form. Citric acid is a weak, colorless, organic acid naturally found in citrus fruits such as lemons, limes, oranges, tangerines, etc.

Of the acids listed, the most preferable for sugar solutions is tartaric acid, as it is stronger than the others, and therefore less is needed. Tartaric acid also reacts immediately when added to the sugar and because of this it can be added at the end of the cooking process. Cream of tartar, on the other hand, needs more time to react and is therefore added at the beginning of the boiling process. For pastillage, I prefer to use vinegar, as it is readily available and user-friendly.

In addition to its use in pastillage, tartaric acid is also used in the recipe for pulling and blowing sugar to make the sugar more elastic. The addition of too much tartaric acid, however, will make the sugar weak and cause your showpiece to collapse.

CONFECTIONERS' SUGAR Used in sugarwork for making pastillage, confectioners' sugar is granulated sugar ground to a fine powder with 3 percent cornstarch added to prevent lumping. It is available in different grades. The higher the number (10–X), the finer the grind of the product.

CORNSTARCH Cornstarch is ground from the endosperm of the corn kernel. Cornstarch gives pastillage a fine, smooth surface, and decreases drying time.

GELATIN Gelatin gives pastillage elasticity: the capability of being shaped and bent. Sheet gelatin must be soaked in cold water prior to use to ensure even hydration and distribution within the sugar dough. Gold gelatin sheets should be used, as the recipes in this book have been formulated using single gelatin sheets with a bloom strength of approximately 200.

GLUCOSE SYRUP A liquid starch, glucose syrup is usually made from wheat, rice, or potatoes. It is used to retard crystallization in a boiled sugar solution. It is available from food service distributors or importers.

ISOMALT Isomalt, also known as hydrogenated isomaltulose, is a bulk sugar replacer made from sugar beets. It comes in many different-size granules. Medium-size granules are recommended.

ROYAL ICING Royal icing is used to crystallize sugar to create rock sugar or to glue pastillage pieces together (see chapter 6).

SUGAR Use the best-quality white cane sugar available to you. Brown and natural sugars are unsuitable for use in sugarwork.

WATER Plain tap water is used for pastillage; specialty water such as distilled or spring water is not required. When working with sugar and Isomalt, tap water can be used if it is not heavy with minerals or other impurities, or bottled spring water can be used if the tap water in your area has a high mineral content.

2

Pastillage

As mentioned in chapter 1, pastillage works very well as a contrasting component alongside any other kind of sugarwork, such as cast, pulled, or blown pieces.

For thin, fine, and detailed work, Pastillage Recipe I works best. When the recipe is mixed by hand without incorporating any air, it will yield a tight, smooth pastillage. The Liquid Pastillage technique (see page 46), which uses Recipe I, is best for casting. Liquid pastillage can be cast in granulated sugar or Isomalt. It will be almost free-form and very white.

For thicker and supporting pieces, use Pastillage Recipe II. Mixing the recipe with a dough hook for 30 to 40 minutes on low speed will incorporate a lot of air and the sugar dough will become warm due to friction from the mixing. Because of this airy texture, it is not possible to roll it out thinly as with Recipe I pastillage, but it is the best choice for thicker and supporting pieces. Since this sugar dough is very airy and warm, it dries fairly fast. To make these thick pieces elegant, the edges can be sanded down.

Pastillage Recipe I

Use this recipe for fine, thin, smooth pieces, and for pieces that require bending. If you work cleanly, the pieces will not need to be sanded. There are three options for coloring pastillage. The color may be added at the beginning of the mixing process along with all the other ingredients, or it can be added once the sugar dough has been mixed, which works well if you wish to color only part of the whole batch. The third option, which is my preference, is to keep the pastillage white and airbrush certain parts of it once the piece has dried.

INGREDIENTS	METRIC	US	VOLUME
Gold gelatin sheets	16 g	0.6 oz	8 sheets
Water, cold	132 g	4.7 oz	½ cup plus 1 tbsp
Confectioners' sugar	850 g	29.9 oz	7 cups
Cornstarch	150 g	5.3 oz	1 cup
YIELD	**1148 g**	**40.5 oz**	

1 Place the gelatin sheets in the cold water and bloom for 5 minutes.

2 Sift the confectioners' sugar and cornstarch into a bowl.

3 Melt the bloomed gelatin and water in the microwave on high.

4 Add the melted gelatin to the dry ingredients and stir by hand to begin to incorporate.

5 As the sugar dough starts to come together, scrape the contents out onto the work surface.

6 Continue to mix, then knead and work the sugar dough until smooth.

7 Use immediately, and store any unused portion in plastic wrap or in a plastic bag with the air expelled to keep it from drying out. →

- Combine the melted gelatin with the sugar and cornstarch.
- Knead the sugar dough by hand until smooth and thoroughly combined.
- It is important to store pastillage sealed in plastic to prevent it from drying out.

NOTE: *This recipe is mixed by hand to limit the amount of air incorporated into the finished sugar dough. The finished sugar dough should appear tight with no air bubbles. The sugar dough will be extremely flexible due to the amount of gelatin used. The sugar dough must be mixed quickly or it will begin to dry. Only make as much sugar dough as you can use within an hour. The sugar dough can be stored, but becomes stiff and difficult to work with. This sugar dough does not need to be refrigerated.*

Rolling, Cutting, and Drying Recipe I

1. Take a small piece of sugar dough from the storage bag. Reseal the bag to prevent the unused portion from drying out. Roll out only what you can immediately cut. The large surface area of the rolled sugar dough, when exposed to air, will dry quickly.

2. For a smooth finish, roll by hand on a smooth surface such as marble, glass, Plexiglas, or granite. The use of a sheeter will release impurities and is not recommended. Gently dust the work surface and the sugar dough with the cornstarch pouch.

3. Use a smooth, plastic rolling pin to roll out the sugar dough. Wooden rolling pins may imprint a grain or texture onto the sugar dough. Move the sugar dough around as you roll it out to be sure that the sugar dough does not stick to the work surface or the rolling pin.

4. Smooth the surface of the sugar dough with the palm of your hand. This closes the pores of the sugar dough and prevents painted color from bleeding.

5. Cut the sugar dough as desired with an exacto knife.

6. Dry the pastillage pieces on a porous surface such as a piece of Styrofoam, wooden or plywood boards, or foam board. Porous surfaces decrease drying time because air flows between the contact surfaces. Pieces can also be dried on cornstarch, which absorbs moisture. To keep pieces flat, they must be turned over after a few hours to allow the sides to dry evenly.

- Use a cornstarch pouch to lightly dust the work surface before rolling out the sugar dough.
- Use a template to cut the sugar dough into the desired shape.
- Place on a flat, porous surface to dry to create flat pieces, or on a curved form to create bent pieces.

7 Forms for bent pieces can be built using foam board or cardboard and poster board.

8 Once the pastillage is dry, it should be stored at room temperature and kept away from dust.

TIPS
When more time is needed to cut a piece you can:
- Place the sugar dough in the refrigerator for 5 minutes. When it is removed from the refrigerator, the pastillage will sweat, which will prevent it from drying out.
- Cut out the pastillage in a walk-in proofer, or place a humidifier in the room.
- Use a travel clothes steamer to remoisten the surface.

Using Recipe I

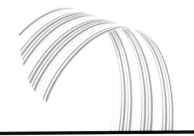

Using a variety of techniques for coloring and texturing pastillage can make a simple, quiet piece more interesting and vibrant. It is also essential to know and understand a range of different techniques for working with pastillage to allow room for creativity.

Marbled Pastillage

Marbled pastillage is mostly used for bases or standing supports because of the way the coloring appears. It is not recommended for use on intricate or airbrushed pieces, as combining the marbled look with playful and colorful pastillage pieces can make a showpiece appear overdone.

1   Color separate portions of pastillage for each color to appear in the marble. For example, to obtain white, red, and pink marbling, take three separate portions of pastillage and color one red and one pink, leaving the third uncolored.

2   Take portions of each color and knead them together. Take care not to overwork the sugar dough (keep in mind that you still have to roll it out) or you will lose the marbled effect.

3   Gently dust the work surface and the sugar dough with the cornstarch pouch and roll out the sugar dough using a smooth, plastic rolling pin.

4   Cut out the desired shapes with an exacto knife.

5   Dry the shapes on a porous surface such as plywood or a shaped drying surface made with foam board and poster board (see steps 6 through 8 on pages 36–37).

- Knead together multiple colors to form marbled pastillage.
- Roll out the sugar dough with a smooth rolling pin.
- Marbled pastillage can be cut as desired for use as a showpiece base or support.

Textured Pastillage

A textured surface can be achieved using molds, textured work surfaces, or textured rolling pins. Before using molds, be sure to lightly dust them with cornstarch.

Using Molds

1 Gently dust the work surface, the sugar dough, and the molds with the cornstarch pouch and roll out the pastillage using a smooth, plastic rolling pin. Cut into the desired shapes.

2 Press the pastillage into the mold using your hands or a rolling pin.

3 Flip the mold and release the pastillage immediately.

4 Dry on a porous surface and store at room temperature.

Pastillage can be pressed into a mold using your hands or a rolling pin.

Using a Textured Work Surface

1   Gently dust the work surface and the sugar dough with the cornstarch pouch. Using a smooth, plastic rolling pin, roll out the pastillage onto a sheet that is stamped with a premolded design, a piece of textured wallpaper or wood, or any other textured surface.

2   Remove the pastillage from the textured surface and cut it into the desired shapes.

3   Dry the shapes on a porous surface and store at room temperature.

Using a Textured Rolling Pin

1   Gently dust the work surface and the sugar dough with the cornstarch pouch.

2   Roll out the pastillage using a textured rolling pin. Rolling pins with various designs are available.

3   Cut out the desired shapes and dry on a porous surface. Store at room temperature.

- LEFT: Roll out pastillage on top of a textured sheet to create a textured surface.
- RIGHT: Pastillage can also be rolled out on a smooth work surface using a textured rolling pin.

Cracked Pastillage

Normally you want to avoid any cracks in a pastillage piece, but you also can create cracks intentionally to force a certain look or style.

1   Roll out a piece of pastillage onto a smooth, cornstarch-dusted surface. Let the rolled-out piece dry for approximately 15 minutes. Only the surface of the pastillage should be dry.

2   Roll over the piece again using moderate pressure. Apply enough pressure to crack the surface of the pastillage, revealing the still moist layer underneath.

3   Cut the pastillage into the desired shapes with an exacto knife, shape it, and place it on the drying surface.

4   Allow to dry for 24 hours at room temperature.

Stones

Pastillage can be shaped and colored to make beautiful "skipping" stones. These can be used as a base for your showpiece, or on a smaller scale as accent pieces.

1   Lightly dust your hands with cornstarch.

2   Flatten a piece of pastillage between your hands.

3   Rub the pastillage in a circular motion between the palms of your hands to shape it.

4   Let the stones dry completely on a flat wooden or Styrofoam surface.

5   Brush at least three colors onto each stone using an airbrush. Start with the lightest color first and then follow with the darker colors, one right after the other.

6   Use a paintbrush to drip or splash denatured alcohol onto the top surface of each stone. This creates a pattern.

7   Dip the stone into boiled Isomalt. For instructions on boiling Isomalt, see Assembling Pastillage, Boiled Isomalt, on page 66.

8   Place on a Silpat mat to dry for about 5 minutes until the Isomalt is completely set. Store at room temperature.

–   Rub the pastillage between your hands to shape it into stones.
–   Airbrush each stone with at least three different colors.
–   Drip denatured alcohol onto each stone to create spots.

Liquid Pastillage

Pastillage can be melted and molded in sugar or Isomalt. This technique creates a playful look that offers a good contrast to straight and more geometric pieces.

1   Prepare a bowl filled with granulated sugar or Isomalt. Create a well, circle, or other shape in the sugar granules.

2   Place the pastillage in a microwave-safe bowl and warm it in the microwave until it becomes liquid. The time will vary based on the wattage of the microwave and the amount of pastillage. For example, 4 oz/½ cup/113 g takes about 20 seconds in a 1300-watt microwave.

3   Pour the liquid pastillage into the molded granules.

4   Immediately cover the exposed pastillage with the granules.

5   Use a spoon or other utensil to shape the pastillage as desired. For example, a section of pastillage can be raised by pushing additional sugar or Isomalt under it.

6   Allow the pastillage to dry for an hour for smaller pieces or half a day for larger pieces and remove it from the granules.

7   Store the shaped pastillage at room temperature away from humidity.

–   Warm the pastillage in the microwave until it is liquid.
–   Create a shape in the granulated sugar and pour in the liquid pastillage.
–   Allow the pastillage to dry before removing it from the bowl.

Accent Décor

Vines

1 Do not use cornstarch on the work surface. Lightly moisten the work surface with a damp towel so the pastillage will not slide when it is rolled.

2 Take a small amount of pastillage and roll it with your hand into a pencil shape on the moistened work surface.

3 Use a cake board to roll the vine into the required length and thickness. This will keep the surface of the vine even, without indentations from your fingertips.

4 Immediately shape or curl the vine and place on the drying surface. Because this recipe contains a lot of gelatin, the vine will be flexible and will not break as easily as one made from a recipe containing less gelatin.

5 Allow to dry for 24 hours at room temperature.

Feathers

1 Roll out a piece of pastillage onto a smooth, cornstarch-dusted surface.

2 Use an exacto knife to cut a feather shape out of the rolled pastillage.

3 Use a smooth-edged paring knife to score lines around both sides of the feather. The cuts should make an indent near the center of the feather and cut through the pastillage at the outer edge. This is easily accomplished if the blade of the knife is curved toward the tip.

4 Immediately shape the feather with your fingers and place on the drying surface.

5 Allow to dry for 24 hours at room temperature.

Circle Noodles

1 Roll out a piece of pastillage onto a smooth, cornstarch-dusted surface.

2 Cut out a circle using a round cutter.

3 Remove the center of the circle using a cutter one size smaller than the first cutter to create a ring.

4 Cut out additional rings from the same center piece using incrementally smaller cutters.

5 Immediately shape and bend each piece as desired and place on the drying surface.

6 Allow to dry for 24 hours at room temperature.

LEFT: Feathers. RIGHT: Circle Noodles.

Wavy Triangles

1   Roll out a piece of pastillage onto a smooth, cornstarch-dusted surface.

2   Use a chef's knife to cut long, thin triangular pieces.

3   Immediately shape and bend each piece as desired and place on the drying surface.

4   Allow to dry for 24 hours at room temperature.

Modeling

Pastillage can be modeled into different shapes if you work quickly. Otherwise the surface will wrinkle or crack. If modeling a shape with multiple pieces, allow each piece to dry independently before attaching so that the pieces dry faster and more completely. After the pieces are dry they can be carefully sanded and painted or airbrushed. If perspiration is a problem, lightly dust your hands with cornstarch before rolling and shaping the pastillage.

1 Roll or shape the pastillage into the desired shape quickly.

2 Then roll or shape any smaller pieces you intend to attach, for example a fin for a fish, and allow the smaller piece to rest on the freshly molded main piece (in this case, the fish body) just long enough to set, 3 to 5 minutes.

3 Carefully remove the smaller molded piece from the main piece and allow to dry completely.

4 Once all the pieces are fully dry, they can be attached to one another using Boiled Isomalt (page 66) or Royal Icing Glue (page 68).

Pastillage Flowers

Cutout Flower

These flowers are similar to gum paste flowers in that each petal is cut and shaped individually. However, pastillage dries much faster than gum paste, and therefore you have less time to handle each petal. For this reason, flowers made of pastillage have to be simple.

1   Roll out a piece of pastillage onto a smooth, cornstarch-dusted surface.

2   Using a round cutter, cut a circle out of the pastillage to use as the base for the flower. Dry on a flat surface.

3   Cut out no more than 4 petals at a time freehand with an exacto knife or using a cutter. The petals must not begin to dry before you are able to shape them.

4   Smooth the edges of each petal on a cell pad using a ball modeling tool.

5   Dry the petals on a curved surface such as a PVC pipe or cardboard tube cut in half lengthwise.

6   Continue rolling out batches of pastillage and cutting and shaping petals until you have all the petals needed for the flower. You will need approximately 15 petals for a medium-size flower. Make extra petals to account for potential breakage as you assemble.

7   Cook Isomalt according to the recipe for Boiled Isomalt (page 66).

8   After the Isomalt is cooked, allow it to stand for 5 minutes. The Isomalt will cool slightly and thicken. Then dip the bottom of a petal in the Isomalt.

9   Place the dipped end of the petal against the base and set the Isomalt with cold spray. It will set immediately.

10   Repeat steps 8 and 9, starting from the center of the flower and working outwards, until all the petals are in place. Allow to dry completely.

11   Airbrush the flower as desired and store at room temperature.   →

– Use a ball modeling tool to shape the edges of each petal.
– Dry the petals on a curved surface.
– Dip the end of each petal into the Isomalt to attach it to the base.

SECOND ROW:
– Use cold spray to set the petals in place immediately.
– Airbrush the completed flower for a finished look.
– A completed cutout flower.

Calla Lily

This is the fastest and perhaps the easiest flower to make using pastillage.

1   Roll out a piece of pastillage onto a smooth, cornstarch-dusted surface.

2   Cut out 1 heart-shaped piece for each flower using an exacto knife or shaped cutter.

3   Pick up 1 heart-shaped piece and, with the pointed end facing away from you, fold the left lobe over the right lobe to form the flower. Let dry.

4   To shape the stamen, roll a very small piece of pastillage into a sphere. Roll the sphere between your hands to make an elongated drop shape. Let dry.

5   Airbrush yellow liquid color onto the rounded end of the stamen. Let dry.

6   Lightly moisten the yellow end of the stamen and dip it into granulated sugar. Let dry.

7   Lightly moisten the pointed end of the stamen and place it into the flower. Royal Icing Glue or Boiled Isomalt can also be used to glue the stamen to the flower (see Assembling Pastillage, page 65). Allow to dry completely.

8   Airbrush the flower as desired and store at room temperature.

–   Use an exacto knife to cut out the heart-shaped petals by hand.
–   Fold the two lobes of the heart shape over one another to form the flower.
–   Wet the pointed end of the stamen and attach it inside the flower.

Rose

This classic flower is beautiful in any medium but can be somewhat tricky when gluing the petals together. You may want to create a flower holder as a support by crumpling aluminum foil together. This can be used to help hold the flower together after assembly while it dries.

1 Roll out a piece of pastillage onto a smooth, cornstarch-dusted surface.

2 Using a round cutter, cut out 1 circle for the center bud.

3 Smooth the edge of the circle on a cell pad using a ball modeling tool.

4 Roll the circle up to form the center bud of the rose. Make sure the top edge is tightly rolled. Press the piece onto the work surface so it stands upright without being held. Allow the center piece to dry.

5 Cut no more than 3 petals at a time using an exacto knife or a shaped cutter.

6 Smooth the edge of each petal immediately on a cell pad using a ball modeling tool.

7 Continue rolling out batches of pastillage and cutting and shaping petals until you have all the petals needed for the flower. For a medium-size flower you will need about 10 to 12 petals.

8 To attach the first petal, lightly moisten the inner bottom edge of the petal with water. Press the left edge against the inner curve of the center bud. Wrap the petal around the center and lightly curl the other edge of the petal toward the back of the petal.

9 To attach the remaining petals, pinch the lower edge of each petal between your thumb and index finger to create a crease from the center of the circle to the edge. Using the thumb and index finger of your other hand, gently curl the top and side edges to the back of the petal. Lightly moisten the bottom edge of the petal and attach it to the center. Repeat until all petals are attached.

10 Allow to dry completely, and then airbrush if desired. Store at room temperature.

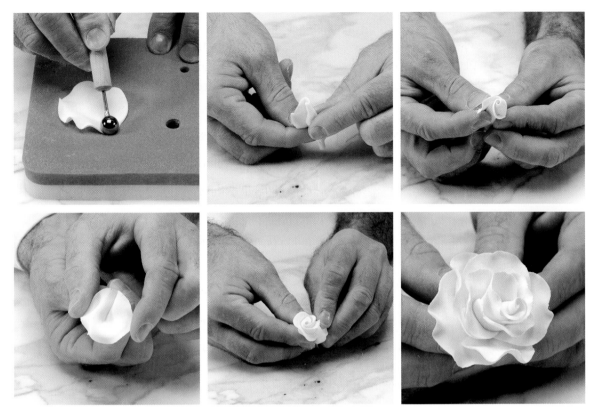

- Use a ball modeling tool to smooth the edges of each petal on a cell pad.
- Cut out a circle and roll it tightly to form the rose's center bud.
- Attach the first petal to the center bud.

SECOND ROW:
- Shape the remaining petals by creasing each at the center and curling the edges back.
- Attach additional petals to the rose, overlapping each petal over the last.
- Continue adding petals until the rose reaches the desired size.

Big Flower

This flower is relatively easy to put together and can be made very colorful and dramatic by airbrushing. The big flower works well as a focus point in larger showpieces.

1   Roll out a piece of pastillage onto a smooth, cornstarch-dusted surface.

2   Cut a large circle out of pastillage with a round cutter. Lay it out flat to dry.

3   Cut 30 to 40 elongated petals freehand with an exacto knife.

4   Immediately after cutting, place the petals on a curved form to dry.

5   Cook the Isomalt according to the Boiled Isomalt recipe (page 66).

6   After the Isomalt is cooked, allow it to stand for 5 minutes. The Isomalt will cool slightly and thicken.

7   Dip the bottom of a petal in the boiled Isomalt.

8   Place the dipped end of the petal against the base and set the Isomalt with cold spray. It will set immediately.

9   Continue dipping and attaching petals, starting from the center of the flower and working outwards, until all the petals are in place.

10 Let the flower dry completely, which should take 3 to 5 minutes, then airbrush it as desired. Store at room temperature.

–   Use an exacto knife to cut out petals freehand.
–   Dry the petals on a piece of curved foam board to create a rounded shape.
–   Airbrush the flower to finish.

Pastillage Recipe II

This recipe is best for heavy, thick pieces like supports. The surface and edges must be sanded to obtain a smooth and elegant appearance. The long mixing time and the use of a dough hook incorporate air and warm the mixture. This causes the mixture to dry quickly in very humid conditions. This type of pastillage should be used immediately; only make as much as you need.

INGREDIENTS	METRIC	US	VOLUME
Gold gelatin sheets	20 g	0.7 oz	10 sheets
Water, cold	220 g	7.7 oz	1 cup
Confectioners' sugar	1700 g	59.7 oz	14 cups
Cornstarch	300 g	10.5 oz	2 cups
Vinegar	30 g	1 oz	2 tbsp
YIELD	**2270 g**	**79.6 oz**	

1   Place the gelatin sheets in the cold water and bloom for 5 minutes.

2   Melt the bloomed gelatin and water in the microwave.

3   Place the melted gelatin mixture and the confectioners' sugar, cornstarch, and vinegar in a stand mixer fitted with the dough hook attachment and mix on low speed for 30 to 40 minutes. The finished product should be light, airy, and warm. Use immediately.

Rolling, Cutting, and Drying Recipe II

1   Take a small piece of sugar dough from the mixing bowl. Leave the unused portion in the mixer bowl on low speed to prevent it from drying out. You may need to add small amounts of water if the sugar dough in the mixer starts to dry. Roll out only what you can immediately cut. The large surface area of the rolled sugar dough that is exposed to air will dry quickly.

2   For a smooth finish, roll by hand on a smooth surface such as marble, glass, Plexiglas, or granite. Gently dust the work surface and the sugar dough with the cornstarch pouch.

3   To achieve an even thickness, roll the pastillage between metal bars. Use a smooth, plastic rolling pin to roll out the sugar dough. Wooden rolling pins may imprint a grain or texture onto the sugar dough. Move the sugar dough around as you roll it out to be sure that the sugar dough does not stick to the work surface or the rolling pin.

4   Cut the sugar dough as desired. The surface and edges of the cut piece will be rough and can be sanded after the piece is completely dry. Return the trimmings to the mixer bowl; the trimmings can be remixed and reused. If the pastillage becomes dry, just mix in a little water to bring it to the original consistency.

5   Dry the pastillage pieces on a porous surface such as a piece of Styrofoam, wooden or plywood boards, or foam board. Porous surfaces decrease drying time because air flows between the contact surfaces. Pieces can also be dried on a cornstarch-dusted surface, which absorbs moisture. To keep pieces flat you must turn the pieces over after a few hours to allow the sides to dry evenly. Forms for bent pieces can be built using foam board or cardboard and poster board.

6   If the pastillage has any big air holes or gaps, fill them in with Royal Icing Glue (page 68) using a piping bag before the pieces dry.

7   Once the pastillage is dry, sand the surface and edges of the piece until smooth.

8   Store the finished pieces at room temperature and away from dust.

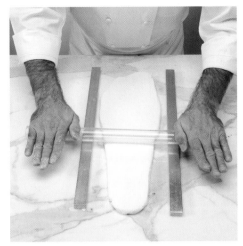
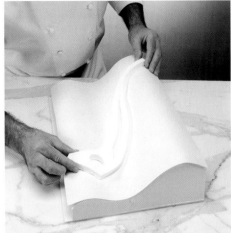

FIRST ROW:
- Roll out pastillage between metal bars for an even thickness.
- Cut out the desired piece and dry it on a curved foam board.

SECOND ROW:
- Sand to smooth any rough edges.

Using Recipe II

Pastillage Recipe II contains a large amount of air, and therefore is ideal for creating rock pastillage. The air in the pastillage expands as it is heated in the microwave, causing the pastillage to grow in size and resulting in the unique rock-like look.

Rock Pastillage

Rock pastillage looks very similar to rock sugar, but it appears white and is lighter. Because of its structure, it can be an eye-catching accent piece to any cutout pastillage piece.

1   Place a small amount of Pastillage Recipe II in a high-sided microwave-safe bowl.

2   Warm the pastillage until it rises up to fill the bowl and does not collapse when the microwave door is opened. The time will vary based on the wattage of the micro-wave and the amount of pastillage. For example, ½ lb/250 g of pastillage will take approximately 160 seconds in a 1300-watt microwave.

3   Remove the bowl from the microwave and allow the pastillage to cool.

4   Remove the cooled pastillage from the bowl and cut it into pieces with a sharp knife. Store at room temperature.

–   Use a small amount of pastillage and a large bowl to allow the sugar dough room to rise.
–   Heat until the pastillage has risen to fill the bowl.
–   Cut the rock pastillage into pieces of the desired shape and size.

Troubleshooting

Because pastillage is very susceptible to the climate and moisture level of the work space, it may be necessary to make adjustments when working with Pastillage Recipe I or Recipe II, particularly in humid or dry areas.

If you work in a very humid area, or you need pastillage to dry quickly, you can add additional acid in a quantity equal to 5 percent of the total weight of the formula. If liquid acid is added, you may have to adjust the quantity of water used. In this case the water quantity should be lowered by an amount equal to the amount of acid being added.

If you work in a dry area, make sure you only roll out very small pieces of pastillage at a time, as the surface may dry out immediately. If you have complicated pieces that need more time, you can use a traveling clothes steamer to moisten the surface of the pastillage, or use a humidifier in the workroom. Alternatively, you can place the rolled-out pastillage in the freezer for a few minutes. When the pastillage is removed from the freezer and starts to come back to room temperature, it will start to sweat, temporarily increasing the moisture level.

Assembling Pastillage

Pastillage pieces made with Pastillage Recipe I or Recipe II can be assembled using Boiled Isomalt, Pastillage Glue, or Royal Icing Glue. Recipes for these three types of glue follow on pages 66–68. The three mediums differ in their setting speeds and in the level of hand skills required for using each method, so it is important to select the right medium for the setting you are working in and the type of piece being created.

Boiled Isomalt

Boiled Isomalt is used for assembling flowers because it sets much faster than Pastillage Glue or Royal Icing Glue. For the same reason, it is also used in timed competitions. It is important to work cleanly, because any drops or gluing mistakes are difficult to clean or scratch off the pastillage.

INGREDIENTS	METRIC	US	VOLUME
Isomalt, medium granule	454 g	16 oz	2¼ cups
Water (optional)	80 g	2.8 oz	⅓ cup
YIELD	**534 g**	**18.8 oz**	

1   Place the Isomalt in a saucepan.

2   Add water; the mixture should resemble wet sand. Water is optional and keeps the Isomalt from burning if it is not stirred regularly when cooked on a hot gas or electric stove.

3   Boil the Isomalt over medium heat to 347°F/175°C. Because it is such a small amount, the Isomalt must be boiled to a high temperature to evaporate enough water to achieve the required strength.

4   Remove the pan from the heat. To stop the Isomalt from boiling, plunge the pan into cold water or pour the Isomalt into a cold pan.

5   Allow the Isomalt to stand for 5 to 10 minutes; it will cool slightly and thicken.

6   To use the Boiled Isomalt to assemble pastillage pieces, dip a pastillage piece into the Boiled Isomalt, place the dipped portion or area against the other pastillage piece, and hold for a few seconds until the Isomalt sets. Pastillage pieces can be dipped directly into the pan or the Isomalt can be poured onto a Silpat mat. If the Isomalt becomes too cool, it can be reheated for reuse.

–   Dip the piece directly into the pan of Boiled Isomalt, or pour the Isomalt onto a Silpat mat.
–   Hold the dipped piece in place to glue it to the base.
–   Pastillage shapes can be assembled with Boiled Isomalt, Pastillage Glue, or Royal Icing Glue.

Pastillage Glue

Pastillage Glue doesn't set as fast as Boiled Isomalt, so the attached pieces have to be supported for approximately 5 minutes. Any mistakes made when using Pastillage Glue can be cleaned off easily.

INGREDIENTS	METRIC	US	VOLUME
Pastillage Recipe 1 (page 33)	40 g	1.4 oz	⅛ cup
YIELD	**40 g**	**1.4 oz**	**⅛ cup**

1   Fill a piping bag or cornet, made of parchment paper, with the pastillage, and fold the open end of the piping bag to close it.

2   Warm the pastillage in the piping bag in the microwave. The time will vary based on the wattage of the microwave. It takes approximately 10 seconds to warm 1.4 oz/40 g of pastillage in a 1300-watt microwave.

3   Using a towel, remove and hold the piping bag. Cut the tip of the piping bag to create a small hole.

4   Pipe the glue onto the pastillage piece and immediately attach the piece to be applied. Support the pieces in place for approximately 5 minutes to dry. Pastillage Glue that becomes too cool can be reheated again and again, as needed, for reuse.

-   Fill a piping bag with pastillage.
-   Fold the bag closed and warm it in the microwave.
-   Apply the warmed glue to the pastillage pieces.

Royal Icing Glue

If Pastillage Recipe 1 is not available, glue can be made using gelatin and royal icing. This glue can be stored for a short period of time. Because of the gelatin, glue that has begun to set can be warmed in the microwave for reuse. Using Royal Icing Glue to attach pieces together requires the least hand skill and it is very easy to clean off any excess. However, Royal Icing Glue takes longer to set than Boiled Isomalt or Pastillage Glue.

INGREDIENTS	METRIC	US	VOLUME
Gold gelatin sheets	10 g	0.35 oz	5 sheets
Water, cold	70 g	2.8 oz	⅓ cup
Confectioners' sugar	450 g	15.8 oz	4 cups
YIELD	**530 g**	**18.95 oz**	

1. Place the gelatin sheets in the cold water and let bloom until the water is absorbed.

2. Melt the bloomed gelatin and water in the microwave. The time will vary based on the wattage of the microwave. It takes approximately 30 seconds in a 1300-watt microwave.

3. Add the confectioners' sugar and mix by hand until incorporated.

4. Fill a piping bag or cornet, made of parchment paper, with the mixture, and fold the open end of the piping bag to close it.

5. Warm the Royal Icing Glue in the piping bag in the microwave. The time will vary based on the wattage of the microwave. It takes approximately 10 seconds in a 1300-watt microwave.

6. Using a towel, remove and hold the piping bag. Cut the tip of the piping bag to create a small hole.

7. Pipe the Royal Icing Glue onto the pastillage and attach the second piece immediately. Keep the glued pastillage pieces supported in place until the glue is completely dry. This may take hours for larger pieces.

Glue for Display-Only, Nonedible Showpieces

If the showpiece is for display only, thick viscosity cyanoacrylate glue can be used with an accelerator. This glue can be found in hobby stores. Using this glue is very easy. You hold the piece in its place and then spray the glue in the spot where you want the piece attached and hold for a few seconds. However, you cannot use this glue in competitions as it is nonedible. It is generally used for display showpieces in hotels because it is fast and easy.

Painting and Airbrushing

Color can greatly enhance the look of a pastillage piece, but remember that size, shape, form, and texture are also essential to the design of a showpiece. Pastillage should look elegant without the application of color, and if the piece is well designed, color may not be necessary. The application of color will not improve the appearance of a poorly designed showpiece. Remember that less is more. There is a tendency to want to do too much with color. If you are not skilled with painting or airbrushing, do not apply color.

To prepare for painting a showpiece, create a mock-up of the piece in poster board or cardboard and work out the painted design on it. The surface to be painted should be smooth and free of imperfections. The paint will run and bleed through cracks and gaps in the surface, and if this happens unintentionally it can ruin the showpiece. If you make a mistake, the paint must be scratched or sanded off.

Scratching and sanding can also be used as a technique to reveal white highlights through color, but this must be done carefully as the piece can break easily.

Painting

Designs to be painted with a brush should always be done before airbrushing. Use powder colors for the best results. Powder can be mixed with water to achieve a strong color, whereas liquid food coloring and airbrush color are often watery and weak in color. The brush must be thick enough to hold the color. Thin brushes like 00 do not hold enough color to paint long lines. I prefer to paint with a 2/0 liner or 10.0 liner; they have more bristles and can hold more color. I advise cutting out an extra piece of pastillage ahead of time and using it first to practice your strokes and techniques. I also recommend that you think twice before actually painting your piece. In 90 percent of all pastillage pieces, it is best not to paint if you have not yet acquired the skill. Pastillage that is elegant enough in its design can do without paint applied as an accent.

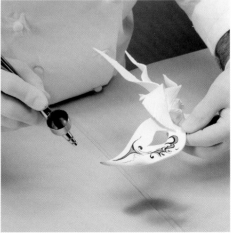

1   Dip the brush into the color. Twirl the brush on a piece of paper to bring the end to a point and to determine how much color is in the brush.

2   Start with easy simple strokes to get the feel of how the color works with the brush. The color will dry and the pastillage will absorb the color immediately.

3   If you make a mistake, you can scratch it off immediately with a paring knife or an exacto knife. If you need to remove color from a very large area, you can use sandpaper. Start with the most difficult part of the painting first because if you make a mistake you can remove it and start over.

Airbrushing

To airbrush pastillage, use liquid airbrush color. Always start with the lightest color first, then add bolder colors as needed, as bold colors cannot be lightened once they have been airbrushed on. Keep in mind that if a finished pastillage piece is held in a humid room, the piece will absorb moisture and the color will get darker and more intense over time.

1   Cover your work surface with newspaper or another absorbent covering. Start by spraying with the airbrush on the paper until you obtain the color intensity and spray pattern that you want, and then move to the pastillage. This allows more control.

2   Spray evenly over the pastillage piece. When applying multiple layers of color, start with the lightest color and work toward the darkest color. The color will dry immediately on the pastillage, so there is no need to wait between layers.

3   Highlights can be revealed through color by carefully scratching the color off with an exacto knife.

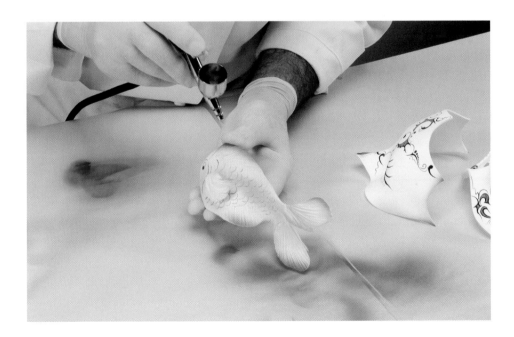

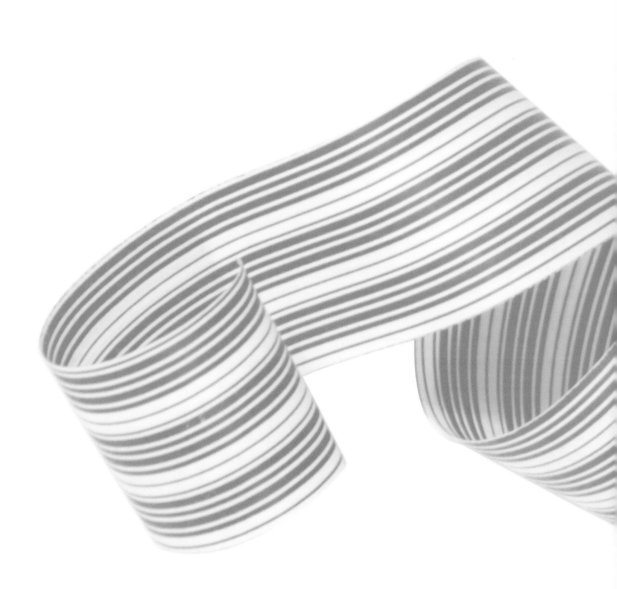

3

Sugar Casting

Casting is the quickest technique for creating a showpiece. A showpiece created from cast pieces can be elegant without the addition of blown or pulled elements. Casting requires good design skills but is less demanding of hand skills than pulling or blowing. Cast pieces are needed in all showpieces for the base and main supports. The base should be the heaviest part of the showpiece. The support pieces must be designed to fit together securely and to handle the weight and balance of the showpiece.

The techniques discussed in this chapter can be used to create a variety of different shapes and textures, which will add interest to your showpiece. Sugar and Isomalt can be cast onto surfaces including oiled marble, vinyl, parchment paper, aluminum foil, Teflon sheets, and Silpat mats. The frame used to create the shape for casting can be made of clay, neoprene, metal bars, silicone molds (spheres), silicone noodles, or foam noodles. Metal bars are primarily used to cast thick, supportive, geometrical base pieces. Noodles are used for simple, rounded, thick shapes. Clay and neoprene allow you to create more complicated two-dimensional shapes. Clay is used for single-use applications, while neoprene is best for shapes that will be reused. Silicone molds can be created from three-dimensional objects and can be used to create décor like leaves, spheres, and angels.

Recipes for Casting

One of the main differences between using Isomalt and plain sugar for casting is that there is no extra ingredient necessary to melt Isomalt. No water is needed. You just pour it into a pot and melt it. Another key difference is that Isomalt, when melted, is very clean and clear. Sugar naturally has a tint to it, so when you add color it is not as clear as when using color with Isomalt. Since Isomalt entered the market in the late 1990s, the trend has been toward showpieces that are clear like glass, since it is easy to achieve this technique using Isomalt. When sugar is used the pieces tend to be more opaque.

Sugar for Casting

When preparing to cast sugar, all ingredients, tools, and work surfaces must be ready before you begin to boil the sugar. The water must be cold. Cold water and low heat allow the sugar to dissolve slowly, so that all impurities are released before the solution begins to boil. Sugar dissolves better without the presence of glucose, so the glucose syrup is added later in the boiling process. The boiled solution must be allowed to stand for 30 to 60 seconds so it cools slightly and thickens. You want the sugar to flow slowly to the edges of your mold so you have a rounded top edge rather than a sharp top edge. There is no acid in this recipe because adding acid would make the sugar softer and weaker. Cast pieces made with sugar with acid added would absorb more humidity and, in the worst case, could lean and fall over.

INGREDIENTS	METRIC	US	VOLUME
Sugar	1000 g	35.25 oz	4⅔ cups
Water, cold	450 g	15.8 oz	1¾ cups
Glucose syrup	200 g	7 oz	½ cup + 2 tbsp
Food coloring (optional)	5–10 drops	5–10 drops	5–10 drops
YIELD	**1650 g**	**58.05 oz**	

1   Place the sugar and cold water into a medium saucepan and stir to combine.

2   Slowly heat the mixture to a boil over low heat. As the mixture heats, impurities will rise to the surface. Use a fine-mesh strainer to skim the impurities off the surface.

3   When the solution begins to boil, add the glucose syrup.

4   If coloring the sugar, add the food coloring and return the mixture to a boil.

5   Using a flat brush dipped in water, wash down the inside wall of the pan to remove any sugar crystals that are forming in order to prevent crystallization.

6   Continue to boil the sugar until the mixture reaches 320°F/160°C.

7 Plunge the pan into cold water to stop the sugar from boiling.

8 Place the pan on a towel and let rest until the bubbles have settled and the sugar has begun to thicken, about 30 to 60 seconds. If the sugar is poured too early, it will bubble and come up the sides of the molds, resulting in sharp, straight edges.

9 Cast the sugar using any of the techniques on pages 79–101.

TIP

As the sugar is poured, it will cool and stick to the lip outside of the pan. This stuck-on sugar must not be used. It must be removed from the pan and thrown away. Adding this sugar back to the pan could cause crystallization.

Note: *Water is required for sugar to dissolve. The recipe above is for 35.25 oz/1000 g of sugar. If the recipe is increased to obtain a larger batch, the amount of time needed to boil the sugar to 320°F/160°C will increase. And because more time over the heat will cause the sugar to color, you must decrease the amount of water used in order to decrease the length of time the solution must boil to reach 320°F/160°C. For 35.25 oz/1000 g of sugar, add water at 40 to 50 percent of the weight of the sugar. For batches with more than 35.25 oz/1000 g of sugar, add water at 35 to 40 percent of the weight of the sugar.*

– Heat the sugar and water together, skimming impurities off the surface.
– Wash down the inside wall of the pan with water to prevent crystallization.
– Shock the pan in cold water to stop the boiling.

Isomalt for Casting

Isomalt for casting has to be boiled to a higher degree than for pulling and blowing. The cast pieces don't have to be pliable as for pulling or blowing; they must be sturdier and stronger. All ingredients, tools, and work surfaces must be ready before you start to boil the Isomalt. Water is optional, but helps to dissolve the Isomalt granules and prevent the Isomalt from burning if it is boiled on a hot gas stove or strong induction cooktop. The length of the boiling time is crucial. If the boiling time is too short, there will be too much water left in the solution and it will be weak. Pieces made with a weak Isomalt solution may bend over or collapse and will absorb moisture.

INGREDIENTS	METRIC	US	VOLUME
Isomalt, medium granulate	1000 g	35.25 oz	4½ cups
Water, cold (optional)	80 g	0.03 oz	⅓ cup
Food coloring (optional)	5–10 drops	5–10 drops	5–10 drops
YIELD	**1080 g**	**35.28 oz**	

1   Pour the cold water into a large saucepan.

2   Add a small portion of the Isomalt and mix until the mixture looks like wet sand.

3   Over medium heat, dissolve the Isomalt, stirring occasionally. Take care not to splash Isomalt onto the inside wall of the pan. Once the sides of the pan become warm, the Isomalt will stick. Isomalt does not dissolve like sugar so you will not be able to wash it off the inside wall with a brush and water. Keep the inside clean by scraping with a wet, heat-resistant spatula.

4   Once the solution starts to become clear, add more Isomalt. The water will turn milky, which indicates the presence of nondissolved granules. Continue with this process until all of the Isomalt is dissolved.

5   Once all the Isomalt has been added, boil to 340°F/170°C or higher. The end temperature needed will depend on the length of the boiling time. If it takes less than 20 minutes to dissolve all the Isomalt, you must boil the mixture to 360°F/180°C. However, if a large amount of Isomalt is boiled and the boiling time is 30 to 45 minutes, then 330°F/165°C may be high enough. If coloring the Isomalt, add the food coloring anytime during the boiling process.

6   Once the Isomalt reaches the desired temperature, plunge the pan into cold water to stop the cooking process. $\rightarrow$

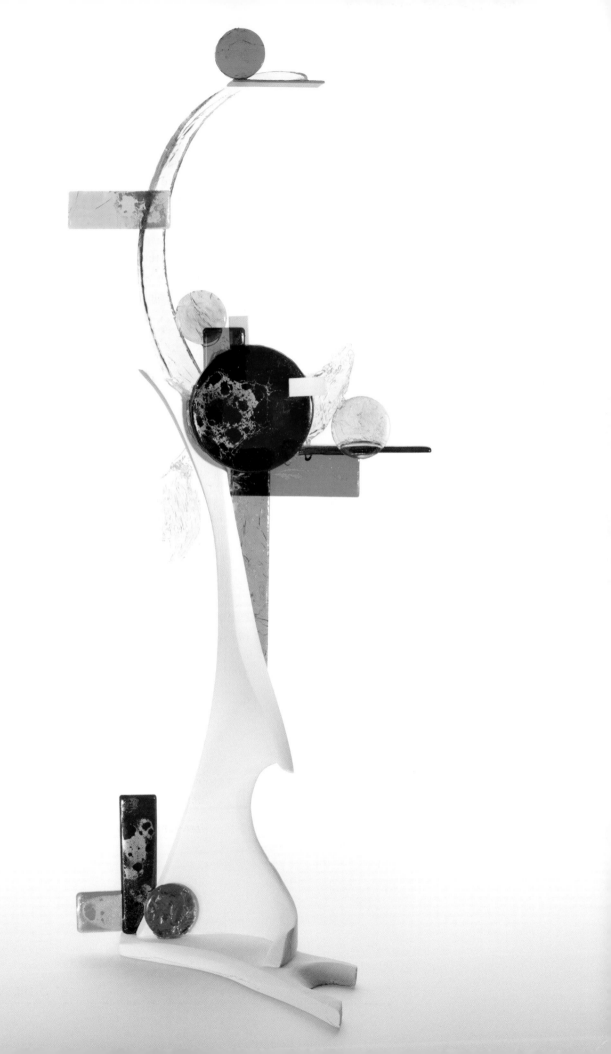

7 Rest the Isomalt in the pan on a towel for at least 10 to 15 minutes until it begins to thicken slightly. Isomalt retains heat longer than sugar so it must rest longer before it is poured into the mold.

8 Cast the Isomalt using any of the techniques on pages 79–90.

– Stir a small portion of Isomalt into the water.
– When undissolved granules are present, the Isomalt will have a milky color. Add more Isomalt when it starts to become clear.
– Let the fully boiled Isomalt rest in the pan.

Casting Techniques

All the casting techniques explained below can be executed using either the Isomalt for Casting recipe or the Sugar for Casting recipe.

Casting into Clay

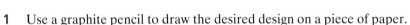

Modeling clay from a hobby store is recommended for single-use, two-dimensional designs. Clay itself can be reused many times, but for each use you will have to roll out the clay and cut out the design. It is the perfect material for an unusual piece that you may not use repeatedly.

1   Use a graphite pencil to draw the desired design on a piece of paper.

2   Prepare the clay. Roll out the clay to the desired thickness using a smooth rolling pin. The clay must be at least 1 in/2.5 cm wider and longer than your drawing. Place the clay onto an acrylic board that has been covered with a piece of parchment.

3   Place the paper drawing-side down onto the clay.

4   Rub over the drawn lines with your hands, using moderate pressure. This will transfer the drawing to the clay.

5   Remove the paper and, using an exacto knife, cut along the drawn lines. Transfer the clay mold onto a sheet of vinyl placed over a piece of parchment paper.

6   Place a piece of clean plastic wrap into the mold. Press the wrap tightly into the corners and along all the edges.

7   Prepare the Isomalt for Casting recipe (page 76).

8   Pour the Isomalt into the mold, staying away from the edges. The Isomalt should be poured so that it flows to the edges of the mold.

9   Use a blowtorch to heat the surface of the Isomalt to remove air bubbles.

10 Allow the Isomalt to cool and harden for 15 to 20 minutes.

11 Remove the modeling clay from the cast Isomalt.

12 Remove the plastic wrap. Compact the clay and store at room temperature for another use.   →

FIRST ROW:
- Place your drawing face down on the rolled-out clay and rub it to transfer the design.
- Cut the shape out along the lines and line the resulting clay mold with plastic wrap.
- Pour the Isomalt into the clay mold.

SECOND ROW:
- Torch the surface of the Isomalt to remove any air bubbles.
- Unmold the Isomalt from the clay mold.
- Remove the plastic wrap from the finished shape.

Casting into Neoprene

Neoprene is recommended for repeat-use, two-dimensional designs. It can be purchased at a pastry supply store.

1   Place the neoprene onto a cutting board. Using a graphite pencil, draw the desired design on a piece of paper, and place the drawing onto the neoprene.

2   Cut through the drawing into the neoprene using an exacto knife, or just cut through the paper and mark the neoprene, then remove the paper and cut through the neoprene.

3   Remove the cutout piece.

4   Set the neoprene mold on parchment paper or on a marble, vinyl, Teflon, or Silpat surface.

5   Prepare the Isomalt for Casting recipe (page 76).

6   Pour the Isomalt into the mold, staying away from the edges. The Isomalt should be poured so that it flows to the edges of the mold.

7   Allow the Isomalt to cool and harden for 15 to 20 minutes. To speed the cooling process, the piece can be moved to cooler parts of the worktable.

8   Pull off the neoprene from the cast piece. It should come off easily. The neoprene may stick to the cast sugar if the cut of the mold is not clean. In this case, you may apply some nonstick baking spray before casting to the cut inside edges of the neoprene. Remove the cast piece from the neoprene mold.

–   Cut through the drawing into the neoprene.
–   Remove the cutout piece of neoprene.
–   Pour the Isomalt into the neoprene mold.

Variation: Patterned Cast Pieces

1   Prepare the mold and cast as described on page 82.

2   Immediately apply gold powder to the surface.

3   Use a blowtorch to heat the surface and create a pattern.

4   Immediately drop titanium dioxide onto the surface of the Isomalt.

5   Swirl the titanium drops with a knife or other utensil.

6   Torch the titanium swirls to dry the liquid whitener.

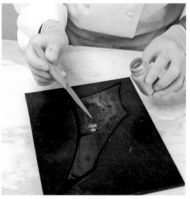

–   Apply gold powder to the surface of the Isomalt.
–   Add titanium dioxide and swirl the titanium drops.
–   Torch the titanium swirls to finish the pattern.

Variation: Bent Cast Pieces

1   Prepare the mold and cast as described on page 82. Let set, and remove the cast piece from the mold.

2   Place the cast piece on a food warmer.

3   As soon as it is warm enough to bend, place it on a form covered with either a Silpat mat or a Teflon sheet and let set until cool.

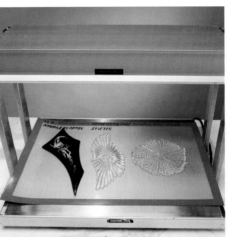

FIRST ROW:
-   Remove the cast piece from the mold.
-   Warm the Isomalt pieces on a Silpat-covered food warmer.

SECOND ROW:
-   Bend the cast pieces and place them on a form covered with a Silpat mat or a Teflon sheet.

Casting into Metal Bars

Metal bars are ideal for casting thick, simple geometric shapes often used as bases and support pieces.

1 Set up the metal bars on marble, vinyl, parchment paper, a Teflon sheet, or a Silpat mat. If the bars are clean and cold, they do not have to be oiled.

2 Prepare the Isomalt for Casting recipe (page 76).

3 Pour the Isomalt between the metal bars, staying away from the edges. The Isomalt should be poured so that it flows to the edges of the bars.

4 Allow the Isomalt to cool and harden for 15 to 20 minutes. To speed the cooling process, the piece can be moved to cooler parts of the worktable.

5 Remove the metal bars.

THE ART OF THE CONFECTIONER

Casting into Noodles with Silicone Insert Molds

Noodles are recommended for simple, rounded shapes. These can be cast thick for use as bases and support pieces.

1 Place a piece of parchment paper on your work surface. Place a piece of clear vinyl over the parchment paper. The parchment paper prevents a vacuum from forming between the vinyl and your work surface, allowing you to move the vinyl after the Isomalt is poured.

2 Arrange the noodles and silicone molds on the vinyl.

3 Prepare the Isomalt for Casting recipe (page 76).

4 Pour the Isomalt in between the noodles, staying away from the edges. The Isomalt should be poured so that it flows to the edges of each mold.

5 Allow the Isomalt to cool and harden for 20 to 30 minutes. To speed the cooling process, the piece can be moved to cooler parts of the worktable.

6 Once it has hardened, remove the noodles from the cast piece.

7 Remove the cast piece from the vinyl.

8 Remove the silicone insert molds from the cast piece.

- Arrange the noodles and silicone pieces on the vinyl.
- Pour the Isomalt into the prepared mold.
- Remove the silicone shapes from the finished piece.

Casting Spheres

Spheres can be used for support on a showpiece as well as to give the showpiece dimension. I also use spheres to support figurines and flowers. Molds for casting spheres can be made by hand, but these days it is also very practical to purchase them. If you do choose to make your own molds, you can purchase glass spheres to use as a model (see Making the Molds, page 92). When working with sugar, only silicone molds should be used.

1   Line the molds up on the worktable in the order in which you plan to cast them.

2   Prepare the Isomalt for Casting recipe (page 76). You will need to prepare two batches of Isomalt, one clear and one colored.

3   Pour the clear Isomalt into the bottom mold to fill it a little less than half full. Let set for 3 to 5 minutes.

4   Pour the colored Isomalt over the clear Isomalt in the mold.

5   Add pieces of gold leaf, if desired.

6   Lock the top mold onto the bottom mold.

7   Pour the remaining clear Isomalt into the closed mold until it is full.

8   Let set until cool and hardened, 20 to 30 minutes, depending on the size of the mold.

9   Unmold the spheres by removing the top piece of the mold.

10 If the sphere looks dull due to tiny air bubbles on the surface, use a blowtorch to melt the surface. This will make the sphere shiny.

11 If you want to add decorative surface cracks to the sphere, spray for a few seconds with cold spray. The temperature difference will cause the Isomalt to crack. If you want the cracks to be deeper, place the sphere in a freezer for 3 to 5 minutes. Then remove and apply heat briefly with a blowtorch.   →

FIRST ROW:
- Pour clear Isomalt into the bottom mold.
- Add the colored Isomalt.
- Place pieces of gold leaf on top of the Isomalt in the molds.

SECOND ROW:
- Close the mold and fill it with clear Isomalt.
- Allow to harden, then unmold the finished spheres.
- Spray with cold spray to crack the surface of the sphere.

Casting into Silicone Molds

Casting in silicone molds is more popular now than it has ever been. A high level of hand skills is not required to fabricate sugar pieces using a mold. Molds allow the user to make multiple copies of an item that will be identical to the original. Making copies from a mold takes much less time than if the copies were made manually, and making your own silicone molds allows you to create a custom design for casting.

To make a one-sided mold of a simple object is very easy. Silicone is the only material that can be used to make a mold for sugar because it can withstand the high temperature of the sugar syrup when it is poured into the mold. The object to be molded can be made of any type of material—porcelain, metal, etc. If a mold of a more complicated three-dimensional object is needed, it is best to find a company to make it. And ready-to-use molds are widely available.

To get started, you will need an acrylic base, a utility or exacto knife, marzipan modeling tools to create the design, marzipan to create the side walls around the object to be molded, and a soft silicone prepackaged mix. The silicone used must be a food-grade product if the items made with the mold will be consumed.

Making the Molds

1   Place an acrylic base on the work surface. The base must be longer and wider than the final desired size of the mold.

2   Roll out a thick layer of marzipan over the acrylic base.

3   Cut the marzipan to the shape and dimensions of the final desired piece.

4   Create a design in the marzipan with modeling tools. You will need to work in reverse. Indentations in the marzipan will create raised areas in the final piece. Raised areas in the marzipan will create indentations in the final piece.

5   Roll out an additional piece of marzipan and wrap it around the designed piece to create side walls. The height of the marzipan will dictate the thickness of the final cast piece.

6   Mix the silicone according to the package directions.

7   Pour the silicone into the cavity of the modeled marzipan.

8   Allow the silicone to set completely for 12 to 24 hours.

9   Remove the marzipan from the silicone mold and clean the mold. The mold is now ready for use.

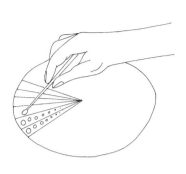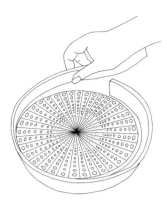

Create a design in the marzipan. Create a ring of marzipan. Pour silicone into the cavity.

Silicone casting molds and a silicone impression mold.

Casting

1 Line the silicone molds up on the table in the order in which you plan to cast them.

2 Prepare the Isomalt for Casting recipe (page 76). Let the Isomalt cool down until it appears a little thicker before casting it into the mold. This will reduce the number of air bubbles that will appear on the surface.

3 Pour the prepared Isomalt into the mold.

4 Let set until cool and hardened.

5 Pull off the mold to remove the piece from the mold.

6 Use a blowtorch to heat the surface of the piece to clear any tiny air bubbles. If the heat from the blowtorch removes fine details from the molded piece, see the Variation on page 97.

7 If desired, bend the molded piece by warming it under a food warmer and then carefully bending the shape.

8 Place onto a bent form to cool, or hold in front of a hair dryer on the cool or cold setting.

9 Airbrush the piece, if desired, while it is still slightly warm. The color will dry immediately.

– Pour the Isomalt into the mold.
– Carefully unmold the Isomalt.
– Torch the surface of the piece to remove air bubbles.

→

 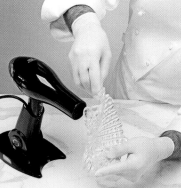 

- Hold the Isomalt under a food warmer to bend the shape.
- Hold the piece in front of a hair dryer on the cool or cold setting to set the bent shape.
- Airbrush the piece while it is still warm.

Variation: Pressing into Silicone Molds

If you are casting a mold with delicate detailing (small facial details, for example), it is recommended that you press the Isomalt into an impression mold.

Making an Impression Mold

Any type of object can be used to create an impression mold. Simple objects, like the leaf shown on page 98, work best. The silicone for an impression mold must be hard, and if the items made with the mold will be eaten, the silicone must be food-grade. When the object to be molded is flexible, plaster of Paris is used as a base to create the shape and movement in the final impression mold.

1   Place the acrylic base onto the work surface. The base must be longer and wider than the final desired size of the mold.

2   Mix the plaster of Paris according to the package instructions.

3   Place the plaster of Paris mixture onto the acrylic board and spread it out at least as long and wide as the object you are using to create the mold. The thickness it is spread to does not matter.

4   Place the object onto the plaster with the side you want the mold to reflect downward.

5   If the object is flexible, use your knife to move the plaster under the object to form the final desired shape.

6   Trim the excess plaster from around the object with a utility or paring knife.

7   Allow the plaster to dry for 1 hour.

8   Once the plaster is completely dry, use rolled-out marzipan, modeling clay, or modeling chocolate to create a rim around the sides of the plaster and the object. The rim must extend above the object by the same height that you want the mold to be—a height of about 1 in/2.5 cm is recommended.

9   Mix the silicone according to the package directions.

10 Pour the silicone into the cavity.

11 Allow the silicone to set completely for 12 to 24 hours or according to the package directions.

12 Remove the marzipan from the silicone mold and plaster. Use a paring knife to clean off the sides if necessary.

13 Remove the plaster and the object from the silicone mold. Wash or brush the surface of the silicone mold clean.

14 Apply petroleum jelly to the surface of the impression side of the mold. $\longrightarrow$

15 Place the mold impression side up and use marzipan to create a rim around the mold. The marzipan must extend above the surface of the mold by 1 in/2.5 cm.

16 Mix the silicone according to the package directions.

17 Pour the silicone into the cavity.

18 Allow the silicone to set completely for 12 to 24 hours or according to the package directions.

19 Remove the marzipan from the mold. Peel the silicone molds apart. The mold is now ready for use.

FIRST ROW:
– Spread the plaster onto an acrylic board.
– Place the object for your mold onto the wet plaster.
– Shape the plaster beneath the object.

SECOND ROW:
– Trim excess plaster from the sides.
– Create a marzipan rim around the shape.
– Pour silicone into the cavity.

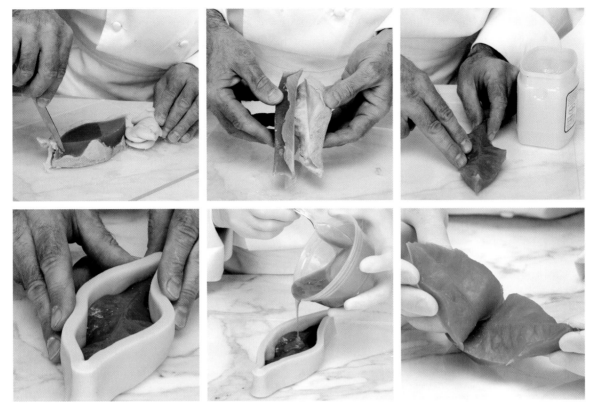

- Remove the marzipan rim.
- Release the plaster and the object from the silicone mold.
- Apply petroleum jelly to the surface of the mold.

SECOND ROW:
- Once again, create a marzipan rim around the mold.
- Pour silicone into the petroleum jelly–coated mold.
- Peel the finished molds apart.

Pressing

1 Prepare the Isomalt for Casting recipe (page 76) and pour the Isomalt onto a Silpat mat.

2 Once the Isomalt is cool enough to handle, fold it over a few times to build up height. Do not incorporate air in the folds.

3 Press the folded Isomalt firmly into the mold, removing all air pockets.

4 Let set until cool and hardened (the time will vary depending on the size of the molds), then remove the cast piece from the mold. The cast piece will not have surface air bubbles and will not need to be torched.

Casting Opaque

Opaque sugar is used to achieve contrast or create a focus point in a showpiece. To achieve the opaque effect, you have to add titanium dioxide to the boiling sugar. Years ago, the use of opaque sugar was much more common, but the trends for showpieces have changed, especially when Isomalt came on the market. If the entire showpiece is opaque, then the piece will appear too heavy, but using just a little opaque sugar can make a showpiece appear lighter and more elegant.

1   Prepare the work surface (oiled marble, vinyl, parchment paper, Teflon, or Silpat) and molds. For this example neoprene molds are used, and the work surface is marble that is covered with parchment paper.

2   Prepare the Isomalt for Casting recipe (page 76). During the boiling process, add about 4 drops of titanium dioxide to the Isomalt (1 to 2 drops titanium dioxide per 1 lb/450 g Isomalt); it will mix under completely as the mixture boils. Or, alternatively, add the titanium dioxide to the finished boiled Isomalt and stir it underneath completely to create a cloudy look.

3   Pour the Isomalt into the mold, staying away from the edges. The Isomalt should be poured so that it flows to the edges of the mold.

4   Allow the Isomalt to begin to set. If desired, paint a design onto the surface with powder color dissolved in water while the Isomalt is still warm. The water will immediately evaporate.

5   When the Isomalt is only slightly warm, remove the neoprene from around the piece. Be careful when removing the neoprene, because if the Isomalt is too warm, the surface will wrinkle. Airbrush the piece, if desired. The heat will force the color to dry immediately.

Variation: Casting Opaque and Clear Pieces Together

Opaque and clear pieces can be cast together for a unique look. In the example shown here, a neoprene cutout with three distinct sections was used to create one piece cast with opaque and clear portions. The three sections include the inner heart, the outer heart, and the main support piece. The outer heart is cast opaque, while the inner heart and main support are cast clear. To use a multi-component mold, cast and decorate the opaque piece and then replace the neoprene around the casting. Remove the neoprene pieces for the additional components and cast with clear Isomalt. Let set until cool and hardened.

FIRST ROW:
- Add titanium dioxide to the prepared Isomalt.
- Pour the opaque Isomalt into the mold.
- To add a design, paint the Isomalt while it is still warm.

SECOND ROW:
- Remove the piece from the mold and airbrush it while still warm.
- For a different look, cast the support pieces using clear Isomalt.
- Use boiled Isomalt to assemble the finished pieces.

Assembling Cast Sugar Pieces

It is recommended that you create and assemble your cast showpiece in one session on the same work surface. This keeps the cast pieces at the same temperature. If the cast pieces are made and then moved to a different work surface and stored for a period of time, the new surface may be cooler and the cast pieces may become cold. If the piece is too cold, it can crack when it is dipped into the hot Isomalt for assembly. If a cast piece does become too cold, a hair dryer can be used to warm it before it is dipped.

1 Prepare the Isomalt for Casting recipe (page 76). If you plan ahead, you can boil a little extra when you prepare the Isomalt for the cast pieces and then use the extra boiled Isomalt for assembly.

2 To assemble the pieces, pour the boiled Isomalt onto a Silpat mat.

3 Dip the support piece into the Isomalt.

4 Attach the support piece to the main piece and hold it for a short time to make sure the piece adheres and stands straight. This will take a few seconds.

5 Dip the bottom of the main piece into the Isomalt.

6 Place the main piece onto the base and hold in place for a few seconds, until the Isomalt "glue" sets.

TIP

Keep the pieces to be assembled close together and close to the boiled Isomalt. When a piece is dipped you won't have to move it far to attach it to another piece. This will prevent drips on your work surface.

4
Sugar Pulling

Pulled sugar inspires thoughts of woven baskets, delicate flowers, and bright, colorful ribbons. Simple flower petals are a great introduction to sugar pulling for the beginner confectioner. Once you have mastered the basic techniques for pulling petals, you will be able to build on those skills to create a wide variety of sugar flowers, from classic roses and daffodils to lilies and orchids. Pulled ribbons and bows utilize similar hand skills, and provide a festive accent to any sugar piece.

Sugar Pulling Basics

For the beginner, it is most important to master the technique without concern about shine. Isomalt is best for beginners because it does not crystallize as easily as sugar and, therefore, is more forgiving when reused. Sugar, on the other hand, is less expensive than Isomalt and creates a better shine because sugar cools down faster than Isomalt. Early crystallization is a constant concern when pulling sugar, and is most often caused by mishandling. Contaminants from tools, surfaces, and hands can get worked into the Isomalt and force crystallization. To prevent this, make sure all work surfaces and tools are clean, wear gloves, and warm only the amount of Isomalt you immediately need. Take care when warming the Isomalt, as very intense heating can cause crystallization. Placing the Isomalt in the microwave or under a heating lamp for too long will also cause it to melt. The Isomalt must then be cooled by pulling and turning it on marble. Be cautious, as the Isomalt can become overworked and crystals will form. When overworked, the Isomalt will first turn opaque in appearance, then will stiffen in consistency; and granulates will visually appear, the whole piece will set up like a rock and crumble. Overworked sugar will appear opaque in color, and granulates will visually appear and continue to grow until the whole mass sets up like a rock. Due to the high probability of crystallization in used sugar, new sugar should not be mixed with old sugar while pulling and blowing. When you are done with the Isomalt, immediately cool it on your work surface and place it in a storage container.

Once the technique has been mastered, then your focus can move to shine. Shine is obtained by working the Isomalt at as cold a temperature as possible, and is dependent on the length of time it takes for the Isomalt to cool. When the Isomalt is boiled, the initial time taken to cool the Isomalt must be short. As Isomalt retains heat longer than sugar, it is more difficult to obtain and retain the shine when using it. Take care when reheating the Isomalt, because the shine can be lost by over-warming it. The more practice you get and the more hand skills you learn, the colder the Isomalt you can work with, as you will not need as much time to achieve the desired shape for petals, ribbons, and so on.

Sugar for Pulling and Blowing

There are three different sugar recipes below for pulling and blowing, plus a recipe for Isomalt on page 110. I have worked and given demonstrations in many different pastry shops, hotels, and schools both nationally and internationally, and have found that sometimes glucose is available in liquid form or in powder form, and sometimes it is not available at all. To be comfortable in any situation, I have included recipes for all three options below.

Sugar Recipe I for Pulling and Blowing

INGREDIENTS	METRIC	US	VOLUME
Sugar	1000 g	35.25 oz	4⅔ cups
Water, cold	400 g	14 oz	1¾ cups
Glucose syrup	200 g	7.05 oz	¾ cup
Tartaric acid	10 drops	10 drops	10 drops
Water-dissolved powder color (optional)			
YIELD	**1600 g**	**56.3 oz**	

Sugar Recipe II for Pulling and Blowing

INGREDIENTS	METRIC	US	VOLUME
Sugar	1000 g	35.25 oz	4⅔ cups
Water, cold	400 g	14 oz	1¾ cups
Cream of tartar	2.5 g	0.08 oz	½ tsp
Water-dissolved powder color (optional)			
YIELD	**1402.5 g**	**49.33 oz**	

Sugar Recipe III for Pulling and Blowing

INGREDIENTS	METRIC	US	VOLUME
Sugar	1000 g	35.25 oz	4⅔ cups
Glucose powder	160 g	5.64 oz	1 cup
Water	440 g	15.52 oz	2 cups
Tartaric acid	10 drops	10 drops	10 drops
YIELD	**1600 g**	**56.41 oz**	

1   Place a Silpat mat on a marble or granite work surface.

2   Combine the sugar and cold water in a medium saucepan over low heat. If using Recipe II, add the cream of tartar to the sugar and mix well before adding the water. If using Recipe III, add the glucose powder to the sugar and mix well before adding the water. This will prevent the cream of tartar or glucose powder from lumping up with the water.

3   Slowly bring the mixture to a boil over low heat. As the mixture heats, impurities will rise to the surface. Use a fine-mesh strainer to skim the impurities off of the surface.

4   For Recipe I, when the sugar begins to boil, add the glucose syrup and tartaric acid.

5   Dissolve water-soluble powder color in water and add to sugar, if using color. If making a batch for practice use, color is not necessary.

6   Boil the sugar to 320°F/160°C. This should not take less than 20 minutes. If the sugar is boiled too rapidly, there may be sugar crystals left in the syrup.

7   Pour the syrup onto the Silpat mat.

8   The syrup will cool first on the outside edges. As you see the edges cool, use your fingertips to push and fold the outside edges toward the center of the pool.

9   Continue to push and fold the edges toward the center until all of the sugar has been incorporated.

10   Knead the sugar. Pick up one edge of the sugar, fold it in half, and set it down on a cool spot on the Silpat. At this point, when it is folded, the sugar is still warm enough to fall in on itself. Repeat this step, moving the sugar to cooler areas of the Silpat, until the sugar holds its shape.

11   Start pulling and twisting the sugar. Hold one end against the Silpat while pulling the other end to stretch it.   →

−   Add the glucose syrup and tartaric acid to the boiling syrup.
−   To color the syrup, add water to water-soluble powder color and dissolve before adding to the syrup.
−   Pour the syrup onto the Silpat.

12 Twist it twice and fold it in half. Press the ends together. Repeat this step until the sugar develops lighter stripes and a silky sheen.

13 Pull the sugar flat. Pull it and fold it in half three times without twisting. Use cool scissors to cut the sugar into pieces. Push the sharp corners down to prevent them from cutting the storage bag.

14 Place the pieces in a storage container or bag with a small container of a hygroscopic drying agent, like limestone. Make sure the container or bag is kept closed. The drying agent will prevent the sugar from absorbing humidity.

15 To prepare the sugar for use, remove it from the storage container and place it on a food warmer or under an infrared lamp until warm enough to work.

Isomalt for Pulling and Blowing

Because Isomalt is less hygroscopic than sugar, it is easier to work with in humid areas, where sugar would be very sticky and difficult to work with.

INGREDIENTS	METRIC	US	VOLUME
Isomalt	1000 g	35.25 oz	4⅔ cups
Water, cold	100 g	3.5 oz	½ cup
Water-dissolved powder color (optional)			
YIELD	**1100 g**	**38.75 oz**	

1 Place a Silpat mat on a marble or granite work surface.

2 Pour the cold water into a medium saucepan set over medium heat.

3 Add a small amount of the Isomalt. Using a heat-resistant spatula, stir occasionally until the Isomalt dissolves. Repeat this step until all of the Isomalt is dissolved. Take care not to splash Isomalt onto the inside wall of the pan. Once the sides of the pan become warm, the Isomalt will stick. It does not dissolve like sugar, and cannot be washed off the inside wall with a brush and water. Keep the inside wall clean by scraping it down with a wet, heat-resistant spatula.

4 Dissolve water-soluble powder color in water and add to the Isomalt, if using color. If making a batch for practice use, color is not necessary.

5 Boil the syrup to 330°F/165°C minimum, 340°F/171°C maximum. The end temperature needed will depend on the length of the boiling time. Isomalt needs →

to be boiled for at least 20 minutes to make sure all the granules are dissolved. If you are boiling over very high heat, the boiling time will be shorter and therefore the end temperature must be higher. Otherwise too little water will evaporate, so the Isomalt may not be strong enough and the pulled pieces may not hold up. If boiling over lower heat, the boiling time will be longer, so the end temperature can be lower. Be careful not to boil the Isomalt for too long or to too high a temperature, as this will cause too much water to evaporate. The more water contained in the finished Isomalt, the more elastic it will be. If there is not enough water present, the finished Isomalt will be brittle and difficult to work with.

6   Pour the Isomalt onto the Silpat mat.

7   The Isomalt will cool first on the outside edges. As you see the edges cool, use your fingertips to push and fold the outside edges toward the center of the pool.

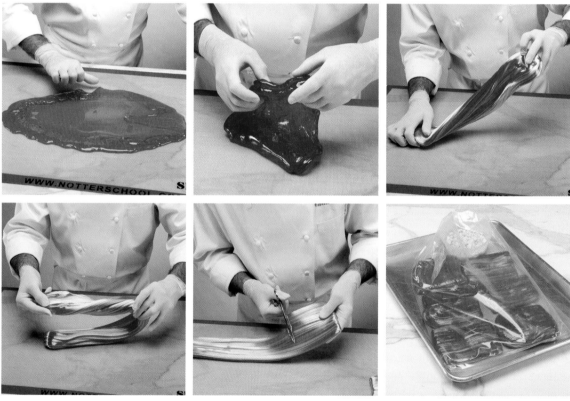

FIRST ROW:
- Pour the Isomalt onto the Silpat and fold the outside edges in toward the center.
- Pick up one edge of the Isomalt and fold it in half.
- Pull and twist the Isomalt.

SECOND ROW:
- Twist the Isomalt twice and fold it in half.
- Cut the Isomalt into pieces for storage.
- Place a hygroscopic drying agent in the storage bag with the Isomalt pieces.

8 Continue to push and fold the edges toward the center until all of the Isomalt has been incorporated.

9 Knead the Isomalt. Pick up one edge of the Isomalt, fold it in half, and set it down on a cool spot on the Silpat. At this point, when it is folded, the Isomalt is still warm enough to fall in on itself. Repeat this step, moving the Isomalt to cooler areas of the Silpat, until the Isomalt holds it shape.

10 Start pulling and twisting the Isomalt. Hold one end against the Silpat while pulling the other end to stretch it.

11 Twist it twice and fold it in half. Press the ends together. Repeat this step until the Isomalt develops lighter stripes and a silky sheen.

12 Pull the Isomalt flat. Pull and fold it in half three times without twisting. Use cool scissors to cut the Isomalt into pieces. Push the sharp corners down to prevent them from cutting the storage bag.

13 Place the pieces in a storage container or bag with a small container of a hygroscopic drying agent, like limestone. Make sure the container or bag is kept closed. The drying agent will prevent the Isomalt from absorbing humidity.

14 To prepare the Isomalt for use, remove it from the storage container and place it on a food warmer or under an infrared lamp until warm enough to work.

Pulling Techniques

Preparing for Pulling

All of the techniques that follow can be completed using either Isomalt or sugar. All necessary tools must be in place before you begin working. Remove the Isomalt or sugar from the storage container and place it on a food warmer or under an infrared heating lamp. Warm only those pieces that you will immediately use. The Isomalt must be warm enough to pull, but not so warm that it loses its shine and begins to melt. If the Isomalt melts, and two colors pool together, separate them and work any excess light color into a dark color. Do not leave part of a dark color on a light color and work them together, because the lighter color will be changed and will not match what you may have already used on your project. Pull the pieces directly under the heat lamp so the Isomalt or sugar stays warm and elastic while you are working with it.

Pulling Flowers—Hedge Rose

Because of the size and simple shape of the petals, the hedge rose is the ideal flower to begin with when learning pulling techniques.

Create the First Row of Petals

1. Prepare the Isomalt or sugar by heating it on a food warmer or under an infrared heating lamp (see Preparing for Pulling, above).

2. Work part of the Isomalt or sugar evenly upwards from the main piece using your thumb and index finger.

3. Grip each side of the upper edge between your thumbs and index fingers and pull it apart to create a thin edge.

4. Flip the Isomalt or sugar so that the thin edge is pointing toward you. In the center of the piece, place your thumb on top of the thin edge, and your curled index finger underneath the thin edge.

5. Slide and pull the Isomalt or sugar toward you to create a petal.

6. Pinch the base of the petal with the fingers of your other hand while you wiggle the petal off of the main piece.

7. With the petal still on your thumb, press the center of the petal into the palm of your other hand and twist it a few times. This will shape the petal and loosen it from your thumb.

8. Remove the finished petal from your thumb. Set the petal aside on a cool surface close to the lamp and repeat steps 2 through 8 until you have 5 petals.   →

Create the Second Row of Petals

9   Work part of the Isomalt or sugar evenly upwards and create a thin edge as you did for the first row of petals above.

10 Using the fingernails of your thumb and index finger, pinch the center of the outer edge, bringing the petal to a point.

11 Slide and pull the Isomalt or sugar toward you to create a petal, remove the petal from the main piece, and press the center of the petal into your palm to shape it as you did for the first row of petals in steps 5 through 7 above.

12 Remove the petal from your thumb. Bend the pinched end slightly backwards. This will cause the petal to bend away slightly from the petal in front of it, keeping the flower open.

13 Repeat steps 9 through 12 until you have 6 petals for the second row.

Create the Stamen

14 Use room-temperature scissors to score off a small sphere from the Isomalt or sugar and cut it away from the main piece. It is important not to warm the scissors, as this will cause the Isomalt or sugar to stick and will make it impossible to cut.

15 Sculpt the sphere into a drop shape and flatten the wide end.

16 Use cool scissors to crimp the edges of the flattened end. This will create a crown and give the stamen definition and texture.

Assembly

17 Hold the stamen upside down between the thumb and index finger of one hand. Hold a first-row petal by the outer edge in the other hand. Melt the bottom edge of the petal over an alcohol burner until the sugar starts to melt.

18 Attach the petal to the stamen just underneath the crown and hold it in place for a second.

19 Attach the remaining first-row petals using the same technique. Each petal must slightly overlap the previous petal. The last petal should overlap the previous petal and fit just in front of the first petal.

20 Melt the bottom edge of a second-row petal and attach it so that it overlaps and falls in between two petals in the first row. The petal should be angled slightly away from the first row of petals, opening the flower.

21 Attach the remaining second-row petals using the same technique. Each petal must slightly overlap the previous petal. The last petal should overlap the previous petal and fit just in front of the first petal.

22 Store the completed flower in an airtight container or plastic bag with limestone, calcium carbonate, or silica gel. $\rightarrow$

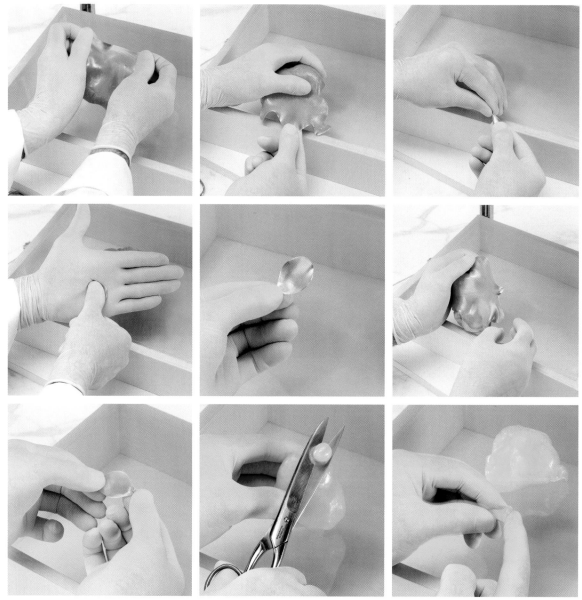

FIRST ROW:
- Pull the upper edge of the Isomalt apart to create a thin edge.
- Pull the center of the thin edge toward you to create a petal.
- Wiggle the petal to remove it from the main piece of Isomalt.

SECOND ROW:
- Press into your palm to shape the petal.
- Remove the shaped petal from your thumb.
- Pinch the center of the thin edge for the second-row petals.

THIRD ROW:
- Bend the pinched end backward slightly.
- For the stamen, cut a small sphere of Isomalt away from the main piece.
- Model a drop shape and press on the wide end to flatten it.

THE ART OF THE CONFECTIONER

FIRST ROW:

- Use scissors to shape the stamen.
- Heat the bottom of the petal before attaching it to the stamen.
- Attach the first row of petals, with each petal slightly overlapping the last.

SECOND ROW:

- The first petal of the second row should be placed in between two petals from the first row.
- Place the last petal so that it overlaps the previous petal and fits just in front of the first petal in the row.
- The finished hedge roses.

Pulling Flowers—Rose

The sugar rose is a must for every pastry chef. No other flower is more requested than the rose. The techniques are built from those used to create the hedge rose.

Create the Petals

1 Prepare the Isomalt or sugar by heating it on a food warmer or under an infrared heating lamp (see page 115).

2 Work part of the Isomalt or sugar evenly upwards from the main piece using your thumb and index finger.

3 Grip each side of the upper edge between your thumbs and index fingers and pull it apart to create a thin edge.

4 Flip the Isomalt or sugar so that the thin edge is pointing toward you. In the center of the piece, place your thumb on top of the thin edge, and your curled index finger underneath the thin edge.

5 Slide and pull the Isomalt or sugar toward you to create a medium-size petal. This will become the center bud.

6 Pinch the base of the petal with the fingers of your other hand while you wiggle the petal off of the main piece.

7 With the petal still on your thumb, press the center of the petal into the palm of your other hand and twist it a few times to shape the petal and loosen it from your thumb.

8 Roll the petal to form the center of the rose. The top should be narrower and the bottom should be wider. Do not roll the center too tightly, as the rosebud should show some volume. Set the center bud aside.

9 For the first row of petals, pull 3 long, narrow petals using your thumb and the tip of your index finger and set aside.

10 Pull 5 more rows of petals with 3 petals each. For each successive row of petals, pull petals that are slightly wider than those from the previous row. To pull a wide petal, bend your index finger and place it underneath the Isomalt or sugar with your thumb on top. Set the finished petals aside.　　　　　→

11 For the sixth row, pull 4 petals slightly wider than those for the fifth row. After the petals are removed from your thumb, curve the right side of each petal backwards slightly and set aside.

12 For the seventh row, pull 6 larger petals. Curve both sides of each petal backward and set aside.

13 If a bigger rose is desired, continue to create additional rows of petals, increasing the size and number of petals for each successive row and bending both sides of each petal backward.

Assembly

14 Take a small portion of the Isomalt or sugar and cut a short stem, using room-temperature scissors. Attach this to the bottom of the rosebud by melting one end of the stem and attaching it to the wider part of the rosebud. You will hold the rose by the stem at a downward angle as the petals are attached.

15 Hold the stem angled down toward your work surface. Melt the bottom of one of the first-row petals over an alcohol burner, attach it to the base of the rosebud, and hold it in place for a second. Keep the petal angled close to the rosebud.

16 Attach the remaining 2 first-row petals, overlapping each petal over the last.

17 Attach the second through fifth rows of petals using the same technique, keeping the rose angled down toward your work surface. These rows should be angled close to the center.

18 Add the sixth row of petals, with one edge curved back, using the same technique. With this row, the petals start to open, angling slightly away from the center.

19 Add the remaining rows using the petals with both edges curved back. Widen the angle more with each row that is added until the rose reaches the desired fullness.

20 Store the completed flower in an airtight container or plastic bag with limestone, calcium carbonate, or silica gel.

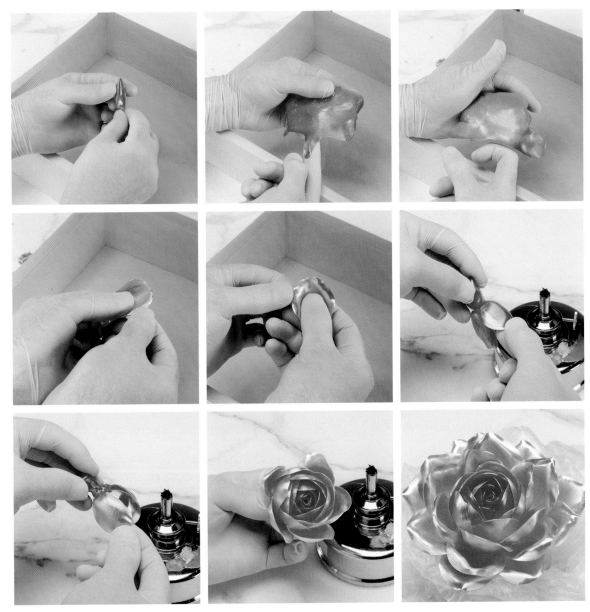

FIRST ROW:
- Create a medium-size petal and roll it to form the center of the rose.
- Pull three long, narrow petals for the first row.
- To pull a wide petal, bend your index finger and place it underneath the Isomalt with your thumb on top.

SECOND ROW:
- For the middle rows, begin to curve the petals backward slightly. Start by curving back only the right side.
- As you continue to add rows, curve both sides of each petal backward.
- Hold the rosebud angled downward and melt the bottom of each petal before attaching it to the bud.

THIRD ROW:
- Continue attaching petals in rows, keeping the flower angled down toward your work surface.
- For the outer rows, angle the petals slightly away from the center of the rose.
- Continue to add rows until the flower reaches the desired size.

Pulling Flowers—Daffodil

The daffodil is an ideal flower for Easter. A very interesting and unique technique is employed to create the bell.

Form the Bell

1 Prepare the Isomalt or sugar by heating it on a food warmer or under an infrared heating lamp (see page 115).

2 Flatten the Isomalt or sugar by pulling it a little. The Isomalt should not be flattened too thin, or the bell will become very thin when you push the wooden dowel through it.

3 Push a wooden dowel or spoon handle into the flat, pulled piece of Isomalt or sugar to create a bell shape.

4 Use room-temperature scissors to cut the excess Isomalt or sugar away from the bell shape.

5 Remove the bell from the dowel or spoon handle before the Isomalt or sugar sticks to the wood.

6 Use cool scissors to curve the open edge of the bell outwards while scoring the edge.

Create the Petals

7 Prepare another piece of Isomalt or sugar and work part of it evenly upwards from the main piece using your thumb and index finger.

8 Grip each side of the upper edge between your thumbs and index fingers and pull it apart to create a thin edge.

9 Flip the Isomalt or sugar so that the thin edge is pointing toward you. In the center of the piece, place your thumb on top of the thin edge, and your curled index finger underneath the thin edge.

10 Slide and pull the Isomalt or sugar toward you to create a medium-wide, elongated petal.

11 Pinch the base of the petal with the fingers of your other hand while you wiggle the petal off of the main piece.

12 With the petal still on your thumb, press the center of the petal into the palm of your other hand and twist it a few times. This will shape the petal and loosen it from your thumb.

13 Repeat the steps above to pull a total of 6 medium-wide, elongated petals.   →

Assembly

14 Hold the bell upside down. Melt the bottom of each petal over an alcohol burner and attach it to the bottom of the bell, slightly overlapping each petal over the last.

15 Store the completed flower in an airtight container or plastic bag with limestone, calcium carbonate, or silica gel.

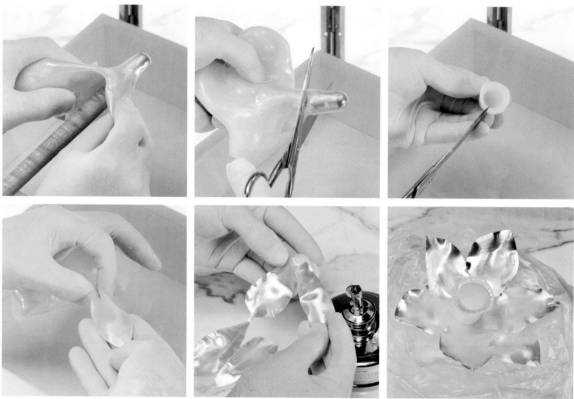

FIRST ROW:

- Push a wooden dowel into the Isomalt to create a bell shape.
- Cut away the excess Isomalt.
- Score the outer edge of the bell shape with scissors.

SECOND ROW:

- Pull an elongated petal and pinch it off the main piece.
- Melt the bottom of each petal and attach it carefully to the bottom of the bell shape.
- Each petal should slightly overlap the previous one.

Flowers—Orchid

Four colors of Isomalt are needed to create this flower. In this example, white is used for the center, yellow for the tongue, pink for the petals, and red for the petal edge.

Create the Two-Color Petals

1 Prepare the Isomalt or sugar by heating it on a food warmer or under an infrared heating lamp (see page 115).

2 To create a two-colored petal, press a thin piece of darker Isomalt or sugar onto one edge of the main piece.

3 Grip each side of the upper edge where the darker Isomalt or sugar has been attached between your thumbs and index fingers and pull it apart to create a thin edge.

4 Flip the Isomalt or sugar so that the thin edge is pointing toward you. In the center of the piece, place your thumb on top of the thin edge, and your curled index finger underneath the thin edge.

5 Slide and pull the Isomalt or sugar toward you to create a petal.

6 Elongate the petal by gently sliding and pulling the petal between your index finger and thumb. Pinch the base of the petal with the fingers of your other hand while you wiggle the petal off of the main piece.

7 Pinch the rounded end of the petal.

8 Push the ends of the petal toward each other to create waves—this is known as an accordion fold. The waves break the light, increasing the petal's shine.

9 Repeat the steps above to pull 2 more elongated two-color petals.

Create the Tongue

10 Using a contrasting-color Isomalt or sugar, repeat the steps above to pull a petal longer and wider than the two-color petals.

11 Pinch the rounded end and push the ends of the petal toward each other to create an accordion fold.   →

Create the Center and Side Petals

12 Using white Isomalt or sugar, repeat the steps above to pull another petal shorter than the two-color petals.

13 At the end where the petal was pinched off of the main piece, roll the edges toward each other. Bend the petal gently backwards.

14 Using the main color from the elongated petals, pull 2 more petals with a wider, rounded end. To create the curve, pull the right side slightly more than the left side.

15 Push the ends of each side petal toward each other to create an accordion fold.

Create the Long Stamen

16 Using the same color as you used for the tongue, gently slide and pull the Isomalt or sugar between your index finger and thumb to pull a rounded, even strip.

17 Fold the strip in half, keeping the two halves from touching one another, and pull from both ends to elongate.

18 Continue folding and pulling the strip two or three more times, keeping the folded-over sections from touching one another, to create stamens.

19 Fold the strips one last time and cut them in half at the fold using cool scissors.

20 Press together the ends that were not cut.

21 Use room-temperature scissors to cut the stamens a little shorter than the length of the white center petal and set aside.

ASSEMBLY

22 Melt the bottom of each of the 3 two-colored petals over the flame of an alcohol burner, attach them to the top of the tongue, and hold in place for a second. Leave the center petal upright. Drape the 2 outer petals along the sides of the tongue.

23 Attach the 2 curved petals to each side behind the two-color petals.

24 Attach the center white petal right into the middle of the other petals.

25 Using a fine-tipped brush, liquid food coloring, and a small amount of water, paint red dots onto the center petal. Too much water will cause the color to bleed.

26 Melt the bottom of the stamens where they are gathered together and attach the long stamen just above the center petal.

27 Store the completed flower in an airtight container or plastic bag with limestone, calcium carbonate, or silica gel.

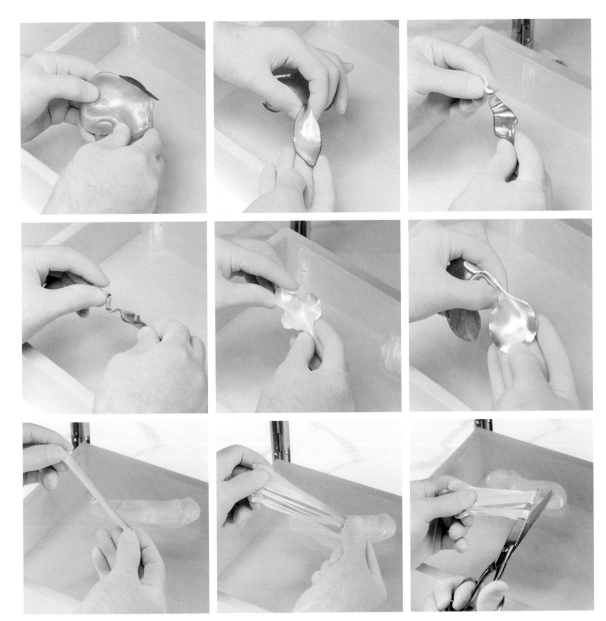

- Add a thin piece of darker Isomalt to one edge of the main piece. Pull the two-colored petal from this edge.
- Elongate and shape the petal.
- Pinch the rounded end of each two-colored petal.

SECOND ROW:
- Push the ends together to create an accordion fold.
- Use a contrasting color to create the tongue.
- Pull the side petals with wider, rounded ends.

THIRD ROW:
- Pull a rounded strip for the stamen.
- Fold the strip in half several times, without touching the halves together.
- Cut the folded strips in half with scissors.

→

FIRST ROW:
- Cut the stamens to the right length.
- Attach the three two-colored petals to the top of the tongue.
- Attach the two curved petals to each side.

SECOND ROW:
- Attach the center white petal.
- Paint very small dots onto the center petal.
- Attach the stamen above the center petal to finish the orchid.

Flowers—Blooming Flame

For the center of this flower, you will need a sphere attached to a half-sphere base. These can be created using the casting techniques on pages 88–91.

Create the First Row of Petals

1   Prepare the Isomalt or sugar by heating it on a food warmer or under an infrared heating lamp (see page 115).

2   Work part of the Isomalt or sugar evenly upwards from the main piece using your thumb and index finger.

3   Grip each side of the upper edge between your thumbs and index fingers and pull it apart to create a thin edge.

4   Flip the Isomalt or sugar so that the thin edge is pointing toward you. In the center of the piece, place your thumb on top of the thin edge, and your curled index finger underneath the thin edge.

5   Slide and pull the Isomalt or sugar toward you to pull a narrow, elongated petal into a point. Pinch the base of the petal with the fingers of your other hand while you wiggle the petal off of the main piece.

6   Pinch the rounded end and push the pointed end upwards.

7   Repeat the steps above to pull 7 more narrow, elongated petals.

8   Melt the bottom of each petal over an alcohol burner and attach it to the center sphere, leaving a gap between each petal where the sphere can be seen. Hold each petal in place for a second to attach.

Add Additional Rows of Petals

9   For the second row of petals, the color of Isomalt or sugar can be lightened. Pull 15 to 20 petals using the same technique as for the first row, making the petals slightly wider and longer.

10   Attach the second row of petals in between the petals of the first row. The ends of the petals should be angled slightly away from the sphere.

11   If desired, continue to pull additional rows of petals. For each additional row, 15 to 20 petals will be needed. The petals for each new row will need to be slightly longer than the last row.

12   Attach the third and fourth rows of petals to the sphere, gently bending each petal around the petal in front of it. Place the petals for each row in between the petals of the previous row for a staggered look.

13   Store the completed flower in an airtight container or plastic bag with limestone, calcium carbonate, or silica gel.   →

- – Pull a narrow, elongated petal into a point.
- – Pinch the wide end and push the other end upwards.
- – The center sphere should be visible between the first row of petals.

SECOND ROW:

- – Attach the second row of petals, which should be slightly wider than the first.
- – Center the petals of each new row in between the petals of the prior row.
- – A finished blooming flame flower.

Flowers—Lily

The lily has fewer petals than any other flower, and because of the pointed end of the flower, it is easy to place anywhere on a showpiece.

Create the Petals

1 Prepare the Isomalt or sugar by heating it on a food warmer or under an infrared heating lamp (see page 115).

2 Work part of the Isomalt or sugar evenly upwards from the main piece using your thumb and index finger.

3 Grip each side of the upper edge between your thumbs and index fingers and pull it apart to create a thin edge.

4 Flip the Isomalt or sugar so that the thin edge is pointing toward you. In the center of the piece, place your thumb on top of the thin edge, and your curled index finger underneath the thin edge.

5 Slide and pull the Isomalt or sugar toward you to pull a wide petal.

6 Pinch the base of the petal with the fingers of your other hand while you wiggle the petal off of the main piece.

7 Push the edges of the petal upward. Curve the petal backwards.

8 Holding the petal by each end, push the petal together slightly to create an accordion fold.

9 Repeat the steps above to pull 5 more wide petals.

Create the Long Stamen

10 Gently slide and pull a piece of Isomalt or sugar between your index finger and thumb to pull a rounded, even strip.

11 Fold the strip in half, keeping the two halves from touching one another, and pull from both ends to elongate.

12 Continue folding and pulling the strip two or three more times, keeping the folded-over sections from touching one another, to create stamens.

13 Fold the strips one last time and cut them in half at the fold using cool scissors.

14 Press together the ends that were not cut.

15 Use room-temperature scissors to cut the stamens a little shorter than the length of the petals and set aside.

Assembly

16 Warm the narrow ends of 3 petals over the flame of an alcohol burner and attach each petal to the next, keeping the bottom of the flower open.

17 Push the bottom of the flower closed by attaching the first and third petals together.

18 Melt the narrow ends of the second row of petals and attach them to the flower, placing each petal in between and behind 2 petals of the first row.

19 Melt the end of the stamens where they are gathered together and attach the stamen in the center of the flower.

20 Store the completed flower in an airtight container or plastic bag with limestone, calcium carbonate, or silica gel.

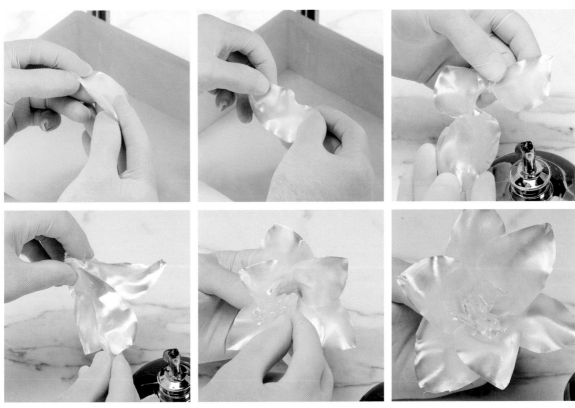

FIRST ROW:
-   Shape each petal by pushing the side edges upward and curving the petal back.
-   Push the ends together to create an accordion fold.
-   Attach the first three petals together, keeping the bottom of the flower open.

SECOND ROW:
-   Add the last three petals in a second row, placing them in between the first three.
-   Attach the stamen in the center of the flower.
-   The finished lily.

Making a Ribbon

Ribbons can be made of one or multiple colors. In this example, the primary color is red, with a yellow accent line and a green border.

1 Prepare the Isomalt or sugar by heating it on a food warmer or under an infrared heating lamp (see page 115).

2 Pull a short, round length of Isomalt or sugar by sliding and pulling an even, rounded piece between your index finger and thumb, and cut it with room-temperature scissors.

3 Pull a second round length of Isomalt or sugar, and leave it attached to the main piece. Place it next to the first cut piece and press the 2 pieces together side by side to form a wider strip. Cut to match the length of the first piece.

4 Repeat step 3 until you have 6 pieces of Isomalt or sugar pressed together, changing the color of the Isomalt, if desired. In this example, a green border is on one outside edge, followed by three lengths of red, one length of yellow, and a final length of red.

5 Stretch the piece to a length of approximately 12 in/30 cm and fold it to bring one of the long edges together. In this case the red edge is folded to the inside, with the green border color kept to the outside. Firmly press the inside edges together and flatten the upturned end.

6 Stretch and fold the strip two more times. With the last stretch and fold, press the inside edges together and leave the center fold upturned.

7 Cut the fold with room-temperature scissors and press the ribbon flat.

8 Holding one edge of the ribbon, pull the Isomalt or sugar to the final desired length.

9 Place the ribbon on the cutting surface. Using a blowtorch, heat the edge of a bench scraper, an old knife, or a putty knife and use the hot edge to cut the ribbon into pieces.

10 To shape the pieces of ribbon, warm each piece briefly under a heating lamp and shape as desired.

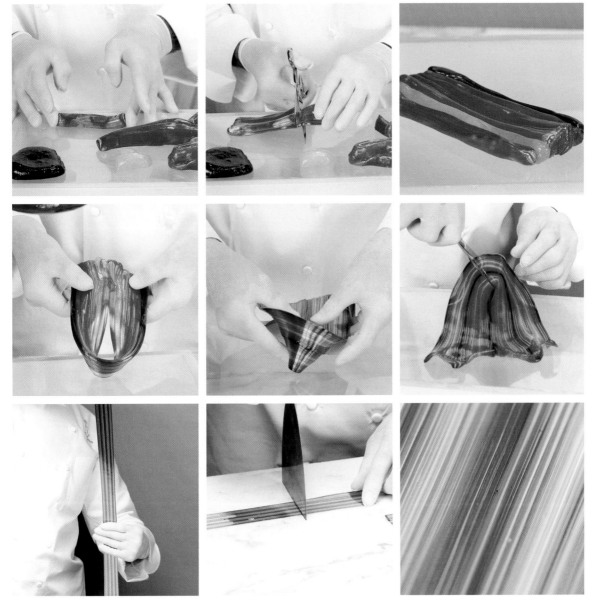

FIRST ROW:
- Cut a short, round length of Isomalt off of the main piece.
- Pull a second strip, place it next to the first, and cut to the same length.
- Continue to pull and cut additional pieces of Isomalt to create a wide, multicolored piece.

SECOND ROW:
- Stretch and fold the piece in half, pressing the inside edges together.
- With the last fold, press the inside edges together and leave the center fold upturned.
- Cut the fold and press the cut ends of the ribbon flat.

THIRD ROW:
- Pull the ribbon to the final length.
- Cut the ribbon into pieces with a heated bench scraper or knife.
- Use multiple colors of Isomalt for a striped ribbon.

Making a Two-Sided Ribbon

This technique creates a ribbon with two distinct sides. In this example, one side is striped and the opposite side is silver. The silver color can be achieved using white Isomalt or sugar, which takes on a shiny, silvery look after pulling.

1 Prepare the Isomalt or sugar by heating it on a food warmer or under an infrared heating lamp (see page 115).

2 Pull a short, round length of Isomalt or sugar by sliding and pulling an even, rounded piece between your index finger and thumb, and cut it with room-temperature scissors.

3 Pull a second round length of Isomalt or sugar, using a different color if desired, and leave it attached to the main piece. Place it next to the first cut piece and press the 2 pieces together side by side to make a wider strip. Cut to match the length of the first piece.

4 Repeat step 3 until you have 6 pieces pressed together.

5 Repeat steps 1 through 4 to create the same number of strips out of white Isomalt or sugar and press them together.

6 Place the block of white strips on top of the block of colored strips and press them firmly together.

7 Stretch the piece to a length of approximately 12 in/30 cm and fold it to bring one of the long edges together. Firmly press the inside edges together and flatten the upturned end.

8 Stretch and fold the strip two more times. With the last stretch and fold, press the inside edges together and leave the center fold upturned.

9 Cut the fold with room-temperature scissors and press the ribbon flat.

10 Holding one edge of the ribbon, pull the Isomalt or sugar to the final desired length.

11 Place the ribbon on the cutting surface. Using a blowtorch, heat the edge of a bench scraper, an old knife, or a putty knife and use the hot edge to cut the ribbon into pieces.

12 To shape the pieces of ribbon, warm each piece briefly under a heating lamp and shape as desired.

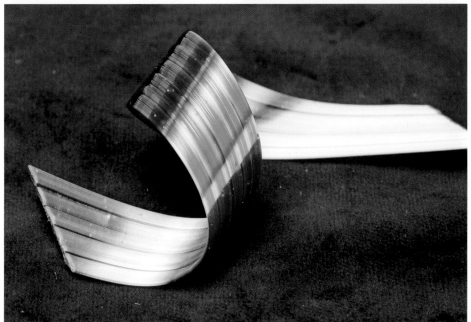

FIRST ROW:
- Press two contrasting colors of sugar or Isomalt firmly together to create a two-sided ribbon.
- Stretch and fold the ribbon three times.

SECOND ROW:
- The finished ribbon will be striped on one side and silver on the other.

Making a Bow

As important as it is to be able to create a flower, it is equally important to be able to pull a ribbon or a bow. A bow always makes a showpiece very festive. You can make a bow with a single- or double-sided ribbon.

1   Make a ribbon and cut 6 long pieces, 4 medium pieces, and 1 short piece (see pages 138–141). The longer the pieces, the larger the finished bow will be.

2   Briefly warm 1 of the long pieces under a heat lamp. Wrap the piece around a tube or dowel and hold it, pressing the ends together, until cool. Slide the bow loop off the dowel and set aside. Repeat with all the remaining ribbon pieces.

3   Melt the bottom edge of each long piece over an alcohol burner and attach them in a circle.

4   Melt the bottom edge of each medium piece and attach them to the center of the base ring, in between the first ring of bow loops.

5   Melt the inside edge of the short piece and attach it to the center of the second ring to complete the bow.

6   Store the completed bow in an airtight container or plastic bag with limestone, calcium carbonate, or silica gel to keep it dry.   →

FIRST ROW:

- Form bow loops by holding the ribbon pieces around a tube until cool.
- Attach the largest six loops together to form a circle.
- Melt the bottom of each medium-size loop and attach.

SECOND ROW:

- Place the medium-size pieces staggered on top of the first ring of loops.
- Attach the shortest loop in the center of the bow.
- The completed bow.

Making a Basket

To make a woven basket with a handle, you will need shaped wire for the basket handle, four pieces of wire for the basket handle supports, and a basket form, which you can purchase at a pastry supply store. You can fill the basket with blown fruit, as shown here, with blown eggs for Easter, or with spun sugar, or fill it with paper and then add a layer of chocolates or other confections.

Weave the Basket

1 Prepare a large piece of Isomalt or sugar for pulling by heating it on a food warmer or under an infrared heating lamp (see page 115).

2 Begin to pull a "rope" by gently sliding and pulling an even, rounded, strong piece off the main piece of Isomalt or sugar, leaving it attached to the main piece.

3 Twist the end of the rope around 1 of the support pieces to attach the rope to the bottom of the basket form support.

4 Elongate the rope, still attached to the main piece of Isomalt or sugar, and weave it back and forth between the supports.

5 Continue pulling the rope and weaving between the supports, pressing the rope down into place as you weave. It is important to keep the rope even in diameter as you continue to pull it from the main piece.

6 When the basket is complete, cut the rope with room-temperature scissors and hide the cut end inside of the basket.

7 Pull a piece of Isomalt or sugar the same height as the basket and approximately ¼ in/5 mm wide. This will be used as an interior support for the basket. Press this piece against the inside of the basket.

8 Pull 3 more interior support pieces and attach them, spacing them evenly along the interior of the basket.

9 Let the basket cool completely, then carefully remove each of the metal basket form supports.

10 Pull a long rope and remove it using room-temperature scissors from the main piece of Isomalt or sugar. Fold the rope in half and twist it together.

11 Turn the basket upside down and attach the twisted rope to the bottom edge of the basket. Warm the rope at approximately 2-in/5-cm intervals using an alcohol burner, then gently press to the bottom edge to attach.

12 Turn the basket right side up. Pull thin strips of Isomalt or sugar slightly shorter than the height of the basket and thin enough to replace the wire supports from the basket form. Insert one strip into each of the openings left by the metal basket form supports.
$\rightarrow$

13 Form another twisted rope using the same technique as in step 10 above, and attach it to the top rim of the basket. Warm the rope at approximately 2-in/5-cm intervals using an alcohol burner, then gently press to the top rim to attach.

Create the Basket Handle

14 Pull a thin rope of Isomalt or sugar, leaving it attached to the main piece.

15 Attach the rope to one end of 1 of the 4 basket handle support wires. Roll the Isomalt or sugar around the wire, continuing to pull from the main piece as you go, and evenly cover it from end to end. Cut with room-temperature scissors when you reach the end of the wire.

16 Repeat the steps above to cover the remaining 3 handle support wires.

17 Pull another rope of Isomalt or sugar, attach it to the basket handle wire, and roll the Isomalt or sugar around it, evenly covering it from end to end. Cut with room-temperature scissors when you reach the end of the wire.

18 Attach a small piece of Isomalt or sugar along the outside of each end of the basket handle.

19 Warm the small pieces of Isomalt or sugar over the flame of an alcohol burner and immediately attach the handle to the basket by adhering the small pieces of Isomalt or sugar at the ends of the basket handle to the inside of the basket.

20 Attach small pieces of Isomalt or sugar to both ends of each basket handle support.

21 Warm the small pieces of Isomalt or sugar over the flame of an alcohol burner and attach the handle supports to the basket and handle. Attach 2 of the supports to each side of the basket, placing the top ends of the supports together on either side of the handle and the bottom ends on the basket rim to create a triangle support.

22 Pull 8 thin pieces of Isomalt or sugar and cover each of the attachment points.

Fill the Basket

23 If items are to be placed in the basket and the basket is too deep, the cavity can be partially filled with a blown sphere (see Blowing a Basic Sphere, page 158). Begin to blow the sphere outside the basket, and when it nears the appropriate size, place the sphere into the basket and finish blowing it until it reaches the desired size, then remove the sphere from the tube (see page 163).

24 Cool the sphere using a handheld hair dryer on the cool or cold setting.

25 Once the sphere is completely cool, fill the basket with the desired items. In this example, blown fruit is used (to create blown fruit shapes, see pages 183–189).

Finish the Basket

26 To decorate the basket handle, create 2 long pieces of pulled ribbon (see pages 138–141) and 1 bow (see Making a Bow, page 143). →

FIRST ROW:
- From back to front: a basket form, wire for the basket handle supports, and shaped wire for the basket handle.
- Attach the rope to the bottom of a basket form support and begin to weave.
- Press the rope down into place as you weave between the supports.

SECOND ROW:
- It is important to keep the entire rope even in diameter as you pull.
- Hide the cut end of the rope inside the basket.
- Press the interior support pieces against the inside of the basket to attach.

THIRD ROW:
- Remove the metal basket form supports from the cooled basket.
- Pull a long rope and fold it in half before twisting.
- Attach the rope to the bottom edge of the basket.

FIRST ROW:
- Pull Isomalt strips and insert them into the openings left by the basket form supports.
- Attach another twisted rope to the top rim of the basket.
- Evenly cover the basket handle and basket handle support wires with Isomalt rope.

SECOND ROW:
- Attach a small piece of Isomalt to each end of the basket handle.
- Warm the small pieces of Isomalt over a flame.
- Attach the handle to the inside of the basket.

THIRD ROW:
- Attach the handle supports to the handle and basket rim.
- Cover each attachment point with a thin piece of Isomalt.
- Finish blowing the sphere inside the basket.

27 Melt the end of the first piece of ribbon over the flame of an alcohol burner and attach it to the basket handle at the place where you will want to attach the bow.

28 Drape and wrap the ribbon around the handle, continuing until you reach the basket rim. The support pieces can be partially hidden under the ribbon.

29 Repeat with the second ribbon on the other side of the handle, starting where the first ribbon was attached.

30 Attach a small piece of Isomalt or sugar to the bottom of the bow. Melt this piece over the flame of an alcohol burner and attach the bow to the handle at the point where the two ribbons meet.

31 If desired, attach additional ribbon pieces by melting the ends and attaching them beneath the bow.

FIRST ROW:
- Place blown fruits on top of the sphere to fill the basket.
- Attach the ribbon to the part of the handle where you want to place the bow, and drape the ribbon around the handle.
- Wrap the ribbon around both sides of the handle all the way down to the basket rim.

SECOND ROW:
- Attach the bow over the point where the two ribbons meet.
- Attach additional ribbon curls below the bow.
- A completed fruit basket.

5

Sugar Blowing

It is a prerequisite that you become proficient in the chapter 4 techniques of pulling petals and ribbons before you begin chapter 5.

Think back to the objects created with the pulling technique in chapter 4: petals, stamens, ribbons, and rope. The pulled objects have to be assembled to create a three-dimensional piece such as a flower, bow, or basket. When Isomalt or sugar is blown, however, the object created is already a three-dimensional piece, like the sphere. Pulling techniques can then be applied to the blown object to change the basic sphere into other shapes, like a teardrop and an oblong shape.

The blowing technique is used to create larger objects. The air supports the walls of the larger object, allowing you to obtain the desired shape without the piece disfiguring. Smaller items such as arms and legs can be modeled from a cut piece of Isomalt and do not have to be blown.

Sugar Blowing Basics

It can be difficult to determine when the Isomalt or sugar is at the right temperature and consistency to be placed on the tube for blowing. If the Isomalt or sugar is too warm, it will lose its shine and will not hold its shape when air is added. Uneven temperature within the Isomalt or sugar will cause warmer areas to stretch more than cooler areas as the air is added. This will cause disfigurement, and holes will break the Isomalt where it becomes too thin as it is overstretched. If the Isomalt or sugar is too cool, it will not stretch when air is added and will shatter when you try to shape it. When you first begin to blow Isomalt, you will need to work with warmer Isomalt, because it takes more time for the beginner to model the Isomalt into the final shape. The final piece will not have as much shine because it was fairly warm when you started the piece. As you practice and develop faster hand skills, you will be able to work with Isomalt that is cooler. This will lend more shine to the final piece.

One rule to remember: The simpler the design, the cooler the Isomalt or sugar can be when it is put on the tube. When making a more complex figure, it is easier to make it in multiple pieces and attach them than to make it all from one piece of Isomalt.

Be mindful that this technique is more about modeling than about adding air. There are four basic steps to commit to memory. First, before you add air you must be sure you are holding the tube and not the Isomalt. Where the hand touches the Isomalt or sugar, it causes it to cool. If the Isomalt or sugar is being held when air is added, it will stretch irregularly. Second, hold the Isomalt or sugar at eye level. This allows you to clearly see the effect of the added air. Third, always add air in very small amounts. Fourth, use one or both hands to mold the shape. If the Isomalt or sugar begins to deflate, use your hands or a hair dryer on the cool or cold setting to cool the area just enough for the piece to hold its shape. If an area becomes too rigid, place it under a heat lamp for a short period of time until the area becomes flexible again. When room-temperature scissors are used to make cuts or indentations, the Isomalt or sugar must be warm enough to give way without shattering.

If another piece will be attached to the object you are blowing, you must consider where the other piece will be attached. The attachment point must be thick enough to handle the weight of the other piece and the heat needed to meld the two pieces together. In addition, if you have made a piece earlier in the day or week, and you want to attach another piece to it, you must rewarm the older piece. If you attach a warm piece to a cold piece, the cold piece will crack or shatter. A hair dryer on the low heat setting can be used to rewarm the older piece.

When you have finished a piece and want to lacquer it, keep in mind that the spray from the lacquer is often cold and it can cause the piece to crack. Try to keep the can at a distance from your finished piece and apply multiple light coats.

Before you begin to make the objects illustrated in this chapter, you will need to memorize all of the steps under Preparing Isomalt or Sugar for Blowing (see page 157), Blowing a Basic Sphere (see page 158), and Removing the Blown Piece

Equipment needed for blowing sugar includes, left to right: hair dryer, alcohol burner, scissors, sugar pump, wooden frame with vinyl sheet.

from the Tube (see page 163). These steps are required for all blown pieces and will not be repeated under each section.

Master the simple shapes, such as spheres and teardrops, before moving on to more complex pieces. Take the time to develop your hand skills to be able to work the Isomalt quickly into shape. This will reduce frustration when you move on to the more complex figures.

Preparing Isomalt or Sugar for Blowing

1   Prepare the Isomalt or sugar using any of the recipes for pulling and blowing on pages 108–113.

2   Assemble all the basic equipment needed for blowing. You will need a heat lamp, a pump with a one-way valve, a tube (I prefer pear or cherry wood, but copper or aluminum is also fine), cool, room-temperature scissors, an alcohol burner, denatured alcohol, and a hair dryer with a cool or cold setting.

3   If the final piece is going to be painted, white Isomalt or sugar works well. If the final piece will not be painted, then use colored Isomalt or sugar.

4   Set the Isomalt or sugar piece(s) under the heat lamp until warm enough to work. If the Isomalt or sugar loses its shine because it becomes too warm, cool it on the marble and pull it until the shine returns.

5   Under the heat lamp, the top of the Isomalt or sugar will become warmer than the bottom. Knead the Isomalt or sugar to redistribute the warmer areas among the cooler areas and even the temperature throughout the piece.

6   Hold the Isomalt or sugar with both hands, with your thumbs together on top. Apply pressure with the length of your thumbs and rotate your wrists to stretch the Isomalt or sugar outward. Push upward with your fingers as you stretch and fold the Isomalt.

7   Move your thumbs back to the starting position and repeat the movement two or three more times. The result will be a smooth, shiny surface on the top of the Isomalt or sugar.

Press down with your thumbs and push upward with your fingers to work the Isomalt into a smooth ball.

Blowing a Basic Sphere

This is the basic technique for blowing. The sphere is the starting point for most blown pieces, and can be modified to create additional shapes. Practice this shape until you have mastered it. Then move on to the teardrop shape (see Clown Head, page 164).

1   Prepare the Isomalt or sugar for blowing and form a smooth, even-temperature ball (see page 157).

2   Use room-temperature scissors to cut the ball away from the main piece.

3   Press your index finger into the bottom of the ball (where it was cut off from the main piece) to create a short hole. It is important to push your finger deep enough into the ball to ensure a consistent thickness around the sides and top of the hole. If the hole is too shallow, the Isomalt or sugar at the top of the sphere will be thicker than the sides and the sphere will not stretch evenly as air is added.

4   Quickly warm the edges of the hole over the flame of an alcohol burner. Place the Isomalt or sugar onto the edge of the tube. There must be space between the end of the tube and the end of the hole to hold the air that you will pump into the sphere.

5   Close the edges of the hole firmly against the tube to prevent air from escaping.

6   If you are right-handed, hold the Isomalt or sugar in your right hand and the pump in your left hand. If you are left-handed, hold the Isomalt or sugar in your left hand and the pump in your right hand. Squeeze to pump a small amount of air into the sphere.

7   Rotate the sphere and check to make sure that it is stretching evenly on all sides. If the temperature and thickness of the Isomalt or sugar is even throughout the sphere, it will stretch evenly. If not, the sphere will stretch more at the places where the Isomalt or sugar is warmest and thinnest. For example, if the Isomalt or sugar is cooler/thicker at the top and warmer/thinner near the tube, the sphere will stretch more at the bottom. To correct a temperature difference, cool down the warmer areas with your hand. If an area is too thin, you will have to remove the Isomalt or sugar from the tube and start over.

8   Pump another small amount of air into the sphere. Pull or push the sphere away from the tube at least ½ in/1 cm, creating enough distance to be able to cut the object away from the tube without damaging the final piece.

9   As you continue to slowly add air, use your hands to model the shape into a sphere.

10 Once the sphere has reached the desired shape and size, cool and remove the sphere from the tube (see Removing the Blown Piece from the Tube, page 163).   →

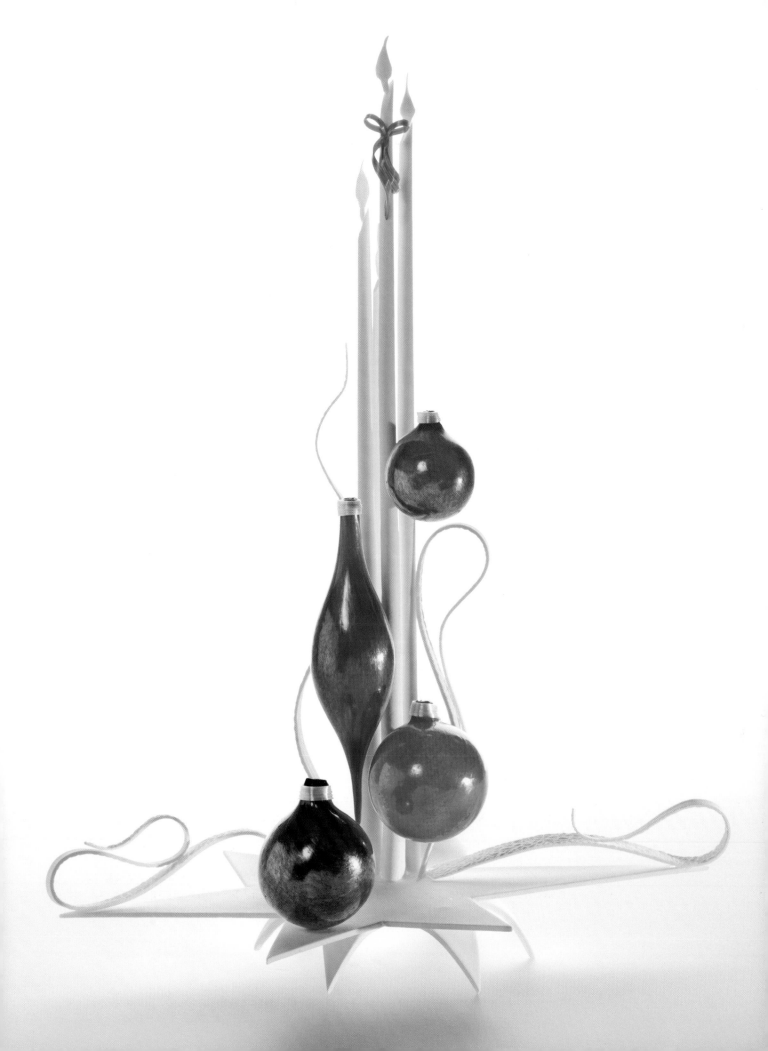

11 Close the hole either by modeling it with your hand or attaching it to a base.

12 Finished blown pieces can be stored in an airtight container or plastic bag with limestone, calcium carbonate, or silica gel.

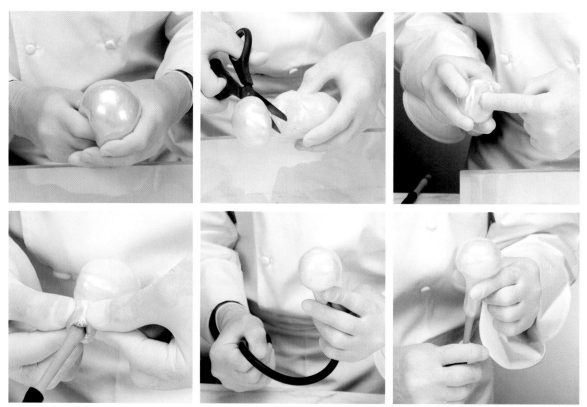

FIRST ROW:
- Prepare a smooth ball for blowing.
- Cut the ball away from the rest of the Isomalt.
- Press a hole into the bottom of the ball.

SECOND ROW:
- Place the tube into the hole and press the Isomalt firmly around the tube to seal.
- Pump a small amount of air into the ball.
- Work the ball away from the tube while pumping more air in.

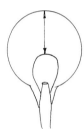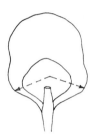

FIRST ROW:
- Use one hand to model the sphere shape.
- The finished sphere should be smooth and evenly shaped.
- After the sphere is removed from the tube, it can be attached to a base to close up the hole.

SECOND ROW:
- If the temperature and thickness of the Isomalt is even throughout, the sphere will stretch evenly.
- If the Isomalt is thinner and warmer near the tube, the sphere will stretch more at the bottom and will have an uneven shape.

Removing the Blown Piece from the Tube

1 Cool the blown piece using a fan or a hair dryer set on the cool or cold setting. Be aware of the piece as it cools, correcting any changes in its shape before it hardens. The piece must be completely cool when removed from the tube, or it will not retain its shape. You can check the coolness of the piece by lightly touching different areas to your cheek. If an area feels warm, continue to cool it.

2 Locate a point below the piece and before the Isomalt or sugar attaches to the tube. Warm this area over the flame of an alcohol burner, rotating to heat it evenly on all sides, until it becomes pliable.

3 Use room-temperature scissors to cut the piece away from the tube. Finish modeling the opening according to the instructions given for the piece you have made, for example, by modeling it with your hand or attaching it to a base.

4 Immediately clean the tube. Use the flame of an alcohol burner to warm the Isomalt or sugar that is still adhered to the tube. Catch one edge of your scissors under the warmed Isomalt or sugar and pull it off of the tube. Continue to warm and remove the Isomalt or sugar until the tube opening is clear. If the tube is wood, do not soak it in water, as this opens the pores in the wood. Instead, wipe with a damp cloth if needed. Pump the valve to make sure the air is flowing freely.

- Cool the piece with a hair dryer on the cool or cold setting.
- Heat the air channel over a flame until it becomes pliable.
- Cut the piece from the tube and close up the hole.

Blowing Shapes and Figures

The sphere is the most important blowing technique, as every piece you blow will first start out as a sphere. Taking the time to learn to do this correctly is a core competency in blowing figures of any kind.

Clown Head—Teardrop Shape

The teardrop shape is the second shape to master after you have become skilled at blowing a basic sphere. The teardrop is really just an elongated sphere, and can be used as the base for creating other blown shapes, such as the heart shape.

1   Begin to blow a sphere (see Blowing a Basic Sphere, steps 1 through 8, page 158).

2   Continue to slowly add air while using your hands to model a teardrop shape by narrowing the end nearest the tube. This narrow end of the teardrop will form the clown's hat. Allow for extra length so you will be able to cut the head and hat away from the tube.

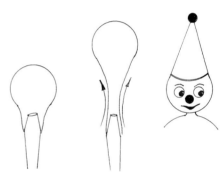

3   Cool and remove the head from the tube (see Removing the Blown Piece from the Tube, page 163), closing the open end of the hat.

4   To attach the finished head to a body or support base, warm a very small piece of Isomalt or sugar over an alcohol burner and attach it to the base of the head, then warm it again and attach it to the body or support base. It is important to use a small piece of Isomalt or sugar in between the head and the base; otherwise you would lose the shape of the head by warming it directly over an alcohol burner.

5   Paint the facial features using a fine-tipped brush and water-soluble powder color dissolved in water.

6   The hat needs a brim to separate it from the face of the clown. Pull a narrow ribbon or thin rope longer than the circumference of the hat (see Making a Ribbon, page 138). Warm the ribbon under a heat lamp until flexible, then over the flame of an alcohol burner melt one end of the ribbon and attach it to the center back of the hat. Wind the Isomalt or sugar around the hat to form the brim. Cool the ribbon or rope and break off the excess. A small piece of Isomalt or sugar can be rolled into a sphere and attached to the top of the hat, if desired.

Elephant Head

The particular technique used to create the elephant head is a little bit trickier than that used for the clown head, but can easily be mastered with some practice. What makes it different is that once you have created the sphere, you will actually need to cut into the sphere to create what will become the trunk.

1   Begin to blow a sphere (see Blowing a Basic Sphere, steps 1 through 8, page 158).

2   Continue to add air until the head reaches the desired size.

3   Use room-temperature scissors to cut into the sphere near its base to create the mouth of the elephant. Pull the cut piece outward to open the mouth slightly.

4   Continue to blow the shape to elongate the Isomalt or sugar tube below the sphere and create the trunk. There will need to be extra length between the sphere and the tube to retain the trunk of the elephant when it is cut away from the tube.

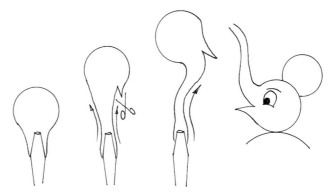

5   Use your hands to bend the trunk upward, away from the open mouth shape.

6   Cool and remove the head from the tube (see Removing the Blown Piece from the Tube, page 163), closing the open end of the trunk.

7   To attach the finished head to a body or support base, warm a very small piece of Isomalt or sugar over an alcohol burner and attach it to the base of the head, then warm it again and attach it to the body or support base. It is important to use a small piece of Isomalt or sugar in between the head and the base; otherwise you would lose the shape of the head by warming it directly over an alcohol burner.

8   Pull 2 ears using the same technique as for pulling a petal (see pages 115–119) and then attach the two ears to the head by melting the pulled-off point of the petal over an alcohol burner.

9   Paint the facial features using a fine-tipped brush and powder color dissolved in water.

10 Store the completed piece in an airtight container or plastic bag with limestone, calcium carbonate, or silica gel.

Dog Head

This technique is similar to the method for making an elephant's trunk. To make the snout of the dog, you will need to use your index finger and thumb to gently pull and slide the sphere into the correct shape.

1 Begin to blow a sphere (see Blowing a Basic Sphere, steps 1 through 8, page 158).

2 Continue to add air until the head reaches the desired size.

3 Model the nose away from the sphere by gently pulling and sliding your thumb and index finger on one side of the sphere.

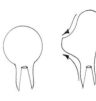 

4 Cool and remove the head from the tube (see Removing the Blown Piece from the Tube, page 163).

5 To attach the finished head to a body or support base, warm a very small piece of Isomalt or sugar over the flame of an alcohol burner and attach it to the base of the head, then warm it again and attach it to the body or support base. It is important to use a small piece of Isomalt or sugar in between the head and the base; otherwise you would lose the shape of the head by warming it directly over an alcohol burner.

6 Pull 2 ears using the same technique as for pulling a petal (see pages 115–119) and then attach the two ears to each side of the head by melting the pulled-off point of the petal over an alcohol burner.

7 Pull hair (see Female Figurine, steps 37 through 42, page 230) and warm over an alcohol burner, then attach to the head and body.

8 To model each eye, using room-temperature scissors, cut off a small ball of sugar or Isomalt and then flatten. Warm one side of the eye over the flame of an alcohol burner, then attach to the head.

9 Store the completed piece in an airtight container or plastic bag with limestone, calcium carbonate, or silica gel.

Snowman

This technique uses basic blown spheres to create the snowman's body. You can customize the snowman in many different ways for any reason or season.

Create the Body

1 Make a large sphere of white Isomalt (see Blowing a Basic Sphere, page 158). Finish step 11 by attaching the large sphere to a base.

2 Make a smaller white sphere for the head using the same technique. Finish step 11 by attaching the smaller sphere to the center top of the large sphere.

Create the Hat

3 Using room-temperature scissors, cut a small ball off of a piece of black Isomalt or sugar.

4 Roll the piece evenly between your hands to form a cylinder. Roll one end of the cylinder between your index fingers so it becomes slightly narrower than the other end. Set aside.

5 To form the brim of the top hat, pull a thick, short, wide petal (see pages 115–119). Remove the brim either by pinching or cutting it, using room-temperature scissors, away from the main piece of sugar or Isomalt. Shape it into a circle slightly wider than the narrow end of the top hat.

6 Warm the narrow end of the top hat over the flame of an alcohol burner and attach it to the brim.

7 Curve the sides of the brim upward.

8 Warm the bottom center of the top hat over the flame of an alcohol burner and attach the hat to the head of the snowman.

Finish the Snowman

9 Using room-temperature scissors, cut a small piece of orange Isomalt or sugar at an angle. Roll it between your fingers to form the snowman's nose.

10 Heat the wide end of the nose over an alcohol burner and attach the nose to the face.

11 Pull a ribbon to use as a scarf (see Making a Ribbon, page 138). Using room-temperature scissors or a heated bench scraper, cut the ribbon to a length sufficient to wrap around the snowman.

12. Warm the ribbon under a heat lamp and wrap it around the neck of the snowman.

13 Using room-temperature scissors, cut a small piece of black Isomalt or sugar. Heat one end over the flame of an alcohol burner. Touch the melted end to the snowman's face to dot on the mouth and the eyes.

→

14 Model additional decorations as desired, and attach them to the snowman. To create the holly and berries shown here, using room-temperature scissors, score the shapes lightly in a small piece of Isomalt or sugar, then once you have achieved the desired shape, using room-temperature scissors, cut the shapes off of the main piece. Warm one side of the holly and berries over the flame of an alcohol burner and attach. To create a heart shape, mold a teardrop shape, then indent the middle of the rounded end using scissors, and press the shape flat.

15 Store the completed piece in an airtight container or plastic bag with limestone, calcium carbonate, or silica gel.

FIRST ROW:
- Cut a small ball of Isomalt for the hat.
- Roll the piece into a cylinder and narrow it at one end.
- Pull a short, wide piece of Isomalt for the hat brim.

SECOND ROW:
- Warm the narrower end of the hat and attach the brim.
- Curve the sides of the hat brim upward.
- Warm the underside of the hat over a flame.

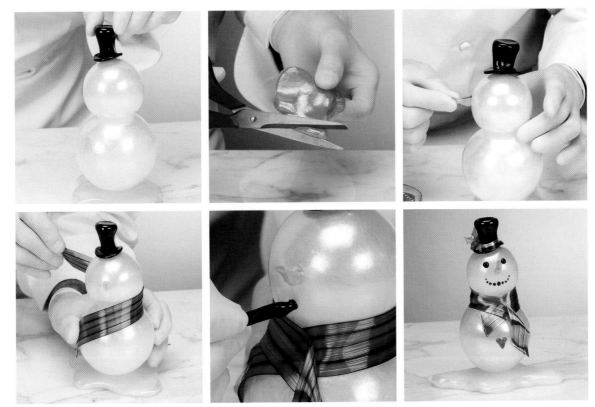

- Attach the warmed hat to the snowman's head.
- Cut the orange Isomalt at an angle for the carrot nose.
- Warm the wider end of the nose and attach it to the snowman.

SECOND ROW:
- Wrap a pulled ribbon around the snowman to create a scarf.
- Melt the end of a piece of black Isomalt and use it to dot on the snowman's mouth and eyes.
- Add a heart and a sprig of holly to finish the snowman figurine.

Swan

Swans have long necks and round heads. The neck is at a right angle to the body. The form is most elegant when the base of the neck is blown a little wider and then tapers gracefully to the head.

1   Begin to blow a sphere (see Blowing a Basic Sphere, steps 1 through 8, page 158).

2   Use your thumb and index finger to work a small ball away from the top of the sphere. This is the swan's head.

3   Pinch the top of the head to create the beak of the swan.

4   Use your thumb and index finger to pull and elongate the swan's neck, sliding your fingers over the neck evenly, keeping an oblong sphere at the base of the neck for the swan's body. Work quickly, as the sugar will cool if it is held in one place too long and will be difficult to smooth. The base of the neck should be thicker than the top.

5   Curve the base of the neck upward.

6   Grasp the beak between your thumb and index finger and bend the head toward the neck.

7   Cool and remove the swan from the tube (see Removing the Blown Piece from the Tube, page 163).

8   Use your fingers to close the open end and shape the tail.

9   Store the completed piece in an airtight container or plastic bag with limestone, calcium carbonate, or silica gel.

FIRST ROW:
- Work a small ball away from the sphere for the head.
- Pinch to form a beak.
- Use your thumb and index finger to elongate the neck.

SECOND ROW:
- Curve the neck upward from the body.
- Grasp the point of the beak between your fingers.
- Gently bend the neck into the desired shape.

THIRD ROW:
- Cool the shape and cut below the body to remove the swan from the tube.
- Use your fingers to shape the tail.
- Add additional details, like a bow or heart, to finish the swan.

Doves

The technique for creating a dove is similar to that for creating a swan, but the dove has quite a different look. Doves have small round heads with short beaks. The neck is short and the chest is full and large. The dove is a universal symbol for love, so these doves holding wedding rings are perfect for a wedding or engagement celebration.

Create the Body

1 Begin to blow a sphere (see Blowing a Basic Sphere, steps 1 through 8, page 158).

2 Use your thumb and index finger to work a small ball away from the top of the sphere. This is the dove's head.

3 Use your thumb and index finger to slightly elongate the dove's neck, leaving a large teardrop shape at the base of the neck for the dove's body. Bend the head to a 90-degree angle.

4 Use your thumb and index finger to roll the head down to touch the neck.

5 Cool and remove the dove from the tube (see Removing the Blown Piece from the Tube, page 163).

6 Pinch the open end closed and rewarm the closed end over the flame of an alcohol burner, then attach a small piece of warm Isomalt or sugar to form the tail.

7 Use your fingers to flatten and widen the tail.

8 Use room-temperature scissors to make indentations in the tail resembling feathers.

$\rightarrow$

 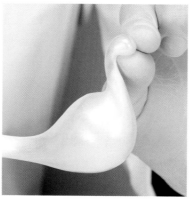 

- Work a ball away from the sphere for the head.
- Bend the head at a 90-degree angle to the neck.
- Roll the head down toward the neck.

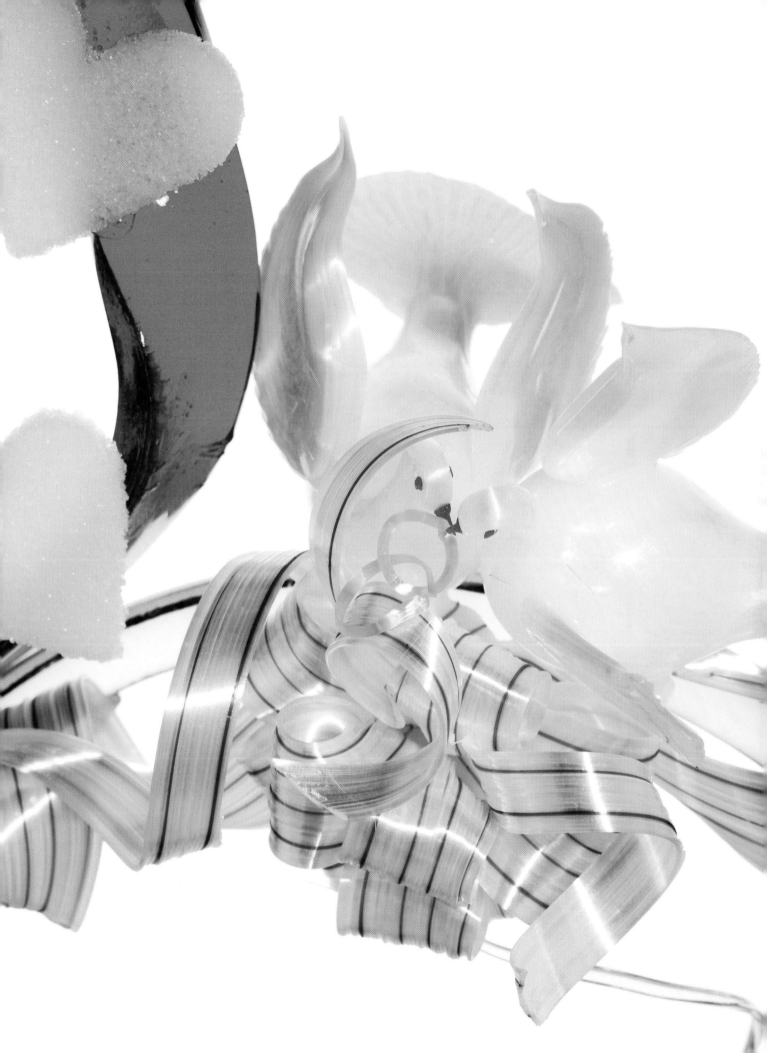

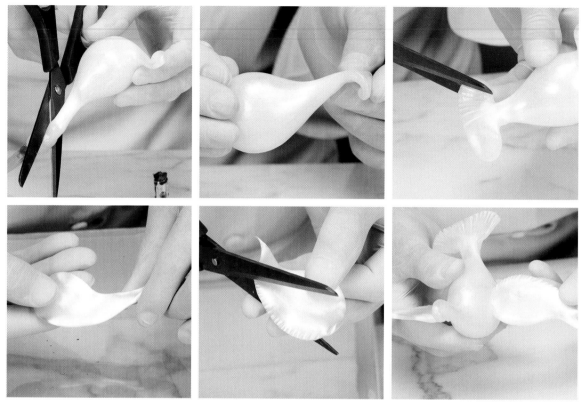

FIRST ROW:
- Cut below the body to remove the dove from the tube.
- Use your fingers to flatten and widen the tail.
- Mark indentations in the tail to resemble feathers.

SECOND ROW:
- Pull a petal with one side longer than the other to form a wing.
- Mark small indentations in the edge of the wing for feathers.
- Heat and attach both wings to the dove's body.

Create the Wings

9   Pull a wing using the same technique as for pulling petals (see pages 115–119). Pull one side longer than the other to create a curve.

10   Use scissors to make short indentations in the long edge of the wing. Set aside.

11   Pull a second wing and use scissors to mark it with feather indentations.

12   Melt the wide edge of each wing slightly over the flame of an alcohol burner.

13   Attach the wings to the dove, facing downward, then bend the wings upward.

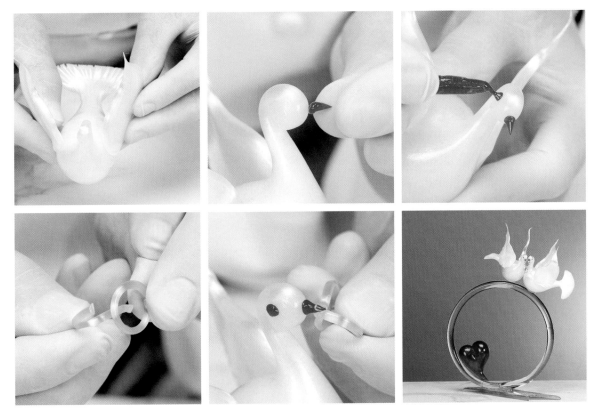

FIRST ROW:
- Fold the wings upward and set in place.
- Attach a small piece of Isomalt to the head to form the beak.
- Use a melted piece of Isomalt to dot an eye on each side of the head.

SECOND ROW:
- Link the two rings together and close the open ring.
- Immediately attach the rings to the bird's beak.
- Combine a pair of doves with a blown heart shape for a beautiful symbol of love.

Finish the Dove

14 Use room-temperature scissors to cut a small triangle from a piece of red Isomalt or sugar. Warm the triangle over the flame of an alcohol burner and attach it to the head to form the beak.

15 Cut a small piece of red Isomalt or sugar and melt one end over the flame of an alcohol burner. Use the melted end to create eyes by dotting each side of the head.

Create the Rings

16 Pull a thin, short piece of Isomalt or sugar by pulling and sliding it between your index finger and thumb. Cut it off from the main piece using room-temperature scissors, then warm both ends over the flame of an alcohol burner and bring the ends together to form a closed ring. $\rightarrow$

17 Pull another thin, short piece of Isomalt or sugar and bend it to form an open ring.

18 Place the open ring through the closed ring and join the ends of the open ring to close it and link the two rings together.

19 Using room-temperature scissors, cut a small piece of white Isomalt or sugar and melt one end over the flame of an alcohol burner.

20 Place a small amount of the melted white Isomalt or sugar on the bottom of the dove's beak.

21 Immediately attach the rings to the melted Isomalt or sugar.

22 Store the completed piece in an airtight container or plastic bag with limestone, calcium carbonate, or silica gel.

Heart

The basic teardrop shape forms the base of this heart shape, which accompanies the swan and dove in the photographs on pages 175 and 179.

1   Begin to blow a sphere (see Blowing a Basic Sphere, steps 1 through 8, page 158).

2   Continue to slowly add air while using your hands to model a teardrop shape by narrowing the end nearest the tube.

3   Use one blade of an open pair of room-temperature scissors to crease the top of the sphere, forming the top of the heart. If you add additional air to increase the size of the heart, you may have to use the scissors again to redefine the crease.

4   Elongate the end of the heart that is still attached to the tube and bend.

5   Cool and remove the heart from the tube (see Removing the Blown Piece from the Tube, page 163) and use your fingers to close the open end and bring it to a point.

6   Store the completed piece in an airtight container or plastic bag with limestone, calcium carbonate, or silica gel.

–   Blow a sphere and model it into a basic teardrop shape.
–   Crease the widest part of the teardrop with scissors to create a heart.
–   Pull and bend to elongate the pointed end of the heart.

Fruit

Most fruit can be naturally imitated in Isomalt or sugar using the basic sphere, teardrop, and elongated shapes. An easy way to model the Isomalt or sugar is to have actual fruit on hand from which to copy. Accurate application of color and shading will complete the look. Store the completed fruits in an airtight container or plastic bag with limestone, calcium carbonate, or silica gel.

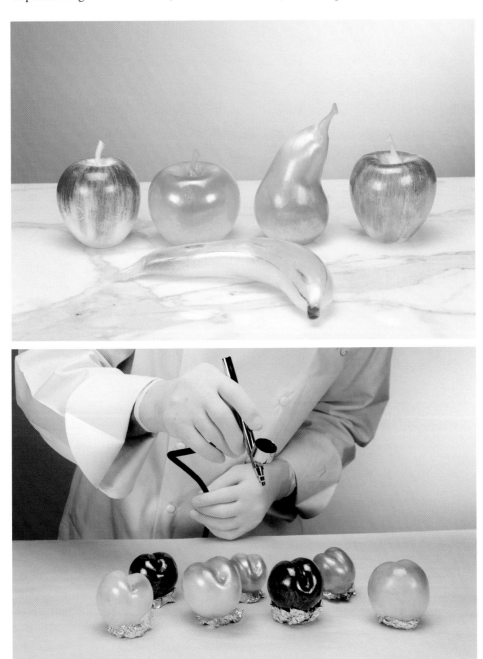

Apple

1   Using yellow Isomalt or sugar, begin to blow a sphere (see Blowing a Basic Sphere, steps 1 through 8, page 158).

2   Add more air while using your hands to form an egg shape first. Then push the whole egg shape down toward the blowing tube to get a more rounded apple shape.

3   When the apple reaches the final desired size and shape, press in the center of the bottom of the apple with one finger. You want to indent the center while leaving a ring upon which the apple will sit.

4   Pull the apple away from the tube so that there is enough additional Isomalt or sugar to form the stem. The top of the apple should appear slightly concave, leaving the shoulder of the apple raised.

5   Cool and remove the apple from the tube (see Removing the Blown Piece from the Tube, page 163), leaving enough Isomalt or sugar attached for the stem.

6   Carefully model the stem from the extra sugar.

7   Paint the apple to finish. Airbrush with green water-dissolvable powder color for a green apple, or paint red color onto the finished apple with a fairly dry brush.

  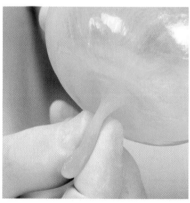

–   Use one hand to form a rounded apple shape while adding air with the other hand.
–   Press with one finger to indent the bottom of the apple.
–   Pinch to model the stem from the excess Isomalt. The top of the apple around the stem should appear slightly concave.

Pear

1   Using light green Isomalt or sugar, begin to blow a sphere (see Blowing a Basic Sphere, steps 1 through 8, page 158).

2   Continue to slowly add air while pulling to elongate the sphere into a teardrop shape by narrowing the end nearest the tube.

3   Pull the neck of the pear slightly.

4   Add additional air to expand the pear until it has reached the desired shape.

5   Cool and remove from the tube (see Removing the Blown Piece from the Tube, page 163), leaving enough Isomalt or sugar attached to form the stem.

6   Pinch and model the stem out of the extra sugar.

7   Airbrush with a light layer of yellow liquid food coloring, then airbrush over the yellow with red to darken.

 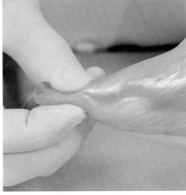 

- Twist the neck of the pear shape.
- Pinch the narrow end to form the stem.
- Airbrush yellow and then red coloring over the green sugar.

Peach

The peach, plum, apricot, and nectarine all share the same basic shape. Differences in color, size, and finish indicate the type of fruit. Plums are generally deep red or purple and shiny. Peaches, nectarines, and apricots are yellow-orange. Apricots are smaller and more oval shaped than the other fruits, and peaches and apricots are fuzzy. The fuzzy appearance can be mimicked by applying talcum powder to the shaped and airbrushed fruit.

1   Using yellow Isomalt or sugar, begin to blow a sphere (see Blowing a Basic Sphere, steps 1 through 9, page 158).

2   Use room-temperature scissors to form an indentation in the sphere running slightly off center from the top to the bottom of the fruit. The indent should be deeper at the top (the end furthest from the tube), and taper off toward the bottom where the fruit attaches to the blowing tube.

3   Cool the fruit, then carefully warm it over the flame of an alcohol burner where the fruit is attached to the blowing tube. Use room-temperature scissors to cleanly remove the fruit from the blowing tube, trying not to leave a seam (see Removing the Blown Piece from the Tube, page 163).

4   Slightly airbrush the top of the fruit with red water-dissolvable powder color.

5   To achieve the slightly fuzzy look of a peach, place the fruit in a bowl of talcum powder immediately after airbrushing. Gently scoop the talcum powder over the peach.

6   Remove the fruit from the bowl and dust off the excess powder.

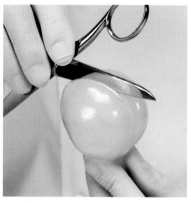  

–   Use scissors to indent the fruit.
–   Coat in talcum powder for a fuzzy look.
–   The fruit on the right was dusted with talcum powder; the fruit on the left was not.

NECTARINE: Follow the steps for creating a peach, but stop at step 4 and do not cover with talcum powder.

APRICOT: Blow a smaller and more oval-shaped fruit, and after airbrushing with red color, place the apricot in a bowl of talcum powder to cover, then remove and blow off any excess powder.

PLUM: Use purple or deep red Isomalt or sugar. Follow the steps for creating a peach, but stop at step 4 and do not cover with talcum powder. Airbrush the plum with red water-dissolvable powder color.

Banana

1   Using yellow Isomalt or sugar, begin to blow a sphere (see Blowing a Basic Sphere, steps 1 through 8, page 158).

2   Pull to elongate the sphere into the shape of a banana, continuing to add small amounts of air while you model the shape with your hands.

3   Pull the banana away from the tube to create a narrower piece that will become the banana stem.

4   Cool and remove the banana from the tube (see Removing the Blown Piece from the Tube, page 163), leaving enough excess Isomalt or sugar to form the stem.

5   Model the stem with the sugar left from removing the fruit from the blowing tube.

6   Using a fine-tipped paintbrush and black liquid food coloring, add black lines to the top of the banana.

7   Lightly airbrush the top half of the banana with green liquid food coloring.

 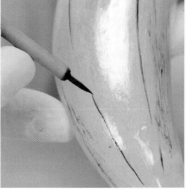 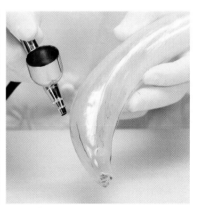

–   Add small amounts of air while shaping the Isomalt into a long banana shape with your other hand.
–   Hand paint black lines onto the banana with a fine-tipped paintbrush.
–   Lightly airbrush green coloring onto the top half of the banana.

Cluster of Grapes

Create the Support Structure

1   Using the same color Isomalt or sugar as will be used for the grapes, begin to blow a sphere (see Blowing a Basic Sphere, steps 1 through 8, page 158).

2   Continue to slowly add air while forming the sphere into a reverse teardrop shape, with the widest portion closest to the tube. Elongate the shape to just slightly shorter than the length you want the finished grape cluster to be.

3   Grasp the narrow end of the teardrop shape and push both ends gently toward each other to create an uneven S shape.

4   Cool and remove the shape from the tube (see Removing the Blown Piece from the Tube, page 163).

5   Set aside until ready to use.

Create the Individual Grapes

6   Prepare a basket weaving stand for use.

7   Cut a short piece off a drinking straw, and place it onto the tube.

8   Place a small ball of red or green Isomalt or sugar onto the end of the straw, using the same technique as for placing Isomalt or sugar on the tube to blow a sphere (see Blowing a Basic Sphere, steps 1 through 6, page 158).

9   Pump a tiny amount of air into the ball to form an individual grape.

10 Remove the straw from the tube and place it with the grape still attached onto one of the supports of the basket weaving stand.

11 Cool the grape using a fan or hair dryer on the cool or cold setting.

12 Repeat to form enough grapes to cover the support structure, cooling the grapes as you go.

Assembly

13 Using room-temperature scissors, remove each cooled grape from its straw.

14 Heat the open end of one grape over the flame of an alcohol burner.

15 Attach the grape to the support structure.

16 Continue heating and attaching grapes until the support structure resembles a complete bunch of grapes.

17 Airbrush the grapes to finish. Both red and green grapes should be airbrushed with red liquid food coloring.

- Elongate the sphere and narrow the end farthest from the tube.
- Gently push the ends together to form an uneven S shape.
- Blow a tiny sphere on the end of a straw.

SECOND ROW:
- Place the straws on the basket weaving supports and use a hair dryer on the cool or cold setting to cool the grapes.
- Heat the open end of each grape and attach it to the base.
- Airbrush red coloring onto the grapes to finish.

Penguin

The penguin figurine is very unique, because it is blown using two colors at once.

Create the Body and Head

1   Prepare black and white Isomalt or sugar for blowing (see Preparing Isomalt or Sugar for Blowing, page 157), and cut an equal-size ball from each color.

2   Press the two spheres together and roll into one half-black, half-white sphere.

3   Begin to blow a sphere with the hole for the tube centered in between the two colors of Isomalt or sugar (see Blowing a Basic Sphere, steps 1 through 8, page 158). Continue to blow air into the sphere while elongating it with your hands to form an oval shape.

4   Use your thumb and index finger to work a small ball away from the top of the sphere to form the penguin's head. The top of the head should be black and the bottom of the head should be white.

5   Form the beak by pinching the top of the head with your thumb and index finger. The top of the beak will be black and the bottom of the beak will be white.

6   Elongate the body, adding a small amount of air if needed. Lightly pinch the body in the middle to create an indent, defining the separation between the torso and the hips.

7   Cool and remove the penguin from the tube (see Removing the Blown Piece from the Tube, page 163). Warm the bottom of the penguin over the flame of an alcohol burner and press the penguin onto a base. $\longrightarrow$

-   Press the balls of white and black Isomalt together.
-   Elongate the sphere and shape it to form the head and body.
-   Pinch the top of the head to form a beak, and indent the body to shape the torso.

Create the Wings

8   Pull 2 wings from the black Isomalt or sugar using the same technique as for pulling petals (see pages 115–119). Cut the wings on an angle using room-temperature scissors to remove them from the main piece.

9   Warm the cut edge of each wing over the flame of an alcohol burner and attach 1 wing to each shoulder of the penguin at the point where the two colors meet.

Finish the Penguin

10   To create the eyes, melt one end of a small cut piece of white Isomalt or sugar and press to the black top of the head.

11   To create a scarf, pull a small, narrow ribbon (see Making a Ribbon, page 138) and drape it around the penguin's neck.

12   To create a hat, form a small sphere of Isomalt or sugar into a teardrop shape, then into a cone. Pull a small white ribbon to place around the base of the hat. Roll a small white ball of Isomalt or sugar, warm over the flame of an alcohol burner, and attach it to the top of the hat for the pom-pom.

13   Store the completed piece in an airtight container or plastic bag with limestone, calcium carbonate, or silica gel.

- Cut each wing on an angle.
- Attach the wings to the body at the point where the two colors meet.
- A hat, scarf, and other accessories can be added to finish the penguin.

Cat

The same technique can be used to create a cat or an owl; you simply differentiate the two by the way you paint the faces. The eyes are designed with molded sugar for the owl, while the cat's face is simply painted.

Create the Body

1 Begin to blow a sphere (see Blowing a Basic Sphere, steps 1 through 9, page 158).

2 Use your fingers to work the top of the sphere into an elongated shape to create the neck of the cat.

3 To mark the cat's hips and legs, use room-temperature scissors to press gently into the sides of the sphere just at the base of the elongated neck shape on the front of the body, being careful not to cut through all the way.

4 Cool and remove the body from the tube (see Removing the Blown Piece from the Tube, page 163). Warm the bottom of the cat over the flame of an alcohol burner and attach the body to a base.

Create the Head

5 Begin to blow a small sphere using the same color Isomalt or sugar as you used for the body. Pull it slightly away from the tube.

6 Flatten one side of the sphere slightly. This will become the face of the cat.

7 Create the ears by pinching a small amount of Isomalt or sugar between your thumb and index finger to form a small triangle on either side of the face.

8 Cool and, using room-temperature scissors, remove the head from the tube.

9 Warm the base of the head over the flame of an alcohol burner and attach the head to the neck. →

– Pull to elongate the neck from the sphere.
– Use scissors to make indents for the hips and legs.
– Remove the body from the tube and attach it to a base.

FIRST ROW:
- Pinch to shape ears at the top of the head.
- Warm the base of the head and attach it to the neck.
- Blow a small sphere and pull to elongate it into a tail.

SECOND ROW:
- Paint on facial features with a fine-tipped brush.
- Airbrush the ears to finish the cat's head.
- Add a bow and ribbons to finish the cat.

Create the Tail

10 Attach a very small ball of the same color Isomalt or sugar you used for the body and head to the tube.

11 Add a small amount of air to begin blowing a sphere.

12 Elongate the ball with your fingers to form a tail.

13 Cool and, using room-temperature scissors, remove the tail from the tube.

14 Warm the tail under a heat lamp until it becomes flexible. Warm the cut end of the tail over the flame of an alcohol burner and attach the cut end to the body of the cat. Bend the tail into position.

Finish the Cat

15 Using a fine-tipped paintbrush and water-dissolvable powder color, paint the facial details.

16 Airbrush liquid food coloring onto the ears.

17 Pull a length of ribbon (see Making a Ribbon, page 138). Cut a small piece of ribbon using a heated bench scraper and wrap it around the neck of the cat. Cut 2 additional small pieces and form them into loops. Warm over the flame of an alcohol burner and attach them to the front of the neck ribbon to form a bow. Cut 2 longer pieces. Warm each under a heat lamp until it is flexible. Curl each ribbon and warm one end of each ribbon over the flame of an alcohol burner, then attach beneath the loops to finish the bow.

18 Store the completed piece in an airtight container or plastic bag with limestone, calcium carbonate, or silica gel.

Variation: Owl Head

The same technique used to make the cat head can also be used to create an owl head. The head can be attached to a simple sphere shape and wings can be added to create a complete owl figurine.

1 Using white Isomalt or sugar, follow steps 5 through 9 on page 193 to create an owl head.

2 Using room-temperature scissors, cut a small piece of yellow Isomalt or sugar, mold into a beak shape with your fingers, warm over the flame of an alcohol burner, and attach to the face.

3 To create each eyebrow, pull an elongated petal (see pages 115–119) using warm brown Isomalt or sugar. Rewarm the rounded edge of the petal over the flame of an alcohol burner and pinch the rounded edge to a point. Slightly warm the pinched edge of each eyebrow over an alcohol burner and attach the eyebrows above the beak with the points extending toward the ends of the ears.

4 Pull a second pair of black eyebrows a little smaller, using the exact same technique as above. Place them on top of the bigger eyebrows to give the eyebrows a bushier, more three-dimensional look.

5 To model each eye, cut off a small yellow piece of Isomalt or sugar, using room-temperature scissors, and roll it into a small sphere, then press it flat. Warm   →

one flat side over the alcohol burner and attach it to the face underneath the eyebrows. To create the cornea, cut a smaller piece of warm white sugar or Isomalt and roll it into a sphere. Press it flat, warm it over the flame of an alcohol burner, and press it onto the yellow eye.

6   Use brown Isomalt or sugar to model the eyelids. Cut off a piece of warm Isomalt or sugar the same size as the eyes and roll it into a sphere. Press it flat, then immediately cut in half using room-temperature scissors. Warm each eyelid over the flame of an alcohol burner and place it on the top half of the white pupil. Dissolve water-soluble black food coloring in a small amount of water and use a fine-tipped paint brush to paint a black half sphere underneath the eyelid in the center of each eye to resemble the pupil.

7   To create a hat, model a small sphere from a small piece of warm Isomalt or sugar and press it onto the head. Then pull a thicker piece of Isomalt or sugar, using the same technique as for pulling a ribbon (see Making a Ribbon, page 138), and cut it into a square shape using a heated bench scraper. Warm over the flame of an alcohol burner and attach the square to the half sphere to create the hat. To create a tassel, pull a long piece of Isomalt or sugar into a string, then fold the string in half and twist it to create the tassel shape. Warm one end of the tassel over the flame of an alcohol burner and attach it to the center of the hat.

8   For the diploma, pull an elongated piece from white Isomalt or sugar using the same technique as for pulling petals (see pages 115–119). Immediately cut it into a rectangle, rewarm the rectangle under the heat lamp, and roll it into a cone. Warm the pointed side of the cone over an alcohol burner and attach it on the left-hand side of the body.

9   To create the wings, use the same technique as for making a ribbon (see Making a Ribbon, page 138). To avoid cutting off the ends of the wings, use a small amount of Isomalt or sugar and pull as you would a ribbon, but in short folds. While the ribbon is still warm, attach it to the body, overlapping the diploma a little. If the wings don't stick because the sugar became too cold, rewarm the wings over the flame of an alcohol burner and attach them to the body.

10 Airbrush both sides of the head and upper body with yellow liquid food coloring first and then brown liquid food coloring to enhance the characteristics of the three-dimensional figure.

11 Store the completed piece in an airtight container or plastic bag with limestone, calcium carbonate, or silica gel.

Frog

Frogs have increased in popularity and can be made in any color. For a small-size frog, only the body is blown and the rest is molded. When making a larger frog, the legs would be blown as well.

Create the Body

1 Begin to blow a sphere (see Blowing a Basic Sphere, steps 1 through 9, page 158).

2 Use your thumb and index finger to work a small ball away from the top of the sphere to form the head. Shape the neck and elongate it slightly. The head should remain spherical in shape.

3 Shape the bottom part of the sphere into a teardrop shape to create the body. The lower torso should be narrower than the shoulders.

4 Cool and remove the body from the tube (see Removing the Blown Piece from the Tube, page 163).

Create the Legs, Arms, and Toes

5 To create the back leg, working with the same color as used for the body, using room-temperature scissors, cut a piece of Isomalt or sugar at an angle. Cut a larger piece of Isomalt or sugar than you need for the finished leg, and hold onto the excess with one hand while modeling the leg with your other hand.

6 Use your fingers to shape the Isomalt or sugar into a long leg, keeping one end smaller than the other. Flatten the narrow end into a circle.

7 To create the toes, make 2 cuts, using room-temperature scissors, into the flattened circle. Separate and shape the toes.

8 Elongate the leg to the final desired length and shape the upper thigh and hip, which should be wider than the bottom part of the leg.

9 Using room-temperature scissors, cut off all excess Isomalt or sugar at the top of the leg.

10 Bend the leg at the knee, warm the hip of the leg over the flame of an alcohol burner, and attach the leg to the lower body.

11 Repeat steps 5 through 10 above to create and attach the second leg.

12 To create the arm, using room-temperature scissors, cut another piece of the same color Isomalt or sugar at an angle.

13 Use your fingers to shape the Isomalt or sugar into a shorter length than the legs, with one end slightly wider than the other. Shape the shoulder at the wider end. $\rightarrow$

14 Flatten the smaller end into a circle and, using room-temperature scissors, cut the circle twice to create the fingers. Separate and shape the fingers.

15 Bend the arm at the elbow. Warm the shoulder end of the arm over the flame of an alcohol burner and attach it to the top of the frog's torso, just below the neck.

16 Repeat steps 12 through 15 to create and attach the second arm.

17 Take a small piece of black Isomalt or sugar and melt one end over the flame of an alcohol burner.

18 Touch the melted end to each of the toes and fingers, applying a small dot of black Isomalt or sugar to the tip of each.

Finish the Frog

19 To create an eye, roll a very small piece of black Isomalt or sugar into a ball.

20 Pull a thin strip of Isomalt or sugar of the same color used for the frog's body and shape it into a frame around the top and sides of the eye.

21 Warm over the flame of an alcohol burner and attach the eye to the top of the frog's head with the framed side facing toward the back of the frog. Press the frame down against the head to cover the sides and back of the eye. Repeat the steps above to create and attach the second eye.

22 Using a fine-tipped paintbrush and black water-dissolvable powder color, paint the mouth.

23 Finish by airbrushing additional details as desired. For the mouth, use a fine-tipped brush and water-dissolvable powder color. Use an airbrush to color the body, using a darker tint of color to add shading.

24 Attach the frog to the base. Warm a small piece of sugar and attach it to the body, then warm the attached piece of sugar over the flame of an alcohol burner and place where desired on the base.

25 Store the completed piece in an airtight container or plastic bag with limestone, calcium carbonate, or silica gel.

FIRST ROW:
- Work a rounded head from the top of the sphere.
- Model a flat circle at the end of each leg to begin to form the feet.
- Separate and shape the toes.

SECOND ROW:
- Attach the back legs at the narrow end of the body.
- Apply a small dot of black Isomalt to the end of each toe.
- Create a frame the same color as the body around each eye.

THIRD ROW:
- Attach the eyes to the head and press the frames down to cover the back and sides of each eye.
- Add the mouth using a fine-tipped brush.
- Attach the completed frog to a base.

Blue Marlin

To create a realistic wave support for the marlin, as shown here, first cast support pieces in the shape of waves and let cool. Then, using the Clear Blowing technique on page 270, create clear blown pieces resembling water, and press onto the support pieces to cover.

Create the Body and Tail

1 Begin to blow a sphere (see Blowing a Basic Sphere, steps 1 through 9, page 158).

2 Visualize the sphere divided into quarters. Find the center of the upper right quarter and pull a long, narrow piece from that spot to form the sword.

3 Use room-temperature scissors to cut the mouth below the sword.

4 Shape the body of the fish into a curve by rubbing it across your upper thigh. This technique allows an object with a larger surface area to be shaped evenly.

5 Cool and remove the fish from the tube (see Removing the Blown Piece from the Tube, page 163) and close the hole with your fingers.

6 Using room-temperature scissors, cut a ball of the same color Isomalt or sugar, warm it over the flame of an alcohol burner, and attach it to the back of the fish where you closed up the hole from the tube.

7 Warm the ball of Isomalt or sugar and flatten it, shaping it into a tail. Use scissors to make indentations in the tail. Let the tail cool and set the fish aside while you make the fins. →

– Pull a long piece for the sword from one corner of the sphere.
– Cut the mouth just below the sword.
– Shape the body into a curve.

Create the Fins

8 To make the top fin, using room-temperature scissors, cut a medium piece of the same color Isomalt or sugar used for the body and pull a ribbon (see Making a Ribbon, page 138).

9 Fold the ribbon in half, placing the two halves side by side and pressing the edges together well. Continue to fold and compress until you have reached the correct length for a long fin. The fin must be long enough to fit on the fish from the back of the head to within the start of the tail. Pull to elongate it, if necessary.

10 Using room-temperature scissors, trim the bottom straight across and trim the top into an elongated triangle shape to form the top fin.

11 Warm over the flame of an alcohol burner and attach the fin to the top of the fish, starting with the tallest part of the fin at the back of the head and extending down the back to within the start of the tail.

12 Follow the same steps above using a smaller piece of Isomalt or sugar to create the smaller bottom fin, which should go from the end of the front fin to the beginning of the tail. Warm the fin over the flame of an alcohol burner and attach to the bottom of the fish, toward the tail end of the fish's body.

13 To create the side fins, pull 2 long petal shapes (see pages 115–119). Roll each lengthwise to create a tube that is wide at one end and angles to a point at the other end. Melt the wide end of each tube over the flame of an alcohol burner and attach one fin to each side of the fish, lined up evenly with the starting point of the top fin. Shape the side fins as desired.

Finish the Marlin

14 Using blue Isomalt or sugar, mold 2 small circles for the eyes. Warm over the flame of an alcohol burner and attach one to each side of the fish just in front of and slightly above the side fins.

15 Using blue water-dissolvable powder color and a fine-tipped paintbrush, paint the gills and markings onto the sides of the fish. Set the fish aside and allow the paint to dry.

16 Cut off a piece of white sugar and warm over the flame of an alcohol burner. Attach to the underside of the fish in front of the tail. Rewarm the attached piece of sugar over the flame of an alcohol burner and attach to the top of the wave base. Cover the base with plastic to protect it before airbrushing the fish's body.

17 Airbrush the middle lower portion of the body with yellow liquid food coloring, being careful not to spray any yellow on the top of the body, then spray over the same area using red. Spray blue color on the top of the body and fin, and to achieve a stronger shade, airbrush black liquid food coloring on the very ends of the fins.

18 Store the completed piece in an airtight container or plastic bag with limestone, calcium carbonate, or silica gel.

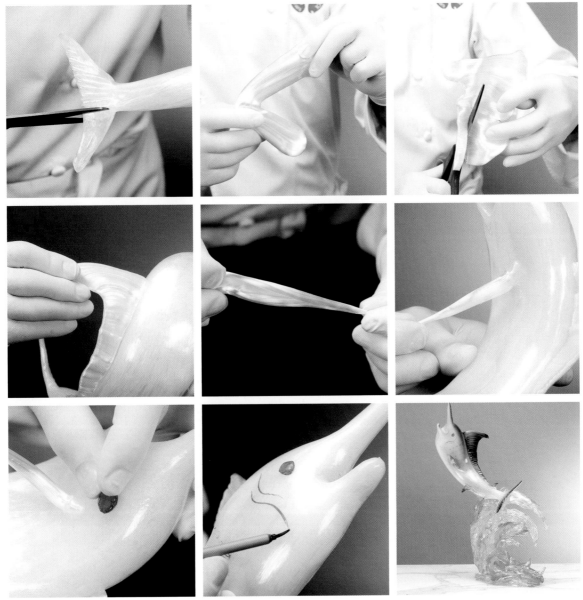

FIRST ROW:
- Flatten the tail and use scissors to mark indentations in the fin.
- Fold the ribbon back and forth in a zigzag pattern for the top fin.
- Trim the top and bottom of the folded ribbon to make the top fin.

SECOND ROW:
- Attach the fin along the top of the fish.
- Pull a petal and roll it to create a long tube with a point at one end.
- Attach the wide end of the tube to the side of the fish for the side fin.

THIRD ROW:
- Attach one eye to each side of the fish, just above the fins.
- Hand paint the gills and other details with a fine-tipped brush.
- Airbrush the marlin to finish and use the Clear Blowing technique to create a water-like base.

Shell

The shell makes a beautiful accent to any marine piece. It can be a difficult piece, but is one worth learning. Precise timing is essential when cutting into the shape, so that you can increase the size and adjust the shape of the shell as desired.

1 Begin to blow a sphere using pink Isomalt or sugar (see Blowing a Basic Sphere, steps 1 through 9, page 158).

2 Form the sphere into a drop shape with your fingers, adding air if necessary, with the narrow end away from the tube. Elongate the narrow end.

3 Using room-temperature scissors, cut into the center of the narrow end of the shape, cutting halfway into the center of the sphere. Be sure to cut the shape early enough in the process, when the sugar is still warm, so that the cut will naturally seal the sugar. Once it is sealed you will be able to increase the shape and size.

4 Twist the two cut ends around each other.

5 Add air to increase the shell to the desired size.

6 Cool and remove the shell from the tube (see Removing the Blown Piece from the Tube, page 163). Using room-temperature scissors, cut the shell from the tube at an angle and pinch to close the open end.

7 Choose a place on the side of the shell opposite the twisted side where the opening should be. Place that spot over the flame of an alcohol burner to create an opening.

8 Cut with room-temperature scissors to widen the opening and roll back the edges on both sides of the opening.

9 Along the bottom edge of the opening, pinch the Isomalt or sugar between your thumb and index finger at even intervals to create spikes.

10 Airbrush the shell to finish. Spray the outside of the shell with yellow, red, and black liquid coloring, but leave the pink Isomalt or sugar on the inside of the shell unpainted.

11 Store the completed piece in an airtight container or plastic bag with limestone, calcium carbonate, or silica gel.

FIRST ROW:
- Pull the sphere into a teardrop shape with the wide end closest to the tube.
- Make a cut in the narrow end that extends to the center of the sphere.
- Twist the two halves around each other.

SECOND ROW:
- Cut at an angle to remove the shell from the tube and close the open end.
- Hold the part of the shell where you want the opening to appear over an open flame to make a hole.
- Use scissors to widen the opening.

THIRD ROW:
- Pinch to form spikes along the bottom edge of the opening.
- Airbrush the outside of the shell to finish.
- Leave the inside of the shell unpainted for a realistic look.

Lobster

The lobster is blown from white Isomalt or sugar and then airbrushed with layers of color. The lobster looks more difficult than it really is, making it a very impressive piece. The most difficult technique used is the method for creating the claws, which is very similar to the technique for blowing a shell.

Create the Body and Tail

1 Begin to blow a sphere (see Blowing a Basic Sphere, steps 1 through 9, page 158).

2 Elongate the sphere into an eggplant shape, adding air if necessary. The body should be narrower at the tube end (tail) and wider toward the head. Curve the body so that the head and tail curve upward.

3 Cool and remove the body from the tube (see Removing the Blown Piece from the Tube, page 163). Close the open end.

4 Using room-temperature scissors, cut a piece of Isomalt or sugar and flatten it into a triangle for the tail support. Warm over the flame of an alcohol burner and attach it to the tail end of the body. This piece will be the support for the tail scales.

Create the Scales

5 To create scales for the tail, pull a long, wide scale, curved evenly on each side, using the same technique as for pulling a petal (see pages 115–119).

6 Using room-temperature scissors, cut the scale from the main piece of Isomalt or sugar and immediately attach it to one side of the tail. If the sugar is too cold, the scale can be warmed over the flame of an alcohol burner and then attached.

7 Create a total of 5 scales using the same technique. Overlap 2 on each side, and lay the center scale on top to cover the tail.

8 To create scales for the body, pull longer scales that are wider in the center and taper off to a point on each end. Each scale must be long enough to completely hide the section of body it covers with the points hanging just below the body on either side. Using room-temperature scissors, cut each scale from the main piece of Isomalt or sugar and immediately attach it while still warm to the body, beginning at the base of the tail and working your way up toward the head. Each scale should slightly overlap the scale behind it. Continue pulling and adding scales until you have reached the middle of the body, where the head scales will begin (approximately 6 body scales should be enough). →

9 The lobster has 2 large head scales, the back of which must be wide enough to cover the lobster's head from the top center line to the bottom. This width should extend halfway down the head scale, and, at the halfway point, the top of the scale curves down so that the front half of the scale is thinner, leaving the top of the lobster's head uncovered. To execute this scale, begin to pull a wide scale, using the same technique as for pulling a petal (see pages 115–119) and allowing a bit more thickness than usual. Allow the scale to become thinner as you reach the center of its length, and retain that thickness until the scale reaches the desired length.

10 Using your thumb on top and your index finger curled underneath, widen the first half of the scale until it is wide enough to cover the back of the head.

11 Using room-temperature scissors, remove the scale from the main piece of Isomalt or sugar and immediately attach while still warm to the head, with the wide part overlapping the last body scale. Repeat the steps above to create and attach the large scale for the other side of the head.

12 The lobster also has 2 small scales layered on the center front of the head. To create these, pull 2 long, narrow scales and immediately attach them to the center front of the head, overlapping the ends of the larger head scales.

Create the Claws

13 Begin to blow a sphere using about half as much Isomalt or sugar as you used for the body.

14 Roll the sphere between your index fingers at a point two-thirds of the way up from the base of the sphere to create an indentation.

15 Elongate the base of the sphere below the indentation until it reaches the desired length for the arm of the lobster.

16 Picture the remaining sphere divided horizontally into thirds and, using room-temperature scissors, cut the sphere along one of the dividing lines to form the claw. Open the claw and shape both pieces with your fingers, shaping the end of each piece into a point.

17 Use scissors to mark segments at equal intervals down the arm.

18 Slowly add air while using your hands to hold the shape of the claws and arm segments. You want to enlarge the top, larger half of the claw, while keeping the lower part of the claw smaller and elongated. You should also add some volume to the arm segments, but be careful to keep the segments well defined. $\longrightarrow$

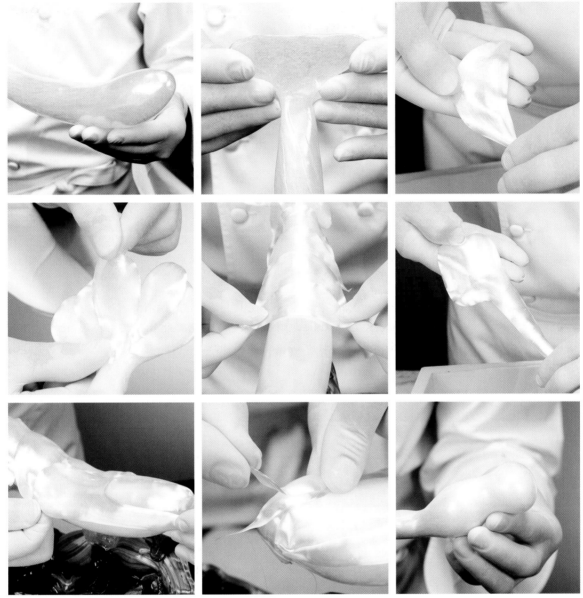

FIRST ROW:
- Begin the lobster with a long eggplant shape.
- Flatten a piece for the tail and attach it to the end of the body.
- Pull long, wide petal shapes for the tail scales.

SECOND ROW:
- Attach the scales on top of the tail.
- Begin attaching the body scales at the base of the tail, and overlap each body scale over the last.
- The head scales should be wider on one end, and narrow to a thinner width about halfway down.

THIRD ROW:
- Place the head scales with the wider part overlapping the last body scale, so the top of the lobster's head remains uncovered.
- Layer the small head scales centered on top of the lobster's head.
- For each claw, roll the sphere between your fingers to create an indentation.

19 Cool and remove the arm and claw from the tube. Warm over the flame of an alcohol burner and attach the arm to the lobster, placing it on the front third of the lobster's body, in between the last square body scale and the front of the head. Leave enough room to place 4 legs between the claws and the square scales.

20 Repeat the same steps to create the second claw, cutting on the opposite dividing line from step 16 to result in a right and a left claw. Attach the second arm to the lobster opposite the first.

Create the Legs

21 Using room-temperature scissors, cut a piece of Isomalt or sugar at an angle.

22 Roll the Isomalt or sugar to form a cylinder that is wider at one end and narrower at the other end.

23 At the narrow end, shape a small circle. Using room-temperature scissors, make a cut in the circle, creating the claw.

24 Use room-temperature scissors to mark the segments of the leg at equal intervals.

25 Warm over the flame of an alcohol burner and attach the leg to the lobster where the back of the head scale meets the body.

26 Repeat the steps above for the other legs. Create 8 legs in all, 4 for each side. Attach the legs one after the other, spacing them evenly between the claws and the last square body scale.

Create the Antennae, Feelers, and Eyes

27 The antennae will attach to the side of each eye, rise approximately 1 in/2.5 cm above the head, and bend back, extending beyond the tail. To create these long antennae, begin by blowing a very small sphere.

28 Pull the sphere to elongate it to the required length. The width of the antenna should be wider at the tube and taper to a point at the far end.

29 Cool and remove the antenna from the tube.

30 Warm the wide end of the antenna under a heat lamp just until it will bend. Approximately 1 in/2.5 cm from the wide end, bend the antenna at an angle just under 90 degrees and curve the remainder upward.   →

FIRST ROW:
- Make a cut two-thirds of the way down the sphere shape to form the claw.
- Use scissors to mark the arm segments.
- Attach the arm to the body in between the last body scale and the front of the head.

SECOND ROW:
- Cut at an angle to begin making a leg.
- Mold a small circle at the end of each leg and cut it to form the claw.
- Score with scissors to mark the leg segments.

THIRD ROW:
- Attach the legs at even intervals, beginning where the back of the head scale meets the body.
- Pull a long antenna that is wider nearest the tube and tapers to a point at the far end.
- Bend the antenna at a 90-degree angle approximately 1 in/2.5 cm from the wide end.

31 Warm over the flame of an alcohol burner and attach the wide end of the antenna to the side of the head scale approximately 1 in/2.5 cm from the front of the head. Repeat to create and attach a second antenna on the other side.

32 To create the feelers, pull 4 thin Isomalt or sugar pieces that taper to a point at one end. Attach the feelers to the face of the lobster, placing 2 on each side just below the antennae.

33 Using room-temperature scissors, cut a small ball of black Isomalt or sugar for each eye. Roll each ball into a small cylinder, then flatten the top to look like the head of a nail. Warm the narrower bottom end of each eye over the flame of an alcohol burner and attach it to the lobster's head, pressing down slightly.

Finish the Lobster

34 Airbrush the lobster with a light spray of red liquid food coloring.

35 Airbrush a touch of yellow liquid food coloring over the red.

36 Airbrush blue liquid food coloring over the yellow to achieve a dark greenish color.

37 Add a final layer of black liquid food coloring, which will darken and intensify the colors.

38 Store the completed piece in an airtight container or plastic bag with limestone, calcium carbonate, or silica gel.

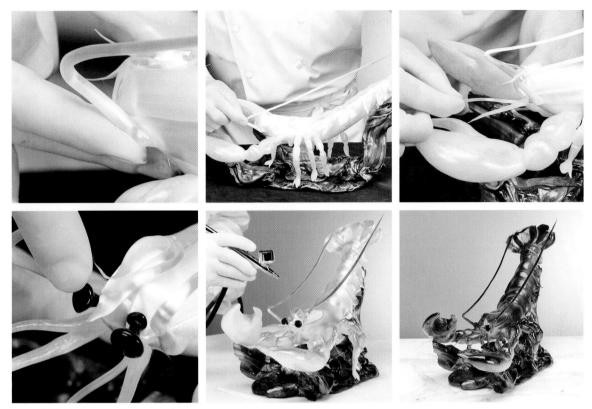

- Attach the wide part of the antenna to the head scale, about 1 in/2.5 cm from the front of the head.
- The antennae should be long enough to rise above the head and then extend all the way back beyond the tail.
- Attach four feelers to the front of the head.

SECOND ROW:
- Attach the narrow end of each eye to the lobster's face, pressing down slightly.
- Airbrush the lobster with red color, then follow with a touch of yellow.
- Add blue and then black airbrushed color to finish the lobster.

Human Figurines

It is extremely difficult to learn to create human figurines by pulling and blowing sugar. The biggest challenge is to make an elegant figurine that has natural movement. It takes much practice and patience. I am sure this is the reason why many professionals do not make figurines at all, and instead use the time to master flowers, ribbons, and casting elements.

The key to creating lifelike human figures is to understand the structure and proportions of the human anatomy. A cartoon-like figurine can result when the proportions are purposely made out of balance. When the effect is unintentional, however, the figure can have an unnatural appearance. There are significant variations in anatomical proportions between male and female figures. See the table below for the distinguishing characteristics of adult males and females.

ANATOMICAL PART	FEMALE	MALE
Hips	Wide	Narrow
Shoulders	As wide as hips	Wide
Waist	Narrow	Narrow
Chest	Small	Wide
Arms	Narrow	Wide
Neck	Narrow	Wide
Facial features	Soft	Hard
Lips	Wide	Narrow

Proportions of the Adult Human

Common mistakes when creating a human figurine include making the head too large and pulling the length of the arms and hands too long. To keep body parts in proportion, use the male and female figure grids shown on page 218 as a guide.

The average adult human figure is 7.5 to 8 heads tall. To account for this, the first seven sections of the male and female figure grids are equal to the height of the head. The bottom section is equal to half of the height of the head. Other characteristics that are common to both males and females include the average proportional length of the arms and hands. When the human body stands upright with arms relaxed at the sides, the fingertips rest at midthigh. The length of the hand is equal to the length of the face from the eyebrows to the chin.

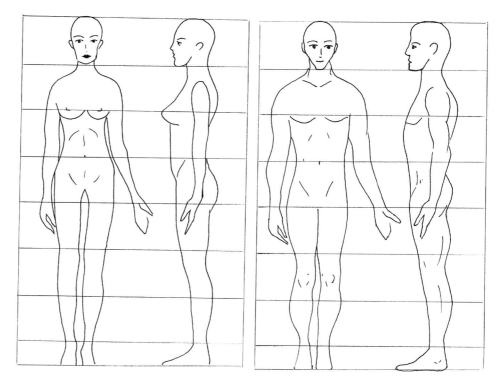

Note that on the female figure, the length from waist to feet is almost two-thirds the total height of the figure. The female adult body shown in the first grid is divided into sections as follows:

1   Top of head to chin
2   Chin to nipples
3   Nipples to belly button/elbow
4   Belly button/elbow to top of thigh
5   Top of thigh to top of kneecaps
6   Top of kneecaps to middle of calves
7   Middle of calves to ankle joint
8   Ankle joint to bottom of feet

Note that for the male figure, the legs are equal to half the total height of the figure, and the body, from shoulders to hips, is equal to two-thirds the length of the legs. The foot is equal to half the length of the shin. The arm length, from shoulder to fingertip, is equal to the length of the leg, and the head is equal to the length of the foot and to the length of the lower arm from elbow joint to wrist. The male adult body shown in the second grid is divided into sections as follows:

1   Top of head to chin
2   Chin to nipples
3   Nipples to belly button/elbow
4   Belly button/elbow to crotch
5   Crotch to top of kneecaps
6   Top of kneecaps to middle of calves
7   Middle of calves to ankle joint
8   Ankle joint to bottom of feet

THE ART OF THE CONFECTIONER

Proportions of the Head and Facial Features

The proportion of the head varies from person to person and changes with age. The shape of the head influences the viewer's impression of the figure. This should be used to your advantage. For example, a narrow, delicate head appears feminine, while a larger head with a square jaw gives the appearance of masculinity and toughness.

The head shown in the facial feature grids below is that of a Caucasian adult. The shape of the head resembles an upside-down egg. To place the facial features, divide the head horizontally into quarters and use the dividing lines as a guide:

- The bottom of the first quarter marks the hairline.
- The bottom of the second quarter marks the line of the eyes, approximately in the middle of the face, and the top of the ears.
- The bottom of the third quarter touches the tip of the nose and the bottom of the earlobes.
- The fourth quarter stretches from the nose to the chin and nape of the neck.

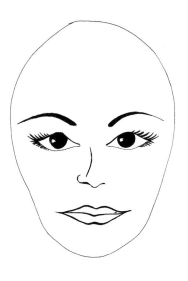 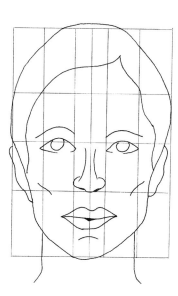 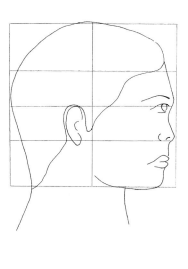

THE ART OF THE CONFECTIONER

Adding Facial Features to a Blown Figure

The face of a blown figure does not need as much detail as you would add when painting a picture. Eyebrows, eyelids, pupils, nose, and mouth are enough to create expression and character. When painting facial features, I prefer to use a fine-tipped paintbrush and water-dissolvable powder color, which can achieve more intense colors than food coloring. Ears are usually hand modeled and attached to the head. They should stretch from the height of the eyebrow to the height of the point of the nose.

EYES

The space between the eyes should be equal to the width of one eye. To determine the size and placement of the eyes, divide the second quarter into five equal portions with vertical lines, and place the eyes within the second and third columns (see grid at left). The steps to paint a female eye are as follows:

1   Start with the line for the bottom edge of the upper eyelid. The line should be medium-wide on the inside edge and then lighten as it curves to the outer corner.

2   Paint a lighter line for the lower eyelid, curved almost to form the shape of an almond.

3   Add another curved line above the top line, following the same shape and painting the line heavier on the inside edge and lighter as you move to the outside, to indicate the top of the eyelid.

4   Add the lashes to the upper lid with a medium thickness. Start the lashes one-third of the way from the inside point of the upper lid, and paint shorter lashes on the inside edge and gradually longer lashes as they approach the outside edge of the eyelid.

5   To add the eyebrow, paint a gentle arch over the eye. Again, the line should be thicker toward the inside edge of the eye.

6   Add the iris (the colored part of the eye) and the pupil (the dark center). Notice that the top of the iris is partially covered by the upper lid. Leaving a spot of white indicates shine.

7   Finish the eye by placing small, light eyelashes on the edge of the bottom lid. The bottom eyelashes should start at the same vertical line as the upper lashes.

The same general technique can be used with minor variations to create a range of

From left to right: a male eye, a closed eye, and an Asian eye.

different types of eyes. The difference between the male and the female eye is the presence of eyelashes and the size of the eyebrow. The male eye is painted without eyelashes and the eyebrow is thicker. A closed eye can be indicated with a heavier curve on the line for the lower eyelid. The Asian eye is narrower and angled upward from the inside point to the outside point. Because the eye is narrower, the pupil naturally takes up more of the space of the eye.

MOUTH

The mouth should be centered vertically between the chin and the nose. The width of the mouth can vary. A general guideline for a relaxed (not smiling) mouth is to have the corners of the mouth meet a vertical line drawn through the center of the eyes. The steps to draw a mouth, working from the bottom lip to the top lip, are as follows:

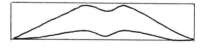

1   The lower lip is generally narrower than the top lip. To get the sizing right, imagine drawing the bottom and top lips within two rectangles, with the lower rectangle slightly narrower than the top rectangle.

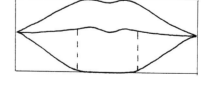

2   To create the line between the two lips, draw a small upside-down V in the center of the bottom rectangle, with the top point of the upside-down V touching the top line of the rectangle. From the two points of the V, extend the lip in an upward curve to the top corners of the bot-

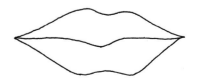

THE ART OF THE CONFECTIONER

tom rectangle, as shown.

3   To finish the bottom lip, draw another upside down V below the first with the bottom two points touching the bottom line of the rectangle. Extend lines from the bottom two points of the V up to the top corners of the rectangle to form the corners of the mouth.

4   To create the upper lip, divide the upper rectangle into three even boxes. In the left box, draw a line from the corner of the mouth to the upper right corner. In the right box, draw a line from the upper left corner down to the corner of the mouth. In the center box, draw a curved line from the upper left corner to the upper right corner to connect the two diagonal lines.

NOSE

The facial features grid on page 220 shows the placement of the nose and nostrils on the face. A vertical line is drawn through the center of the head. The nose is drawn centered over this line. The bridge of the nose should begin at the level of the corner of the eyes, and the tip of the nose should extend to the bottom of the third quarter. If a vertical line is drawn from the edge of each eye down to the chin, the outside edges of the nostrils should touch these lines. The steps to drawing a nose are as follows:

1   Draw a curved line on each side of the center line. This is the bridge of the nose.

2   Add a horizontal curved line below the bridge to create the point of the nose.

3   Draw half circles on either side of the nose, extending from the ends of the bridge to below the curved horizontal line, to create the nostrils.

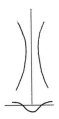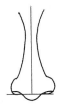

4   I prefer to draw only one side of the nose, as shown in the last step, to indicate the shadow created by light coming from only one side.

Female Figurine

Have the base and support structure assembled and ready to use. Because the individual parts on this figurine are small, the pieces shown here are modeled, not blown. If the figurine were larger, however, the pieces for the torso, limbs, and head would have to be blown, because large objects made out of solid Isomalt would take too long to cool and would lose their shape.

Create the Legs

1   Prepare a piece of Isomalt or sugar in the desired skin color (see Preparing Isomalt or Sugar for Blowing, page 157).

2   Using room-temperature scissors, cut a piece of Isomalt or sugar at an angle to create a wider end and a narrower, pointed end.

3   Fold the pointed end over and shape the ankle and heel from the folded end.

4   Bend the foot at the ankle and form the arch and the base of the toes.

5   Shape the shin so that it widens coming up from the ankle, then narrows slightly again at the base of the knee.

6   Bend the leg at the knee and shape the bottom of the thigh.

7   Shape the top of the thigh, and shape the hip so that it will attach securely to the torso. Cool and set aside.

8   Repeat the steps above to form the second leg.

9   Hold the legs together to determine the desired placement, then heat the inside top of each leg over the flame of an alcohol burner and attach them together.

10   Heat the top of the legs over the flame of an alcohol burner and attach them to the support structure.

Create the Torso

11   Prepare another piece of skin-colored Isomalt or sugar for blowing.

12   Form a smooth ball and, using room-temperature scissors, cut it away from the main piece.

13   Roll the ball between your hands to form an elongated teardrop shape.

14   Use scissors to mark the center line of the torso.

15   Build up the chest by pushing the Isomalt or sugar up with your fingers to create volume, and set aside.

$\longrightarrow$

FIRST ROW:
- Cut an angled piece for the leg and fold it over the pointed end to begin forming the foot.
- Shape the ankle and heel from the folded end and bend the foot at the ankle.
- Model the arch of the foot and the toes.

SECOND ROW:
- Use your thumb and index finger to shape the shin to the base of the knee.
- Bend the leg at the knee and shape the thigh.
- When the legs are both fully shaped, hold them together to determine their placement.

THIRD ROW:
- Heat the inside top of each leg and attach them together.
- Heat the top of the legs and attach them to the support structure.
- Cut a smooth ball away from the main piece of Isomalt.

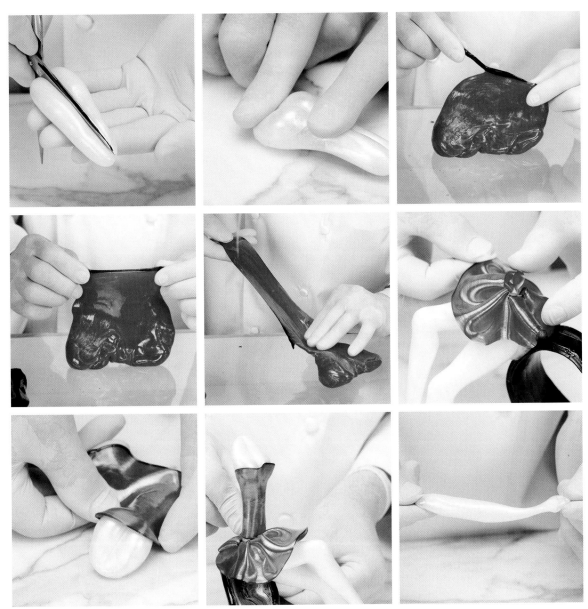

- Roll the ball into a teardrop shape and use scissors to mark the center line.
- Use your fingers to build up the chest.
- Add a contrasting trim color to the Isomalt you want to use for the dress.

SECOND ROW:
- Pull the trimmed edge to thin it.
- Pull a very long petal from the two-color Isomalt.
- Gather the piece into a pleated circle and attach it to the top of the legs to form the skirt.

THIRD ROW:
- Pull another trimmed piece and wrap it around the torso.
- Attach the torso to the top of the skirt and legs.
- Cut an angled piece and shape it to form the hand, wrist, and forearm.

Add the Dress

16 Prepare Isomalt or sugar in the desired color for the dress by heating it on a food warmer or under an infrared heating lamp. Add a thin piece of Isomalt or sugar in a contrasting color to one edge of the main piece, using the same technique as for a two-color orchid petal (see page 127).

17 Pull the edge with the contrasting color to thin it.

18 Pull a very long strip using the same technique as for pulling a petal (see pages 115–119) and, using room-temperature scissors, cut it off from the main piece of Isomalt or sugar.

19 Gather the petal into a circle, shaping it to form a pleated skirt. Warm the top of the skirt over the flame of an alcohol burner and attach it to the top of the legs.

20 From the same two-color Isomalt or sugar, pull a wider strip long enough to wrap around the torso.

21 Using room-temperature scissors, cut the wide strip from the main piece of Isomalt or sugar and wrap around the torso.

22 Warm the bottom end of the torso and attach to the skirt and legs.

Create the Arms

23 Prepare another piece of skin-colored Isomalt or sugar and, using room-temperature scissors, cut a piece at an angle to create a wider end and a narrower end.

24 Roll the narrow end to begin shaping the hand.

25 Shape the wrist and forearm above the narrow end.

26 Use the scissors to mark the fingers and cut the thumb, and pull to separate the thumb from the fingers.

27 Form the elbow and bend the arm.

28 Shape the upper arm and shoulder.

29 Warm the top of the arm over the flame of an alcohol burner and attach it to the torso, leaving it extended downward.

30 Follow the same steps to create the other arm, and attach it with the hand extended up and angled slightly away from the face.

Create the Head and Face

31 Using the same skin color, form and, using room-temperature scissors, cut a small ball from the main piece of Isomalt or sugar for the head. $\longrightarrow$

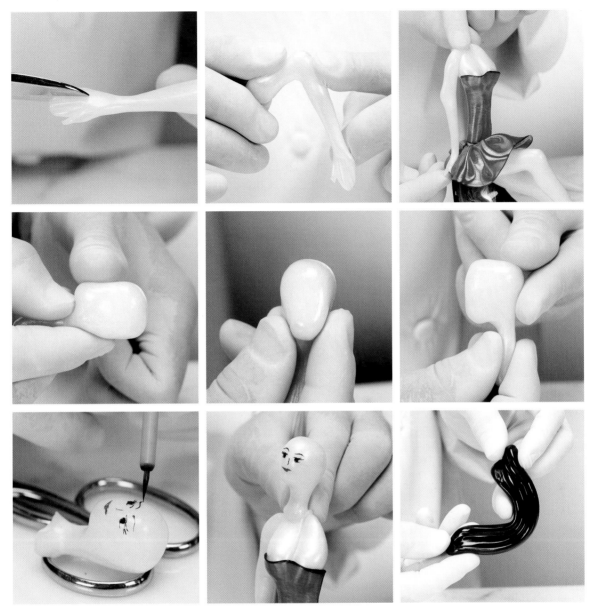

FIRST ROW:
- Use scissors to score the hand for fingers, and cut all the way through to separate the thumb.
- Bend the arm and shape the elbow.
- Attach each arm to the top of the torso.

SECOND ROW:
- Roll a piece for the head and neck and carefully shape the jaw.
- Pinch to shape the chin and sides of the face.
- Pinch the back of the skull at the top of the head to shape it.

THIRD ROW:
- Set the head down on a stable surface and paint on the facial features.
- Heat the bottom of the neck and attach it to the torso.
- Stretch and fold a few times to form a "ribbon" of hair.

SUGAR BLOWING

32 Pull the neck from the head and roll it between your index fingers to smooth.

33 Shape the bottom jaw, the sides of the face, and the chin.

34 Pinch the back of the skull at the top of the head to shape it. Cool until it hardens.

35 Set the head on a stable surface and paint the facial features with a fine-tipped paintbrush and water-dissolvable powder color.

36 Warm the neck over the flame of an alcohol burner and attach the head to the torso.

Add the Hair

37 To create the hair for one side of the head, pull a length of Isomalt or sugar in the desired hair color and, using room-temperature scissors, cut it from the main piece.

38 Stretch and fold the Isomalt or sugar a few times, forming a ribbon wide enough to cover the area extending from one side of the skull to the center of the back of the skull.

39 Using room-temperature scissors, cut the ribbon of hair to the desired length.

40 Warm the hair over the flame of an alcohol burner and attach it just off the center line of the scalp. Fold the hair over the side of the head and shape it.

41 Repeat the steps above to create and attach the hair for the other side of the head.

42 To create bangs, pull a narrower ribbon of hair and cut it using room-temperature scissors. Attach it just above the forehead and shape it as desired.

Create the Fan and Finish the Figurine

43 Using the same edged Isomalt or sugar as was used for the dress, pull a long, narrow strip and, using room-temperature scissors, cut it from the main piece.

44 Pleat the strip into a half circle to form a fan.

45 Warm the fan at the base where the seam appears and attach it to the upraised hand of the figurine.

46 Pull 2 long and very narrow ribbons from the same color Isomalt or sugar and, using room-temperature scissors, cut them away from the main piece.

47 Warm each ribbon underneath the lamp of a food warmer and shape each as desired. Melt one end of each ribbon over the flame of an alcohol burner and attach to the base of the fan to finish the figurine.

48 Store the completed piece in an airtight container or plastic bag with limestone, calcium carbonate, or silica gel.

FIRST ROW:
- Cut the hair to the needed length.
- Attach the first piece of hair to the top of the head slightly off center.
- Fold each piece of hair down and shape it alongside the face.

SECOND ROW:
- Attach a smaller piece to the front of the forehead for the bangs, and bend the bangs into shape.
- Pull a long, narrow, trimmed piece and pleat it into a half circle.
- Attach the pleated piece to the figure's hand for a fan.

THIRD ROW:
- Pull very long, very narrow ribbons.
- Shape and curl the ribbons and attach them to the base of the fan.
- The finished figurine.

Chinese Dragon

The Chinese dragon is very popular, and one of the most impressive blown pieces of all. The most difficult part is the number of different body parts you will need to create, similar to the process for creating the lobster on page 208. The dragon can be blown using white or yellow Isomalt or sugar, but has to be airbrushed later to create the dramatic appearance shown here.

Create the Body

1   Begin to blow a sphere (see Blowing a Basic Sphere, steps 1 through 9, page 158). A larger amount of Isomalt or sugar will be needed for this piece, as it is quite long.

2   Elongate the sphere into a tube that is 1 to 1½ ft/30 to 45 cm long. Bend and shape the body.

3   Cool and remove from the tube (see Removing the Blown Piece from the Tube, page 163). Close the open end of the body.

4   Warm the wider end of the body and the tail end over the flame of an alcohol burner and attach it to the support structure.

Create the Jaws

5   To create the bottom jaw, begin to blow another, smaller sphere.

6   Elongate the sphere into a teardrop shape with the narrow end away from the tube. Flatten the top and bottom of the teardrop shape and curve the jaw upward. Cool and remove from the tube.

7   To create the top jaw, begin to blow another sphere and elongate it into a teardrop shape, as you did for the bottom jaw. The length should match that of the bottom jaw. Flatten the top and bottom. Beginning just before the middle of the jaw, begin to curve the jaw upward. Place the upper jaw against the lower jaw and check the length and that the mouth opens wide enough for teeth to be placed inside.

8   Cool and remove the upper jaw from the tube, closing the open end.

9   Warm the jaw pieces over the flame of an alcohol burner and attach them together very well, keeping in mind that you will have to reopen the end of the jaw later on to be able to insert the neck 3 or 4 in/7.5 or 10 cm into the back of the head. This is important because if you are not able to push the neck far enough into the back of the jaws, the head may fall off.

10   Crumple pieces of aluminum foil and use them to prop up the jaws on your work surface. $\longrightarrow$

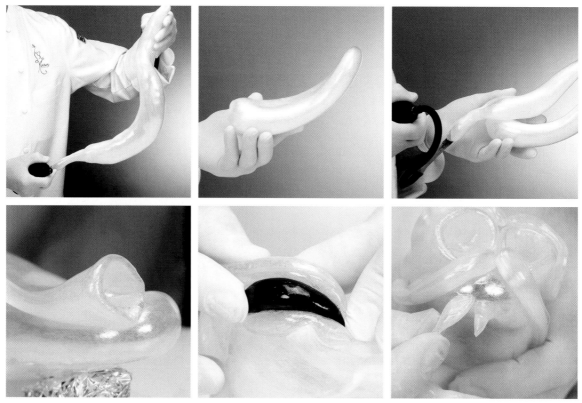

FIRST ROW:
- Blow a very long tube shape and bend and curve it to form the dragon's body.
- Flatten the top and bottom of the teardrop shape and curve it upward for the bottom jaw.
- Before removing the upper jaw from the tube, hold it against the bottom jaw to check the length.

SECOND ROW:
- Attach the wide end of the nostril close to the front of the upper jaw. Lay the tube along the top of the upper jaw and cut it about three-quarters of the way down.
- Attach the lower lid, iris, and finally the upper lid for each eye.
- Attach small triangular pieces along both jaws for the dragon's teeth.

Create the Nostrils

11 Begin to blow a sphere and pull it into an elongated tube that is wider on the end farthest from the tube.

12 Indent the wide end with your index finger to create a nostril. You can use only the open end of the nostril by cutting a shorter piece of the tube, or you can extend the sinus cavity (tube) back toward the eye. Warm the wide end on one side over the flame of an alcohol burner and attach it on one side of the top of the upper jaw, approximately 1 in/2.5 cm from the end. If you are extending the sinus cavity, lay the tube onto the upper jaw surface and extend it approximately three-quarters of the length of the upper jaw. Using room-temperature scissors, cut it from the tube and close the open end.

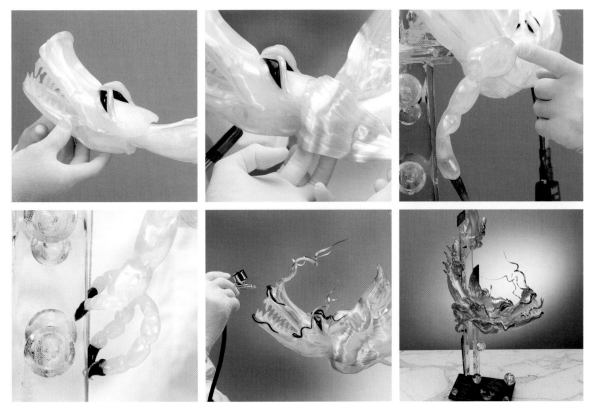

FIRST ROW:
- To attach the head to the body, carefully push the neck into the space between the jaws at the back of the head.
- Attach the mane pieces at the point where the head attaches to the neck.
- Mark segments in each leg and attach the legs to the body.

SECOND ROW:
- Finish each toe with a black, pointed claw and attach four toes to each leg.
- Use an airbrush to paint the dragon with yellow and red color.
- The finished Chinese dragon.

13 Clean the tube and repeat the steps above to create and attach the second nostril.

14 Pull a thin rope of Isomalt or sugar and use it to outline the top of the nostrils. This rope can be extended back to the back of the head, where the eyes will be placed, if desired.

Finish and Attach the Head

15 To create an eye, pull a wide line of Isomalt or sugar the same color as the jaws and place it immediately at an angle toward the back of the head to form the lower lid. Because it is a cut piece of Isomalt or sugar and still very warm, it will stick immediately without warming over an alcohol burner.

16 Using a small piece of colored Isomalt or sugar, mold a crescent-shaped iris. Immediately attach the iris while still warm above the lower lid. $\longrightarrow$

17 Pull another wide line of Isomalt or sugar, using the same color as for the lower lid, and attach it immediately while still warm just above the iris to form the upper eyelid.

18 Repeat the steps above to create and attach the other eye.

19 Pull 4 wide lines of Isomalt or sugar. Using the flame of an alcohol burner, rewarm the pulled lines and attach 2 of them to the upper jaw to form the upper lip, and attach the other 2 to form the bottom lip, placing the ends of each strip at the middle of the mouth.

20 Using room-temperature scissors, cut small triangular pieces of Isomalt or sugar for the teeth, warm the flat ends over the flame of an alcohol burner, and attach them along the upper and lower jaws.

21 To attach the head to the body, warm the back part of the head over the flame of an alcohol burner and carefully open the back of the jaws wide enough so that you can push the neck end of the body into the space at the back of the head. Push it in approximately one-third of the length of the head to ensure that the whole piece is stable.

Create the Spikes and Mane

22 To create spikes and mane pieces, pull a long ribbon (see Making a Ribbon, page 138). Fold the ribbon in half, placing the two halves side by side and pressing the edges together well. Continue to fold and compress them until you have reached the desired length, as for the blue marlin fins (see page 204).

23 Using room-temperature scissors, cut part of the ribbon into spikes and rewarm over the alcohol burner flame before attaching them along the top of the spine, all the way down to the tail.

24 Cut the rest of the ribbon into 5 to 10 triangular pieces for the mane, warm over the flame of an alcohol burner, and attach them around the head at the point where you pushed the head and the body together.

Create the Whiskers

25 Pull 6 long, thin lines of white Isomalt or sugar and cut them all to the same length. Warm over the flame of an alcohol burner and attach 2 on each side of the head near the corners of the mouth, 1 just above the upper lip, and 1 just below the lower lip. Twist and curl the ends of each whisker.

26 Pull another long, thin line of black Isomalt or sugar, warm over the flame of an alcohol burner, and attach it to the upper lip like a mustache. Twist and twirl the ends. Pull 1 more long, thin line, attach it to the lower lip like a mustache, and twist and twirl the ends.

27 Pull 2 whiskers out of black Isomalt or sugar. After twisting them, warm them over the flame of an alcohol burner and attach them to the bases of the white whiskers that were placed just under the lower lip. Angle the black whiskers away from the white ones.

28 Pull 2 more black whiskers and attach them to the inner corners of the upper eyelids. Follow the shape of the upper eyelids and extend the whiskers beyond the eyes, twisting and turning them.

Finish the Dragon

29 To create a leg, blow an elongated, flattened shape and use scissors to mark the segments, as for the lobster legs on page 212. Bend it at the knee or elbow joint. Using room-temperature scissors, cut it from the tube, warm over the flame of an alcohol burner, and attach it to the body. Repeat the same process for the rest of the legs. The back 2 should be attached about three-quarters of the way along the body, and the front 2 should be attached to the front third of the dragon's body.

30 To create the toes, shape 16 small, pointed claws out of black Isomalt and set aside.

31 Using the same color Isomalt or sugar as for the legs and arms, blow a small elongated tube. Warm over the flame of an alcohol burner and attach the wide end of a black claw to the tip of the elongated tube. Use scissors to mark segments at even intervals and bend at each mark to create a toe. Attach the toe to the last segment on a leg or arm.

32 Repeat the same steps to create a total of 8 toes and 8 fingers. Warm each of the toes and fingers over the flame of an alcohol burner and attach 4 toes to each leg and 4 fingers to each arm.

33 Warm the toes and fingers over the flame of an alcohol burner and attach to the support structure or base.

34 Airbrush the completed dragon with layers of yellow and red liquid food coloring.

35 Store the completed piece in an airtight container or plastic bag with limestone, calcium carbonate, or silica gel.

Horse

This is the most difficult figure to model. The entire figure is modeled out of one piece of Isomalt. It is highly recommended that you have a detailed drawing and a good understanding of the anatomy of the horse before you begin this piece. Check your local bookstore or the Internet for drawings to use for reference.

1 Begin to blow a sphere (see Blowing a Basic Sphere, steps 1 through 9, page 158).

2 Use your thumb and index finger to work a small ball away from the top of the sphere to form the head.

3 Begin to shape the head, defining the jaw and muzzle. Flatten the forehead to the top of the muzzle.

4 Just below the head, pull out a piece of Isomalt long enough to begin to form the forelegs.

5 Cut a slit in the muzzle with room-temperature scissors to form the mouth. Open the mouth.

6 Cut a slit in the piece you pulled for the forelegs to separate the 2 front legs.

7 Elongate and shape the front legs. Define the hoof, lower leg, knee, and upper leg on each one.

8 Use your fingers to model the shoulders and the withers (the ridge between the shoulder blades).

9 Farther down the body of the horse, pull a piece of Isomalt about 2 in/5 cm long from the main piece to form the back legs.

10 Cut the pulled piece with room-temperature scissors to separate the back legs.

11 Use your fingers to model the back legs, defining the hoof, lower leg, hock, and upper leg/hip on each one.

12 Use scissors to create the separation between the hindquarters at the back of the horse's body, where the tail will be.

13 Elongate and shape the horse's neck.

14 Use the point of the blade of an open pair of scissors to indent the Isomalt to form a nostril on either side of the muzzle.

15 Cool and remove the body from the tube (see Removing the Blown Piece from the Tube, page 163), closing the open end, before adding the ears, mane, and tail.

16 Using room-temperature scissors, cut 2 very small pieces of Isomalt and form them into the shape of ears. $\longrightarrow$

THE ART OF THE CONFECTIONER

FIRST ROW:

- Pull out a piece about 2 in/5 cm long to begin to form the forelegs.
- Cut a small slit for the horse's mouth.
- Cut to separate the two front legs.

SECOND ROW:

- Elongate and shape each foreleg.
- Pull out another piece toward the back of the horse and cut it to form the back legs.
- Carefully model the back legs and hindquarters.

17 Heat the wider end of the ears over the flame of an alcohol burner and attach the ears to the head just before the poll (the place where the head joins the neck).

18 To create the mane, pull a length of Isomalt and, using room-temperature scissors, cut it from the main piece. Stretch and fold the Isomalt a few times, forming a small ribbon. Cut it to the desired length for a piece of mane.

19 Twist the piece of mane, attach it to the top of the neck, and fold it to one side of the neck. Repeat with additional pieces of Isomalt until the mane is complete.

FIRST ROW:
- Slide your fingers along the neck to elongate and shape it.
- Use the point of the blade of an open pair of scissors to make an indentation for each nostril.
- Fold a small piece of Isomalt for each ear.

SECOND ROW:
- Twist each piece of mane to give it shape.
- Attach the mane pieces to the horse and fold each one to one side of the neck.
- Stretch and fold a wider ribbon for the tail.

20 The tail is made as one piece. Pull a length of Isomalt, cut it from the main piece, and stretch and fold it a few times to form a wider ribbon than you did for the mane. Cut it to the desired length for the tail.

21 Twist the tail to give it shape, warm over the flame of an alcohol burner, attach it to the rump of the horse, and shape it.

22 Store the completed piece in an airtight container or plastic bag with limestone, calcium carbonate, or silica gel.

6

New Trends

When I began to learn sugarwork, we knew only the traditional skills of casting, pulling, and blowing, and did not use many other techniques. The emphasis was on hand skills, and the showpieces highlighted realistic-looking animals, figurines, and flowers. The introduction of Isomalt drastically changed the style of sugar showpieces. Today's showpieces are more abstract and incorporate other techniques that add volume to the piece while saving time. Most of these newer techniques are not as difficult as the traditional pulling and blowing techniques.

It is still essential to be proficient in casting, pulling, and blowing, as these traditional techniques are still used as the basis for the support structure and other focal objects on a showpiece. The other techniques explained in this chapter produce pieces that are different in texture and shape and can be used to change the emotion of a showpiece. You would not want to use every technique from this chapter in one showpiece because the effect would be cluttered and chaotic. Choose the techniques that best convey and complement your theme. Keep the design simple and clean.

Sugar vs. Isomalt

Some of the techniques in this chapter can be accomplished using either Isomalt or sugar, while others are limited to just Isomalt or just sugar. The table below summarizes the techniques covered in this chapter and indicates whether Isomalt or sugar can be used.

TECHNIQUE	SUGAR	ISOMALT
Net Sugar		•
Pressed Sugar	•	
Bubble Sugar	•	•
Ice Casting		•
Rock Sugar		•
Sand Casting	•	•
Spun Sugar	•	•
Vinyl Tubes	•	•
Clear Filling		•
Clear Blowing		•
Straw Sugar	•	•
Saturated Sugar	•	

Net Sugar

The steps and photos below show how to use small portions of Isomalt to make small pieces of net sugar, but you could also cover an entire sheet with Isomalt to make one large piece of net sugar. You can use any combination of colors, or make the net sugar white and airbrush color onto the finished pieces.

1   Place a Silpat mat onto a sheet pan of the same size. Portion Isomalt granules onto the mat, leaving enough space between each portion to allow the Isomalt to spread flat as it melts.

2   Add a tiny pinch of powder color to each portion.

3   Cover the Isomalt with another Silpat mat.

4   Place in a 340°F/170°C oven for at least 10 minutes. The longer it stays in the oven beyond 10 minutes, the larger the holes will become. Check the Isomalt and, once the desired effect has been achieved, remove the pan from the oven.

5   Once cold remove the top Silpat. You may have to press a long ruler or metal bar against the top Silpat as you remove it to prevent the Isomalt from sticking.

6   Remove the finished pieces from the bottom Silpat. If desired, the pieces can be warmed under a heat lamp or on a food warmer and shaped. Store the finished pieces at room temperature in an airtight container with a drying agent like limestone, calcium carbonate, or silica gel.

 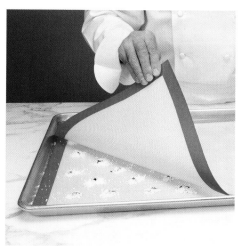

ABOVE:
- Portion the Isomalt onto the Silpat and add powder color to each portion.
- Cover with a second Silpat mat.

OPPOSITE:
- Immediately remove the top Silpat to reveal the finished net sugar.

Pressed Sugar

Pressed sugar is a very simple technique used to create effective accents for a colorful, shiny showpiece. Pressed sugar pieces have an uneven texture and are not shiny, so they contrast well with shinier pieces. The pieces shown here are small and thin, but it is also possible to make thicker and larger pieces. A base can be made of pressed sugar as long as you have a few days to let it dry. Color can be added to the water before it is mixed with the sugar, or color can be airbrushed onto the finished pieces. The sugar can either be pressed into a silicone or plastic mold, or rolled between metal bars and cut into shapes. Suitable molds are available at hobby stores.

1   Place 35.3 oz/1000 g granulated sugar into a mixing bowl.

2   Add 2 oz/¼ cup/50 ml water. If a fine sugar is used, more liquid may be required.

3   Mix well. The mixture should appear like smooth, wet sand.

4   To use a mold, press the mixture firmly into the mold and level the top against a bench scraper.

5   Place the mold onto a flat surface and set aside to dry completely. For a flat cutout, this will take about half a day. Thicker pieces such as a sphere mold, about 1 in/2.5 cm thick, can take up to 2 to 3 days to dry completely, but you can force the drying by placing the piece in a 120°F/48°C oven. Once the sugar is dry, remove the object from the mold.

6   To roll out the sugar between metal bars, place an acrylic base on your work surface and place the metal bars on the acrylic base.

7   Scoop pressed sugar between the metal bars and roll it flat using a smooth, plastic rolling pin.

8   Cut shapes using any type of cookie cutter and set aside to dry completely. This should take about half a day.

9   Once the pressed sugar is dry, separate the shapes from the excess sugar. The excess pieces can be broken down and used in a recipe for casting, pulling, or blowing sugar.

10 Add color to the finished molded or cutout pieces using an airbrush as desired. Store at room temperature.

- Mix the sugar and water until it resembles smooth, wet sand.
- Press the mixture firmly into a mold and level the top against a bench scraper.
- Place the molded sugar on a flat surface to dry.

- Alternatively, roll out the pressed sugar between metal bars and cut shapes with a cookie cutter.
- Gently separate the cutout shapes.
- The pressed sugar shapes on the left were cut from rolled-out sugar; those on the right were pressed into molds.

Bubble Sugar

Bubble sugar is effective and versatile as a background accent. Placed in and around objects in a marine showpiece, it looks like water, and when it is warmed it can be stretched to look like lace. Use it around a flower in place of leaves and ribbons for a different look. The syrup can be colored before it is poured or color can be applied by airbrush after it is shaped and cooled. Bubble sugar can be created using either sugar or Isomalt.

Sugar Recipe for Bubble Sugar

INGREDIENTS	METRIC	US	VOLUME
Sugar	1000 g	35.25 oz	4⅔ cups
Water, cold	350 g	12.75 oz	1½ cups
Glucose syrup	200 g	7 oz	½ cup + 2 tbsp
YIELD	**1550 g**	**55 oz**	

Isomalt Recipe for Bubble Sugar

INGREDIENTS	METRIC	US	VOLUME
Isomalt	1000 g	35.25 oz	4⅔ cups
Water, cold	100 g	3.5 oz	¼ cup + 1 tbsp
YIELD	**1100 g**	**38.75 oz**	

1   Crumple a piece of parchment paper into a ball. Unfold the ball and flatten the paper on your work surface.

2   Combine all the ingredients for the sugar or Isomalt syrup in a saucepan and bring to a boil. Fill a bowl larger than the saucepan halfway with cold water and set aside.

3   If using sugar, boil the syrup to 320°F/160°C. If using Isomalt, boil to 340 to 360°F/170 to 180°C.

4   When the syrup reaches the required temperature, plunge the pan into the bowl of cold water to stop the temperature from increasing.

5   Place the pan on a towel and allow the syrup to cool. Test the consistency by dipping a spoon into the syrup and holding it above the saucepan. The syrup running back into the pan must flow in a steady thread. If the syrup drips, it is not ready.

6   When the syrup has reached the right consistency, pour a thin stream of thickened syrup across the parchment paper approximately ½ in/1 cm from the top edge of the paper.   →

7 Grasp the upper corners of the parchment paper and pick it up. Shake the paper gently to force the syrup to run down the paper. The air trapped in the creases of the parchment creates the bubbles in the final piece. Shaking the paper increases the bubble effect.

8 Place the parchment paper back on the work surface and allow the sugar or Isomalt to harden for about 5 minutes.

9 Place the parchment paper sugar- or Isomalt-side down. Place a ruler against a corner of the paper and pull the paper to release the bubble sugar.

10 Bubble sugar can be warmed with a blowtorch or under a heat lamp and shaped as desired. Color can be added to the finished pieces with an airbrush. Store the finished bubble sugar at room temperature in an airtight container with a drying agent such as limestone, calcium carbonate, or silica gel.

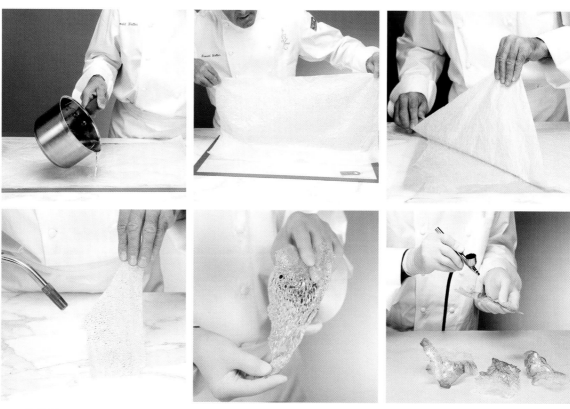

FIRST ROW:
- Pour a thin stream of thickened syrup across the parchment paper.
- Grasp the upper corners of the parchment paper, pick it up, and shake the paper gently to force the syrup to run down it.
- Place a ruler against a corner of the paper while pulling from the corner to release the bubble sugar.

SECOND ROW:
- Warm the bubble sugar with a blowtorch so it can be shaped.
- Finished bubble sugar has a beautiful lacy look.
- The completed bubble sugar pieces can be airbrushed to finish.

Ice Casting

This technique can be used to make coral for a marine showpiece or to use as an accent piece to bring more color and dimension to a showpiece. The viscosity of the syrup is very important. If the syrup is too thick when it is poured into the ice, it will not spread through the ice. If the syrup is too warm, it will spread quickly and become too thin. Pieces cast over ice are not suitable for use as a base. There is not enough smooth surface on which to attach decoration, and the humidity content is too high.

Isomalt Recipe for Ice Casting

INGREDIENTS	METRIC	US	VOLUME
Isomalt	1000 g	35.25 oz	4⅔ cups
Water, cold	100 g	3.5 oz	¼ cup + 1 tbsp
YIELD	**1100 g**	**38.75 oz**	

1 Fill a metal bowl with ice cubes. Place a metal cooling rack over a pan. Set aside.

2 Prepare the syrup. Place the cold water in a medium pan over medium heat. Add a small amount of the Isomalt. Stir occasionally with a heat-resistant spatula until the Isomalt dissolves. Repeat this step until all of the Isomalt is dissolved. Take care not to splash Isomalt onto the inside wall of the pan. Once the sides of the pan become warm, the Isomalt will stick. It does not dissolve like sugar and cannot be washed off the inside wall with a brush and water. Keep the inside clean by scraping with a wet, heat-resistant spatula.

3 Boil to 340 to 360°F/170 to 180°C, then remove from the heat.

4 Add water-soluble powder color, which has been dissolved in water, to the syrup, if desired.

5 Allow the syrup to cool until it begins to thicken. This can take from 5 to 10 minutes, depending on the size of the pan.

6 Pour the syrup over the ice into the metal bowl.

7 Allow to cool until set, about 5 minutes.

8 Wearing gloves, remove the Isomalt piece from the ice and place on the metal cooling rack.

9 Let set at room temperature until the piece is clear of ice. Store the finished cast piece at room temperature in an airtight container with a drying agent such as limestone, calcium carbonate, or silica gel.

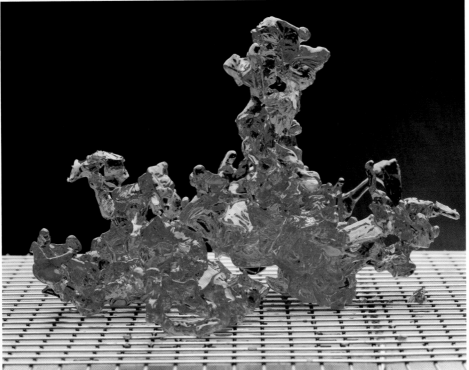

FIRST ROW:
- Pour the syrup over the ice.
- Remove the set piece from the ice and place on a metal cooling rack to drain.

SECOND ROW:
- A finished ice-cast piece.

Rock Sugar

This is similar to the rock sugar created with Pastillage Recipe II in chapter 2 (see page 60). If you want to add color to the mixture, add water-soluble powder color, which has been dissolved in water, to the syrup or use colored royal icing. Rock sugar looks like coral and is attractive on a marine showpiece. Take care when handling and attaching as it crumbles easily. Like pressed sugar, it is dull and contrasts well with shiny sugar or Isomalt pieces.

Sugar Recipe for Rock Sugar

INGREDIENTS	METRIC	US	VOLUME
Sugar	1000 g	35.25 oz	4⅔ cups
Water, cold	300 g	10.5 oz	1⅓ cups
Royal icing	50 g	1.76 oz	2 tsp
YIELD	**1350 g**	**47.51 oz**	

1   Line a bowl with aluminum foil.

2   Combine the sugar and water in a medium saucepan. Fill a bowl larger than the saucepan halfway with cold water and set aside.

3   Bring the sugar and water to a boil over high heat. Boil to 290°F/144°C.

4   As soon as the syrup reaches the required temperature, plunge the pan into the bowl of cold water to stop the temperature from increasing.

5   Add the royal icing and beat well. The mixture will rise and collapse as you beat it.

6   Place the pan back over high heat and stir until the mixture rises to the top edge of the pan.

7   Immediately pour the mixture into the aluminum foil–covered bowl. The mixture will collapse to two-thirds of the original volume.

8   Allow the mixture to cool for about 2 hours.

9   Remove the cooled sugar piece from the bowl and peel off the aluminum foil. Break the sugar into smaller pieces.

10   Shape the individual pieces as desired using a paring knife.

11   Store the finished pieces at room temperature in an airtight container with a drying agent such as limestone, calcium carbonate, or silica gel.

FIRST ROW:

- Add the royal icing to the sugar syrup.
- The mixture will rise and collapse as you beat it.
- Place the pan back over high heat and stir until the mixture rises to the top edge of the pan.

SECOND ROW:

- Immediately pour the sugar into an aluminum foil–covered bowl.
- Remove the cooled rock sugar from the bowl and shape using a paring knife.
- Rock sugar can be broken and shaped into pieces of any size.

Sand Casting

Sand casting is a very interesting and easy technique that can be used as a base or an accent. Due to the unusual technique it will look different every time, with a free-flowing look. I use this mostly on pieces that have a nautical theme, or on pieces that are very geometrical to break the natural lines of the piece.

Sugar Recipe for Sand Casting

INGREDIENTS	METRIC	US	VOLUME
Sugar	1000 g	35.25 oz	4⅔ cups
Water, cold	350 g	12.75 oz	1½ cups
Glucose syrup	200 g	7 oz	½ cup + 2 tbsp
YIELD	**1550 g**	**55 oz**	

Isomalt Recipe for Sand Casting

INGREDIENTS	METRIC	US	VOLUME
Isomalt	1000 g	35.25 oz	4⅔ cups
Water, cold	100 g	3.5 oz	¼ cup + 1 tbsp
YIELD	**1100 g**	**38.75 oz**	

1   Place a layer of granulated sugar about 2 in/5 cm deep into a metal bowl or pan. Create a well in the sugar.

2   Fill a bowl larger than the saucepan that will be used to boil the syrup halfway with cold water and set aside.

3   Prepare the syrup. If using sugar, place all the ingredients in a medium saucepan and boil over medium heat to 320°F/160°C. If using Isomalt, place the cold water in a medium saucepan over medium heat. Add a small amount of the Isomalt and stir occasionally with a heat-resistant spatula until the Isomalt dissolves. Repeat this step until all of the Isomalt is dissolved. Take care not to splash Isomalt onto the inside wall of the pan. Once the sides of the pan become warm, the Isomalt will stick. It does not dissolve like sugar and cannot be washed off the inside wall with a brush and water. Keep the inside clean by scraping with a wet, heat-resistant spatula. Boil the Isomalt mixture to 340 to 360°F/170 to 180°C.

4   As soon as the syrup reaches the required temperature, plunge the pan into the bowl of cold water to stop the temperature from increasing.

5   Place the pan onto a towel and allow the syrup to cool until it begins to thicken. This will take about 1 minute for sugar, or about 5 minutes for Isomalt.

6   Pour the thickened syrup into the well created in the granulated sugar.

7 Cover the syrup with additional granulated sugar.

8 Use the handle of a wooden spoon to adjust the amount of sugar that is underneath the syrup. Adding sugar will raise that section of the finished piece. Removing sugar will lower that section of the finished piece.

9 Allow the syrup to cool completely. This will take 30 minutes to an hour, depending on the thickness of the piece.

10 Remove the finished piece from the granulated sugar and brush off any loose granules of sugar.

11 Apply color to the piece using an airbrush, as desired.

12 Store the finished piece at room temperature in an airtight container with a drying agent such as limestone, calcium carbonate, or silica gel.

FIRST ROW:
- Create a well in the sugar.
- Pour the syrup into the well.
- Cover the syrup with additional granulated sugar.

SECOND ROW:
- Use the handle of a wooden spoon to shape the warm syrup by moving the granulated sugar underneath.
- Remove the finished piece from the granulated sugar.
- Airbrush the sand cast piece to finish.

Spun Sugar

This is an old technique. I used to cut off the end of a whisk, dip the exposed wires into syrup, and fling the syrup over metal bars. It was very messy. This technique using the spun sugar tool is cleaner and more productive. The spun sugar nest is often used for Easter as a bowl to hold flowers and other delicate objects. Spun sugar is highly sensitive to humidity. If it is made ahead of time, it must be stored with limestone; otherwise make it for immediate use.

Sugar Recipe for Spun Sugar

INGREDIENTS	METRIC	US	VOLUME
Sugar	1000 g	35.25 oz	4⅔ cups
Water, cold	350 g	12.75 oz	1½ cups
Glucose syrup	200 g	7 oz	½ cup + 2 tbsp
YIELD	**1550 g**	**55 oz**	

Isomalt Recipe for Spun Sugar

INGREDIENTS	METRIC	US	VOLUME
Isomalt	1000 g	35.25 oz	4⅔ cups
Water, cold	100 g	3.5 oz	¼ cup + 1 tbsp
YIELD	**1100 g**	**38.75 oz**	

1   Fill a bowl larger than the saucepan that will be used to boil the syrup halfway with cold water and set aside.

2   Prepare the syrup. If using sugar, place all the ingredients in a medium saucepan and boil over medium heat to 320°F/160°C. If using Isomalt, place the cold water in a medium saucepan over medium heat. Add a small amount of the Isomalt and stir occasionally with a heat-resistant spatula until the Isomalt dissolves. Repeat this step until all of the Isomalt is dissolved. Take care not to splash Isomalt onto the in-side wall of the pan. Once the sides of the pan become warm, the Isomalt will stick. It does not dissolve like sugar and cannot be washed off the inside wall with a brush and water. Keep the inside clean by scraping with a wet, heat-resistant spatula. Boil to 340 to 360°F/170 to 180°C.

3   As soon as the syrup reaches the required temperature, plunge the pan into the bowl of cold water to stop the temperature from increasing.

4   Place the pan onto a towel and allow the syrup to cool for 2 to 5 minutes for sugar or about 10 minutes for Isomalt. Test the consistency by dipping a spoon into the syrup and holding it above the pan. The syrup running back into the pan must flow in a steady thread. If the syrup drips, it is not ready.

5   As soon as the syrup has cooled to the right consistency, follow the instructions below to create a pulled bird's nest, ladled bird's nest, or fan on page 263, or use the syrup to create any other shape you desire.

Create a Pulled Bird's Nest

1   Wear gloves to keep the hot sugar or Isomalt from contact with your skin.

2   Dip the spun sugar tool into the syrup and allow the syrup to drain back into the pan until you see even streams of syrup.

3   Using a side-to-side motion, grasp the strings of sugar and pull them away from the tool.

4   Keep the sugar strings in your hand and repeat step 3 to pull more sugar strings away from the tool.

5   Repeat this motion until you have enough strings in your hand to shape into a nest of the desired size.

6   Shape the strings into a nest. They will harden immediately.

Create a Ladled Bird's Nest

1   Lightly coat the back of a soup ladle with vegetable oil.

2   Dip a spoon into the syrup and allow the syrup to drain back into the pan until you see even streams of syrup.

3   Use the spoon to apply syrup to the back of the oiled ladle using back-and-forth motions of your wrist. Cover the entire ladle to create the nest. The syrup will harden immediately.

4   Use the spoon to apply additional syrup in a circular motion around the outer edge of the ladle. This strengthens the upper edge of the nest.

5   Trim the edges of the nest with your hands or with room-temperature scissors and remove from the ladle.   →

FIRST ROW:
- Dip your tool into the syrup and allow the syrup to drain back into the pan until you see even streams.
- Using a side-to-side motion, grasp the strings of sugar and pull away from the tool.
- Repeat the pulling motion until you have enough strings in your hand for a nest.

SECOND ROW:
- Arrange the strings into a nest shape.
- For a fan, flick your wrist back and forth to apply the syrup to an oiled plate.
- Trim the excess strings hanging over the edge of the plate.

THIRD ROW:
- Trim the sides of the fan to create a clean edge.
- Remove from the plate and bend to shape the fan.
- A completed spun sugar fan.

THE ART OF THE CONFECTIONER

Create a Fan

1   Lightly coat a metal plate with vegetable oil.

2   Dip a spoon into the syrup and allow the syrup to drain back into the pan until you see even streams of syrup.

3   Use the spoon to apply syrup to the oiled plate using back-and-forth motions of your wrist. Starting in the center of the plate, move your hand to the outer edge, and return to the center of the plate. Continue this motion around the plate to create a fan shape of the desired width. The syrup will harden immediately.

4   Use the spoon to apply additional syrup heavily to the bottom edges for support.

5   Use room-temperature scissors to trim the strings hanging over the edge of the plate and trim the sides of the fan.

6   Remove the completed fan from the plate and shape as desired.

Vinyl Tubes

Vinyl tubes are perfectly suited for Isomalt or sugar. This is a clean technique that creates clean shapes. Be sure to use thin vinyl tubing, as thick tubes are difficult to remove from the cooled Isomalt or sugar. As severe burns can occur, do not hold the tube while it is being filled. Always tape or clamp the tube to a stable object. I recommend that you cast the tube in a straight line and warm it under a heat lamp to bend or shape it. It can be difficult to remove a bent or shaped piece from the vinyl tube without breaking the piece.

Sugar Recipe for Vinyl Tubes

INGREDIENTS	METRIC	US	VOLUME
Sugar	1000 g	35.25 oz	4⅔ cups
Water, cold	350 g	12.75 oz	1½ cups
Glucose syrup	200 g	7 oz	½ cup + 2 tbsp
YIELD	**1550 g**	**55 oz**	

Isomalt Recipe for Vinyl Tubes

INGREDIENTS	METRIC	US	VOLUME
Isomalt	1000 g	35.25 oz	4⅔ cups
Water, cold	100 g	3.5 oz	¼ cup + 1 tbsp
YIELD	**1100 g**	**38.75 oz**	

1 Prepare the vinyl tube by taping or clamping it to the edge of your work space or another stable object. This will allow you to keep your hands off the tube while pouring the hot syrup into it.

2 Fill a bowl larger than the saucepan that will be used to boil the syrup halfway with cold water and set aside.

3 Prepare the syrup. If using sugar, place all the ingredients in a medium saucepan and boil over medium heat to 320°F/160°C. If using Isomalt, place the cold water in a medium saucepan over medium heat. Add a small amount of the Isomalt and stir occasionally with a heat-resistant spatula until the Isomalt dissolves. Repeat this step until all of the Isomalt is dissolved. Take care not to splash Isomalt onto the inside wall of the pan. Once the sides of the pan become warm, the Isomalt will stick. It does not dissolve like sugar and cannot be washed off the inside wall with a brush and water. Keep the inside clean by scraping with a wet, heat-resistant spatula. Boil to 340 to 360°F/170 to 180°C.

4 As soon as the syrup reaches the required temperature, plunge the pan into the bowl of cold water to stop the temperature from increasing.   →

5 Immediately pour the syrup into the tube, being careful not to hold the tube with your hands.

6 Close the ends of the tube tightly with a clamp.

7 Lay the filled tube flat on a work surface and allow to cool until the sugar has hardened completely and does not move when you lift the tube. This can take several hours for a larger tube. Simple shapes can be made with the tube while it is cooling. Complicated forms such as a tied knot will have to be done after the syrup has hardened and been removed from the tube.

8 Use a utility knife to cut lengthwise through one edge of the vinyl tube. Take care not to apply pressure directly to the sugar or Isomalt tube, which could scratch or crack the tube.

9 Wearing gloves, carefully remove the vinyl from the tube.

10 To shape the tube, place it under a heat lamp or on a food warmer until it becomes flexible and then shape it as desired.

11 Store the finished tube at room temperature in an airtight container with a drying agent such as limestone, calcium carbonate, or silica gel.

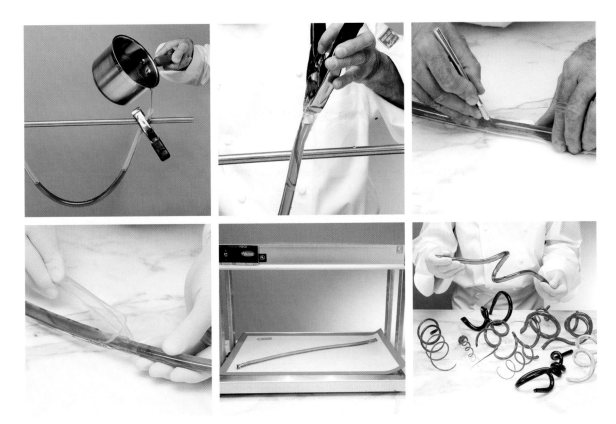

FIRST ROW:
- Attach the tube to a stable object before pouring the syrup in.
- Tightly clamp the ends of the tube.
- Use a knife to cut through the vinyl.

SECOND ROW:
- Carefully peel the vinyl off the tube.
- To shape the finished tube, first place it under heat until it becomes flexible.
- Shape the tube as desired to finish.

Clear Pulling

To get Isomalt as clear as glass, it must be boiled to a high temperature. It is essential to work at a high temperature because the Isomalt cannot be pulled to cool it, but it is a big challenge to work at these temperatures. It is best to make simple, abstract shapes as it is difficult to form shapes with hot Isomalt. Set up a hair dryer turned on at a cool or cold setting to help you shape the Isomalt.

Isomalt Recipe for Clear Pulling

INGREDIENTS	METRIC	US	VOLUME
Isomalt	1000 g	35.25 oz	4⅔ cups
Water, cold	100 g	3.5 oz	¼ cup + 1 tbsp
YIELD	1100 g	38.75 oz	

1   Place a Silpat mat onto a marble or granite work surface.

2   Pour the cold water into a medium saucepan over medium heat.

3   Add a small amount of the Isomalt and stir occasionally with a heat-resistant spatula until the Isomalt dissolves. Repeat this step until all of the Isomalt is dissolved. Take care not to splash Isomalt onto the inside wall of the pan. Once the sides of the pan become warm, the Isomalt will stick. It does not dissolve like sugar and cannot be washed off the inside wall with a brush and water. Keep the inside clean by scraping with a wet, heat-resistant spatula. Boil the Isomalt mixture to 360°F/182°C or higher.

4   As soon as the syrup reaches the required temperature, pour it onto the Silpat. The syrup will cool first on the outside edges. Wearing gloves to keep the hot Isomalt from contact with your skin, use your fingertips to push and fold the outside edge toward the center of the pool as you see the edges begin to cool.

5   Continue to push and fold the edges toward the center until all of the syrup has been incorporated. To keep the Isomalt clear, you must not pull it.

6   Prepare another batch of Isomalt following steps 1 through 5 above, but add powder color to the Isomalt mixture during the boiling process in step 3.

7   Use room-temperature scissors to cut a small piece of the clear Isomalt. Cut a smaller piece of the colored Isomalt. Press the colored Isomalt into the clear Isomalt.

8   Use your hands to pull the Isomalt to elongate and shape it as desired. Use the hair dryer, set on the cool or cold setting, to help achieve the final shape.

9   Let the finished piece cool until it has completely hardened. Store at room temperature in an airtight container with a drying agent such as limestone, calcium carbonate, or silica gel.

→

- For clear pulling, press the colored Isomalt and the clear Isomalt together.
- Pull to elongate and shape the Isomalt.
- Let the finished shape cool until fully set.

Clear Blowing

You will need to be proficient in the technique of blowing a sphere (see Blowing a Basic Sphere, page 158) before attempting this technique. As with the Clear Pulling technique on page 269, to get Isomalt as clear as glass it must be boiled to a high temperature. Because it is a challenge to work at these temperatures, it is best to make simple, abstract blown shapes. Keep a hair dryer turned on at a cool or cold setting to help you shape the Isomalt.

Isomalt Recipe for Clear Blowing

INGREDIENTS	METRIC	US	VOLUME
Isomalt	1000 g	35.25 oz	4⅔ cups
Water, cold	100 g	3.5 oz	¼ cup + 1 tbsp
YIELD	**1100 g**	**38.75 oz**	

1 Place a Silpat mat onto a marble or granite work surface.

2 Pour the cold water into a medium saucepan over medium heat.

3 Add a small amount of the Isomalt and stir occasionally with a heat-resistant spatula until the Isomalt dissolves. Repeat this step until all of the Isomalt is dissolved. Take care not to splash Isomalt onto the inside wall of the pan. Once the sides of the pan become warm, the Isomalt will stick. It does not dissolve like sugar and cannot be washed off the inside wall with a brush and water. Keep the inside clean by scraping with a wet, heat-resistant spatula. Boil the Isomalt mixture to 360°F/182°C or higher.

$\rightarrow$

4   As soon as the syrup reaches the required temperature, pour it onto the Silpat. The syrup will cool first on the outside edges. Wearing gloves to keep the hot Isomalt from contact with your skin, use your fingertips to push and fold the outside edge toward the center of the pool as you see the edges begin to cool.

5   Continue to push and fold the edges toward the center until all of the syrup has been incorporated. To keep the Isomalt clear, you must not pull it.

6   Prepare another batch of Isomalt following steps 1 through 5 above, but add powder color to the Isomalt mixture during the boiling process in step 3.

7   Use room-temperature scissors to cut a small piece of the clear Isomalt. Cut a smaller piece of the colored Isomalt. Press the colored Isomalt into the clear Isomalt.

8   Make a hole in the Isomalt and attach the Isomalt to the tube of a hand pump with a one-way valve.

9   Add air to create a sphere. The sphere does not need to be modeled evenly.

10 Use a blowtorch to create an opening in the sphere.

11 Use your hands to widen the opening and elongate the Isomalt.

12 Set the pump onto the work surface so you can use both hands to shape the final piece as desired. Use a hair dryer on the cool or cold setting to help shape the final piece.

13 Cool the piece and remove it from the tube (see Removing the Blown Piece from the Tube, page 163). Store the finished piece at room temperature in an airtight container with a drying agent such as limestone, calcium carbonate, or silica gel.

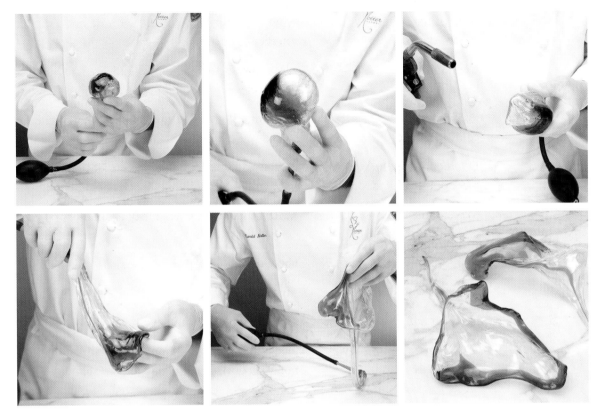

FIRST ROW:

- Make a hole in the Isomalt and attach it to the end of the tube.
- Pump air in to blow a sphere.
- Use a blowtorch to melt an opening in one side of the sphere.

SECOND ROW:

- Pull to widen the opening and elongate the shape.
- Set the pump down and use both hands to finish shaping the piece.
- Cool and remove the finished blown piece from the tube.

Straw Sugar

The idea for straw sugar came from candy making. It resembles driftwood and other organic support shapes. After the ribbon is formed into a tube, it must be pulled quickly a number of times to incorporate enough air into the piece. The air will help it to cool quickly so the final piece is shiny. Without sufficient air worked into the piece, the piece will become dull and heavy looking.

Sugar Recipe for Straw Sugar

INGREDIENTS	METRIC	US	VOLUME
Sugar	1000 g	35.25 oz	4⅔ cups
Water, cold	350 g	12.75 oz	1½ cups
Glucose syrup	200 g	7 oz	½ cup + 2 tbsp
YIELD	**1550 g**	**55 oz**	

Isomalt Recipe for Straw Sugar

INGREDIENTS	METRIC	US	VOLUME
Isomalt	1000 g	35.25 oz	4⅔ cups
Water, cold	100 g	3.5 oz	¼ cup + 1 tbsp
YIELD	**1100 g**	**38.75 oz**	

1 Place a Silpat mat onto a marble or granite work surface.

2 Prepare the syrup. If using sugar, place all the ingredients in a medium saucepan and boil over medium heat to 320°F/160°C. If using Isomalt, place the cold water in a medium saucepan over medium heat. Add a small amount of the Isomalt and stir occasionally with a heat-resistant spatula until the Isomalt dissolves. Repeat this step until all of the Isomalt is dissolved. Take care not to splash Isomalt onto the inside wall of the pan. Once the sides of the pan become warm, the Isomalt will stick. It does not dissolve like sugar and cannot be washed off the inside wall with a brush and water. Keep the inside clean by scraping with a wet, heat-resistant spatula. Boil to 340 to 360°F/170 to 180°C.

3 As soon as the syrup reaches the required temperature, pour it onto the Silpat. The syrup will cool first on the outside edges. Wearing gloves to keep the hot Isomalt from contact with your skin, use your fingertips to push and fold the outside edge toward the center of the pool as you see the edges begin to cool.

4 Continue to push and fold the edges toward the center until all of the syrup has been incorporated.

5 Roll the Isomalt into a rope. It is essential to keep the round rope form in place as you perform the next steps.

6 Pull the rope to lengthen it and fold it in half, then stretch and fold it again.

7 Perform a third stretch and fold. You should now have 8 strands side by side like a ribbon.

8 Curl the ribbon lengthwise to form a hollow tube. Keep the center of the tube open.

9 Press each end closed, keeping the center of the tube open.

10 Quickly perform multiple stretch and folds without compressing the tube. The piece will become shiny and show striations of darker and lighter colors.

11 When the sugar begins to cool too much to work, bend and push it into the desired shape.

12 Cool with a hair dryer set on the cool or cold setting.

13 Store at room temperature in an airtight container with a drying agent such as limestone, calcium carbonate, or silica gel.

FIRST ROW:
- Pull a long rope and fold it in half.
- Curl the ribbon lengthwise to form a tube.
- Press the ends closed, leaving the center of the tube hollow.

SECOND ROW:
- Quickly stretch and fold the tube without compressing it.
- Bend and push the sugar into the desired shape.
- Finished pieces of straw sugar.

Saturated Sugar

In these three saturated sugar techniques, we force crystallization, controlling where the crystallization happens and how large the crystals become. Crystals will grow more quickly if the solution is changed often. I recommend changing the solution once a week to create big crystals. The solution can be colored using water-dissolvable powder color, if desired. Saturated sugar pieces can last forever as humidity does not seem to affect them.

Crystals

Create the Seeding Crystals

1 Mix a solution of 1 part water to 3 parts sugar in a saucepan and place over high heat.

2 Cook at a rolling boil for 1 minute and until the solution reaches a density of 33 to 35 degrees Baumé.

3 Pour the solution into a heatproof container. Let sit uncovered for 1 week; crystals will form.

4 Remove the crystals and dispose of the solution.

Use the Seeding Crystals

5 Attach the crystals to string and suspend them inside a very clean container. The container must be clean so the sugar crystals attach to the seed crystals and not the sides of the container.

6 Mix a solution of 1 part water to 3 parts sugar in a saucepan over high heat.

7 Cook at a rolling boil for 1 minute and until the solution reaches a density of 33 to 35 degrees Baumé.

8 Immediately cover the saucepan with plastic wrap and allow it to cool overnight.

9 Pour the cooled, supersaturated solution into the container with the seeding crystals.

10 Let the crystals sit in the solution, changing the solution weekly until they reach the desired size.

11 Place a cooling rack over a pan.

12 Remove the crystals from the solution and place them on the cooling rack to dry.

13 Store the completed crystals at room temperature in an airtight container. There is no need for any drying agent.

FIRST ROW:
- Suspend the crystals inside a very clean container.
- Pour the supersaturated solution into the container.

SECOND ROW:
- Remove the finished crystals from the container and set on a cooling rack over a pan to dry.

Pastillage Shapes with Sugar Crystals

1 Place a cooling rack on a pan. Set metal bars on the cooling rack.

2 Mix a solution of 1 part water to 3 parts sugar in a saucepan and place over high heat.

3 Cook at a rolling boil for 1 minute and until the solution reaches a density of 33 to 35 degrees Baumé.

4 Pour the solution into a flat pan. Immediately set pastillage shapes onto the surface of the syrup.

5 Let set for about 5 hours until you see crystals inside the pastillage shapes. If they set for too long (more than a day, for example), the crystals will become too thick.

6 Remove the pastillage shapes from the solution. Clean the outer edges with a paring knife.

7 Set the cleaned shapes against the metal bars on the cooling rack to dry.

8 Store the finished pieces at room temperature in an airtight container with a drying agent such as limestone, calcium carbonate, or silica gel.

FIRST ROW:
- Gently set the pastillage shapes on the surface of the syrup.
- Crystals will begin to form inside the pastillage shapes.
- When ready to remove the shapes, set up a cooling rack over a pan and place metal bars on the rack.

SECOND ROW:
- Clean the excess crystals from the outer edges of each shape.
- Lean the cleaned shapes against the metal bars on the rack to dry.
- The sugar crystals are visible inside the finished pastillage shape.

Crystallized Blown Sugar Objects

1 Prepare a clean container. The container must be clean so the sugar crystals attach to the object and not the sides of the container.

2 Attach the blown sugar object to a plate or lid larger than the opening of the container so it can be suspended inside the container.

3 Mix a solution of 1 part water to 3 parts sugar in a saucepan and place over high heat.

4 Cook at a rolling boil for 1 minute and until the solution reaches a density of 33 to 35 degrees Baumé.

5 Pour the solution into the clean container.

6 Place the plate or lid over the container to suspend the blown sugar object in the solution.

7 Allow to sit for 3 to 5 days until the object is covered in crystals.

8 Place a cooling rack over a pan.

9 Remove the object from the solution and detach it from the plate or lid.

10 Place the object on the cooling rack to dry.

11 Store the finished pieces at room temperature in an airtight container. There is no need for any drying agent.

– Attach the blown sugar object to a plate or lid and suspend it in the solution.
– Pull up the lid to remove the object from the solution.
– Set the object on a rack over a bowl to dry.

Pastillage-and-Sugar Geodes

1   Roll out a batch of Pastillage Recipe I (see page 33).

2   Cut out 2 pieces of pastillage and place each inside a half-dome mold.

3   Trim off any excess pastillage at the edges of the molds.

4   With an exacto knife, cut equal-size semicircles into one edge of each dome.

5   Let the pastillage dry for 2 days.

6   Remove the pastillage from the molds.

7   Prepare a batch of Pastillage Glue (see page 67). Glue the two half domes together to form a sphere, with the semicircle cutouts together to form an access hole.

8   Allow the glue to set for about a day.

9   Place the finished dome on a metal ring with the access hole facing up.

10   Mix a solution of 1 part water to 3 parts sugar in a saucepan and place over high heat.

11   Cook at a rolling boil for 1 minute. Add water-dissolvable powder color to the mixture while it boils, if desired. Boil until the solution reaches a density of 33 to 35 degrees Baumé.

12   Immediately cover the saucepan with plastic wrap and allow to cool overnight.

13   Pour the cooled syrup into the pastillage sphere through the access hole.

14   Let set for 3 to 5 days.

15   Use your hands to break the dome open around the access hole at the top and let the remaining syrup run out.

16   Let the domes dry for a day, then break into the desired pieces.

17   Store the finished pieces at room temperature in an airtight container. There is no need for any drying agent. $\rightarrow$

FIRST ROW:
- Press the pastillage into a half-dome mold.
- Trim the excess pastillage.
- Cut semicircles out of each dome, making sure both semicircles are the same size.

SECOND ROW:
- Line up the semicircle cutouts to form a hole and glue the two dome halves together.
- Pour the syrup in through the access hole.
- Break the domes open to reveal the sugar geodes.

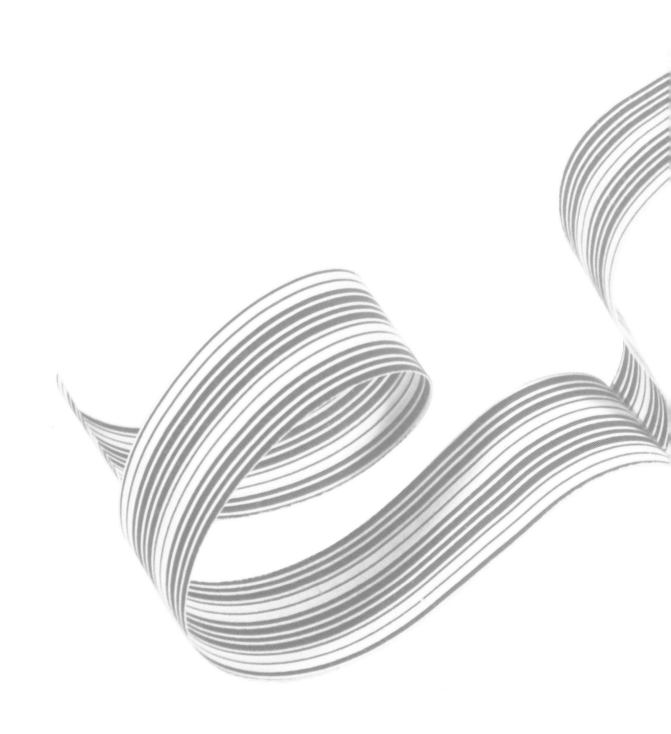

7

Competition

Competing can be one of the deepest learning experiences of your professional career—especially when competing on a team of three, where you have to show, share, and constantly improve your skills. Competing in a pastry competition is very similar to competing in a sport; you are only as strong as the weakest team member. To achieve success, it is essential to be able to work as part of a team, to be critical and to be able to take criticism, and to take hard hits, analyze them, and use them to grow stronger. It is not only about being creative and a good craftsman; it has a lot to do with character, showing up to practice sessions on time, and being helpful and forgiving. It is also about discipline. A session is not finished until the last bowl is washed and dried, and the floor is clean again. A competition is not finished until you have returned home and equipment and supplies are stored and filed away. Too often I have seen competitors prepare only for the competition, thinking the hard work is over once the showpiece is on the table.

Preparing mentally and physically is only the beginning. Are you capable of fixing a broken piece at the last minute? Will you be able to handle a mistake of one of your team members? How will you handle a failure without a lot of excuses? It is simple—attitude is as important as professional skill itself.

It is also essential to build a support network of friends, family, and coworkers. The truth is that the more you give or have given, the more you receive in return.

Preparing to Compete

Competing is fun, but it is also hard work and requires many hours of physical and mental preparation. There are many things to consider when making the decision to compete. Some of the key steps in preparing for the big event include:

1 **SELECTING THE RIGHT COMPETITION:** It is a good idea to attend one or more competitions as a spectator to see firsthand how they are run. Then you must determine what type of competition to train for. In some, competitors bring finished pieces to display for judging, while in others the competitors create their pieces in front of the judges. Whichever type you choose, as a beginner you will probably want to start with one or more local competitions.

2 **GAINING EXPERIENCE:** Volunteering to assist a competition team is an optimal way to get valuable experience and to gain an understanding of what happens during the event. You may be able to find opportunities to volunteer by talking to the organizers of the event or by checking the Internet. It may also be helpful to find a mentor who has trained and competed before and can pass on the knowledge he or she has gained through these experiences.

3 **RESEARCHING THE EVENT:** Learning about the event beforehand is critical. Some essential things to research include the details of the venue, such as what the temperature and humidity of the space will be like, and what supplies you should plan to pack and bring to the event. It is also important to learn about how you can organize your work space at the event, and how you will be able to present the finished showpiece.

4 **GETTING TO KNOW THE JUDGES:** Educate yourself beforehand about the judges—who they are, their tastes in showpieces, and what they would like to see. Try to find out what has made previous winners stand out among the rest, in order to determine trends and decide how best to impress the judges. All of this is very important, and should not be taken lightly or overlooked when preparing for a competition.

5 **UNDERSTANDING THE RULES:** Read the rules carefully and make sure there are no misunderstandings. Most mistakes happen because competitors don't understand the rules or don't follow them correctly. Understanding what kinds of ingredients, molds, and tools are allowed is very important. The rules will also dictate the theme and purpose of the showpiece, and the theme will be the anchor for the piece and the driving force behind your design.

Understanding the Theory of Design

Besides your professional skills and attitude, it is essential to understand the basic elements of the theory of design in order to create an effective competition piece. These elements include colors and their meanings, geometric and natural shapes and their meanings, and size and proportions—using them properly is the key to successfully designing your own original showpiece.

Color

Color is a very important element in showpieces. Used wisely, it can enhance the look of a showpiece and also indicate the piece's meaning. The theme will help determine which colors to choose. Color can evoke a feeling such as cold or warmth, a season such as summer or winter, or even a place such as the tropics. It can also be used to express emotional states like happiness, sadness, hope, aggression, anger, innocence, and love.

Colors in the red, orange, and yellow family, including yellowish greens, are considered warm colors, while purples, blues, and darker greens are considered cold. In general, it is best to use warmer colors in the foreground and colder colors in the background of a showpiece to help achieve an impression of depth and space. Darker colors generally work well for smaller elements in a showpiece, as they attract attention and help to draw the eye to these smaller components. Lighter colors work better for larger elements that would appear too heavy or intense if they were in a darker shade.

The colors can be broken down into several different categories—primary, secondary, tertiary, and complementary—all related to one another through the color wheel.

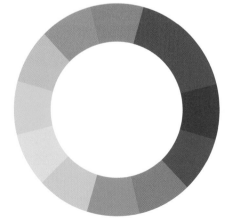

The basic color wheel will give you an understanding of how to choose complementary colors for a showpiece.

Primary Colors

The three primary colors, which are placed opposite one another in a triangle on the color wheel, are red, yellow, and blue. All other colors are made from these three.

Primary colors are the three basic colors from which other colors are derived.

Secondary Colors

Mixing any two of the primary colors together results in one of the secondary colors: orange, green, and purple. The secondary colors are found between the primary colors on the color wheel. Orange is made by mixing red and yellow, green by mixing blue and yellow, and purple by mixing red and blue. Mixing all three primary colors together results in black, gray, or brown, because they absorb all the colors that they cover.

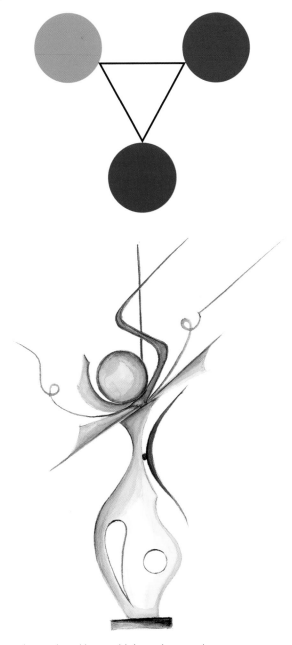

Secondary colors can be produced by combining primary colors.

Tertiary Colors

Tertiary colors fall in between the primary and secondary colors on the color wheel. Each tertiary color is formed by mixing a primary color with an adjacent secondary color. For example, blue and green can be combined to form the tertiary color blue-green.

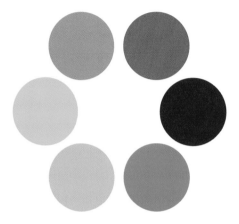

Tertiary colors can be produced by mixing primary and secondary colors.

Complementary Colors

Complementary colors are those colors found opposite one another on the color wheel. When used in equal proportions in a showpiece, they can help bring a perfect balance to the piece. Examples of complementary colors include:

- Yellow and purple
- Blue and orange
- Red and green

White and black, while not technically colors, are also opposites that can be used together to provide balance in a piece.

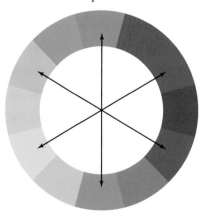

Complementary colors appear on opposite sides of the color wheel.

THE ART OF THE CONFECTIONER

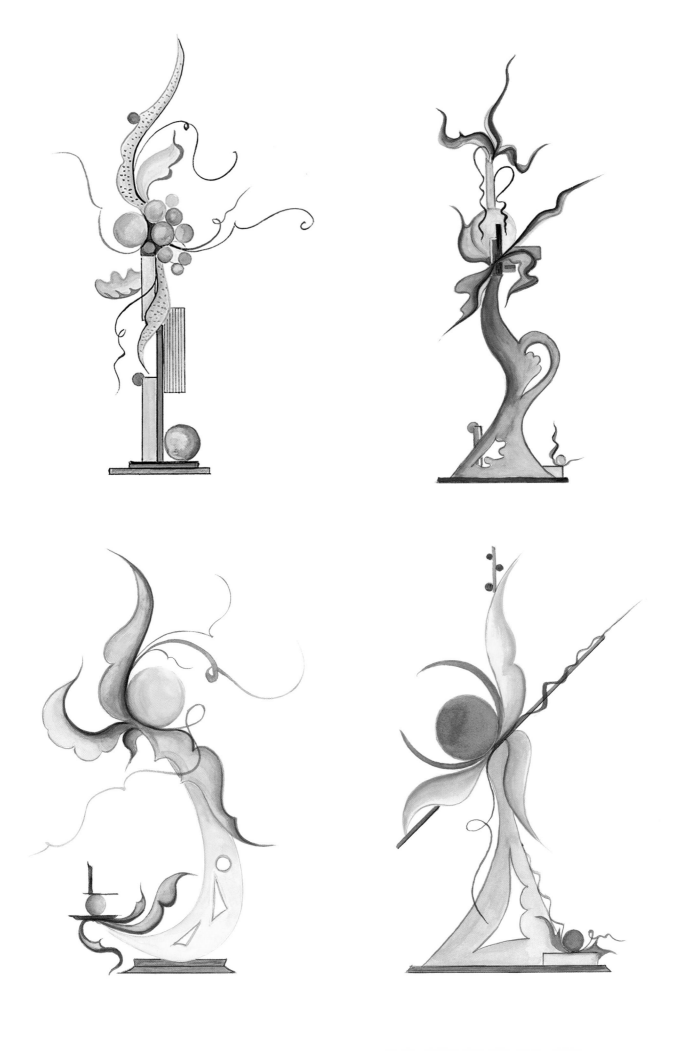

Triadic Colors

Triadic colors are found at the three opposite corners of the color wheel. Green, orange, and violet, for example, are three triadic colors. As with complementary colors, a set of triadic colors can be used together to create balance in a showpiece.

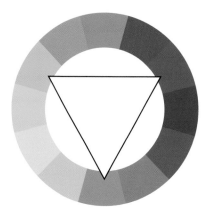

Triadic colors are equally spaced around the color wheel.

Color and Meaning

The following is a range of colors with their traditional meanings:

WHITE: Purity, virginity, truth, innocence, faithfulness, life, peace, the original light

BLACK: Sadness, mourning, the end of things, chaos, silence

RED: Aggression, stimulation, fire, blood, impulsiveness, anger, power, strength, love

GREEN: Hope, renewal, harmony, balance, loyalty, vegetative life, youth, calm

BLUE: Responsibility, spirituality, faithfulness, loyalty, purity, research, rest, quietness, faith, justice

ORANGE: Sociability, sympathy, intelligence, wisdom, idealism, inspiration, enthusiasm

YELLOW: Cleverness, intelligence, openness, creativity, wildness, happiness

PURPLE: Comprehension, generosity, tactfulness, spirituality, modesty, melancholy, truth, suffering, mysticism, royalty

PINK: Regeneration, baptism, birth, softness, prudence, tenderness, modesty, sensual pleasure, love, graciousness

GRAY: Neutrality, warmth, balance, monotony, boredom, mourning

BROWN: Decomposition, dead leaves, treason, mourning

Geometric Shapes

Circles, ovals, squares, rectangles, and triangles are very common shapes that can be seen everywhere. Shapes like these are the most basic elements of design. They are made up of closed contours and can be two-dimensional, as in the case of a flat square, or three-dimensional, as in the case of a cube. Like colors, geometric shapes can be used to convey meanings, and opposite shapes, like opposite colors, can be used to bring balance and creativity to a piece. Three-dimensional shapes, such as cubes and spheres, are an ideal way to gain volume and height in a showpiece and can be used alongside solid, plane bases to provide contrast.

The basic shapes that can be used in showpieces include flat squares and rectangles, circles and ovals, and triangles, as well as their three-dimensional counterparts, such as cubes, spheres, cylinders, and pyramids.

CIRCLE: A circle is the collection of points in a plane that are all the same distance from a fixed point. The fixed point is called the center. A line segment joining the center to any point on the circle is called a radius. A circle is the easiest shape to recognize. But as easy as the shape is to recognize, it is very difficult to draw one accurately by hand, because it has no straight edges. You can observe circles in everyday life—in the shape of a ring, a wheel, or a pastry cutter.

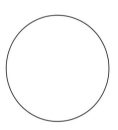

OVAL: An oval is a figure constructed from two pairs of arcs. The arcs are joined at two points that lie on the same line. Any point of an oval belongs to an arc either with a constant, shorter, or longer radius. Put more simply, an oval is essentially an elongated circle. Ovals are commonly seen in everyday life in items such as a mirror, a table, or a cookie.

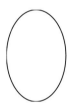

SQUARE: A square is a four-sided polygon with sides of equal length that meet at right angles. The sum of the angles of a square is 360 degrees.

RECTANGLE: A rectangle is a four-sided polygon with all right angles and an oblong shape. Like a square, a rectangular shape has four sides and four square corners, but unlike a square, two of the sides in a rectangle are longer than the other two. The sum of the angles of a rectangle is 360 degrees. It is one of the most commonly seen shapes in everyday life.

TRIANGLE: A triangle is a polygon with three straight sides. The sum of the angles of a triangle is 180 degrees. A triangle is the simplest shape, and can be tall, thin, fat, or short, as long as it has three sides.

Shapes and Meaning

Like colors, geometric shapes often have traditional meanings:

CIRCLE: Unity, wholeness, goodness, feminine spirit of force

OVAL: Creativity, hoarding

SQUARE OR RECTANGLE: Equality, perfection, the shaping of ideas

TRIANGLE: Manpower, trinity

Natural Shapes and Meaning

In designing showpieces, it may also be useful to consider a variety of natural shapes, such as leaves, hearts, and stars, as well as animal shapes like doves, swans, or owls. These kinds of natural shapes or designs often have their own meanings as well, such as:

SUN: Warmth, heat, health, energy, power, light

MOON: Darkness, romance, illusion, vision

STAR: Dreams, hope, celebration, creating your own path

HEART: Love, harmony, passion

LEAVES: Spring, renewal, life, faith, endurance

DOVES: Peace, love

SWAN: Love, purity, grace, elegance, beauty

Size and Proportion

Composing a showpiece is an act of artistic expression, and like any other work of art, a sugar showpiece should have power, harmony, and elegance. An aesthetically correct showpiece must have a focus point that draws the viewer's eyes into the creative composition.

The Golden Ratio

For hundreds of years, visual artists have been studying the best ways to frame their subjects, and have discovered a mathematical phenomenon that can be used to determine the best place to set the focus point for any composition.

The Golden Ratio is the ratio between two segments and the whole, such that the smaller segment (A) is to the larger segment (B) as the larger segment (B) is to the sum of the two segments (A+B). Artists and architects have used the concept of the Golden Ratio for years to determine the proportions of their work, and the same ratio can be used to approximate the ideal height or width of a showpiece and to determine the focus point.

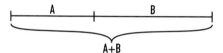

The Golden Ratio can be used to determine a showpiece's height.

The Golden Ratio is represented mathematically by phi (1.618033). To use this geometric relationship to determine the ideal proportions for a showpiece where the base length is known, the length must be divided by 2, then multiplied by 1.618033. For example, if the base of a showpiece is 30 cm long, the golden ratio can be used to figure out the ideal height and width for the piece:

Length: 30 cm

Width: W

(L / 2) × 1.618033 = W

30 cm / 2 = 15 cm

15 cm x 1.618033 = 24.27 cm

Width = 24.27 cm

**Width =
24.27 cm**

30 cm

The ideal width for the showpiece, based on the Golden Ratio.

Once you have determined the width of the showpiece, you can use the Golden Ratio to determine the height based on the length and width. The sum of the length and width, divided by 2 and then multiplied by phi, will give the ideal height for the piece.

Thus, a pleasant size for the showpiece, based on the 30-cm-long base, would be 30 cm long by 24.27 cm wide by 43.90 cm high.

Length: 30 cm

Width: 24.27 cm

Height: H

$((L + W) / 2) \times 1.618033 = H$

30 cm + 24.27 cm = 54.27

54.27 / 2 = 27.135

27.135 × 1.618033 = 43.90

Height = 43.90 cm

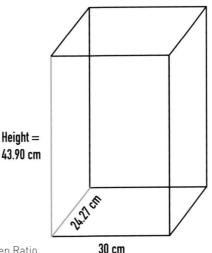

Height = 43.90 cm

24.27 cm

30 cm

The ideal height for the showpiece, based on the Golden Ratio.

Showpieces intended for competition are often created to be much higher than the Golden Ratio might indicate. However, the Golden Ratio is a foolproof way to achieve perfect balance and symmetry in a piece. If the piece described above was created with a 30 cm by 24.27 cm base, but the height was less than 43.90 cm, it would look imbalanced because the base would appear too heavy for the height.

Finding the Focus Point

When glancing at a showpiece, the viewer's eyes will automatically try to extract meaning from the image. There is usually a focus point or "sweet spot" that stands out and draws the eyes to it, and this focus point should indicate what the showpiece is all about. It is very important to consider the placement of the focus point for a showpiece. Although every showpiece is different, and the creator must determine the best design for each, there are basic mathematical rules that can be used to help approximate the best focus point for a piece.

To find the focus point of a showpiece using the Golden Ratio, divide the height of the piece by 1.618033. The result is the ideal height for the focus point. So using the example above of a showpiece whose height is 43.90 cm, the focus point can be determined as follows:

43.90 / 1.618033 = 27.13

Thus, the focus point should be placed 27.13 cm above the base of the showpiece.

If more than one showpiece is being presented on the same table, the size of the table should be used as the "base" and the heights and focus points for the showpieces should be determined based on that table's size. This means the pieces should be taller when being presented in a group on a large table than if they were being presented individually on a smaller base.

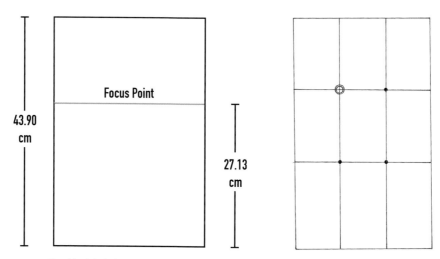

- LEFT: The ideal height for the focus point of the showcase.
- RIGHT: The Rule of Thirds can also be used to find the ideal focus points.

The Rule of Thirds

The "Rule of Thirds" is an even simpler way to identify the ideal focus point for a showpiece. Using both the Rule of Thirds and the Golden Ratio will result in approximately the same focus point, but the Rule of Thirds is much easier to understand. The rule states that if an image is divided into equal thirds both vertically and horizontally, the dividing lines can be used as guides for the focus points of the image.

There is no need to have a degree in mathematics to use the Rule of Thirds. Simply divide your frame into nine compartments as shown above, using two equally spaced vertical lines and two equally spaced horizontal lines. Those lines will intersect in four places, and those intersections represent the ideal focus points for the showpiece.

Using the Rule of Thirds will help prevent the showpiece from appearing too crowded or "busy," as it allows the subject room to breathe. Of course, there are exceptions to any rule, and the same goes for the Rule of Thirds. In some cases, the designer may want to ignore these compositional guidelines in order to convey a feeling of tension in the showpiece.

Creating the Showpiece

Once you have mentally prepared for competition and studied the basic principles of design, it is time to begin the process of actually creating the design for your showpiece. It is important to start with careful research, brainstorming, and sketching to create a plan for the piece before you begin to work with actual equipment and ingredients.

Researching the Theme

Search on the Internet or visit a library to learn more about the theme and its corresponding elements. It can be helpful to jot down a list of key words, colors, and so on that pertain to the theme, to help identify the primary elements for your showpiece. For example, if the theme you are working with is "fall," you might compile a list of key words such as turning leaves, pumpkins, football, harvest, Halloween, Thanksgiving, and turkey, and might note orange and brown as key colors. Meanwhile, an "ocean" theme might inspire a list including water, ships, anchors, shells, coral reefs, fish, waves, sunset, sand, treasure chests, and the color blue. You may even want to write a short essay incorporating the key words in order to bring the theme to life. Then you can use your text to inspire a drawing that incorporates the primary elements of the theme, which will form the basis for your showpiece.

The elements you choose to include in your sketches and in your finished piece should reflect your own personal taste, but should also be balanced and should respect established design concepts. You may choose to work with more realistic elements based on nature that are easily recognizable to the viewer, but can be difficult to copy well, or with more abstract elements that may be easier to create but can be difficult for the viewer to identify. Keep in mind that in your final design, all the elements must be balanced and in harmony with one another, and should be easy for the viewer to understand.

Designing the Piece

Shape, proportion, and color are as important to the design of a showpiece as a carefully researched theme. You can create wonderful, modern pieces using mainly simple geometric shapes and a few natural shapes. Begin by sketching the design on paper, keeping the following elements in mind:

HEIGHT AND PROPORTION. In competition, the pieces are always taller than they would be if designed using the Golden Ratio as a guide. The taller the piece and the narrower the base, the more elegant the piece may appear. Still, it is essential to have a beginning, a focus point, and an ending for your piece. Use the Rule of Thirds to determine the focus point, and don't forget that the piece has to be strong enough to be moved.

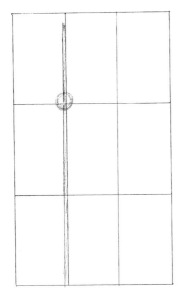
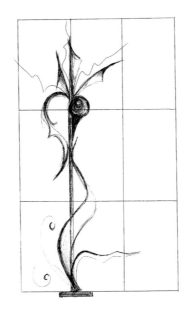

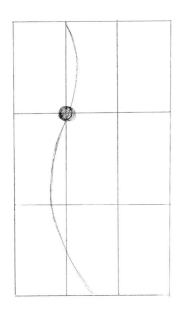
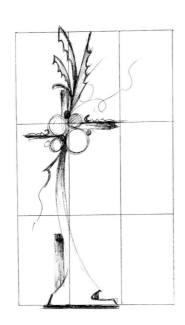

OPPOSITE SHAPES AND TEXTURES. You may start to design the piece with a straight or curved line, or you can begin with a simple geometric shape like a square, rectangle, triangle, circle, or oval. If the base is square, rectangular, or triangular, you should use opposite shapes like a ring, circle, or oval piece to gain height and provide contrast.

Use the rule of thirds to place the focus point, and start placing simple elements or shapes first. If using a lot of small pieces, group them together so they are related, rather than spacing them out throughout the piece, which would make the piece look busy and unorganized. Keep in mind that the piece must have a beginning and an end and should show a sense of movement, appear light, and be pleasing to the eye. The eye should not only be able to travel from the beginning to the end, but also be able to read the piece. As you start to fill in pieces, empty space will start to appear. This negative space is very important to make the piece look elegant and not too heavy. The biggest challenge will be knowing when to stop. If the structure of the piece is elegant and simple, then there is no need to overcrowd the piece.

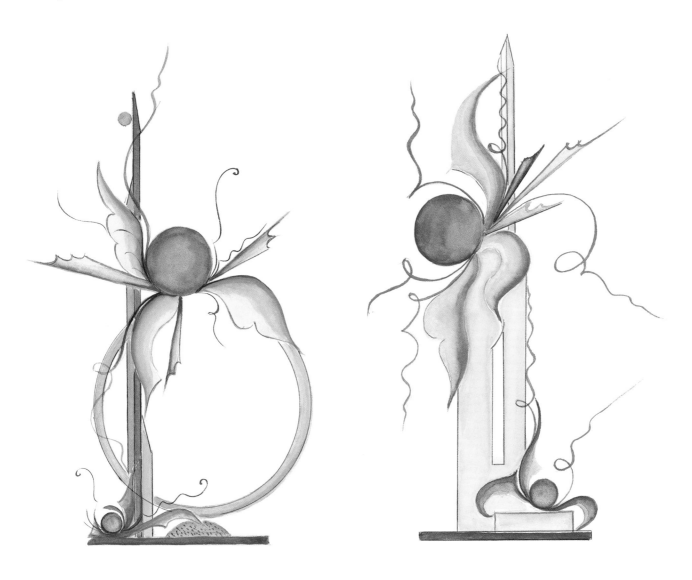

A GOOD COLOR COMBINATION. Once you have a complete sketch of the piece, make a new, clean version of the sketch and fill in the colors. To go a step further, you may also want to create a model made out of cardboard and paper to help visualize how the finished piece will appear, and airbrush the pieces to get a sense of how the color will work. This will give you a good idea of how the final showpiece will look before you begin working with any real ingredients, which can be very costly, especially if using Isomalt.

The colors can be the most important elements of a showpiece. Once the theme has been established, choosing the color becomes almost second nature. A main color is generally selected to complement the theme, and this main color is usually a primary color. To make sure that the piece does not become too colorful or too busy, use only one main color. Based on that main color, choose a secondary color to use more sparingly in the piece. Complementary colors work without fail; it is always a good idea to choose colors that are opposite one another on the color wheel. Black and white are not technically colors, and they can both be used as desired throughout the piece. Remember that when it comes to color, there is often a tendency to want to do too much. Less is more, and the application of color will not improve the appearance of a poorly designed showpiece.

Once you have completed your initial design, think about how to translate it into a finished sugar piece. If you still have basic geometric shapes planned for the focus point, you may be able to change the shapes to better represent the theme, for example, by using blown hearts, birds, flowers, instruments, or other thematic shapes.

To bring your sketch to life with sugar, replace the straight or curved support line with a cast tube or pulled straw sugar. The simple supporting elements can be built with cast sugar or pastillage. For any smaller décor elements around the focus point, you can use ribbons, pastillage, bubble sugar, net sugar, clear pulled sugar, or pastillage pieces.

Assembling the Showpiece

Before you begin to work with sugar, decide carefully which colors and techniques will work best for each of the elements you plan to create. The same showpiece can look very different depending on whether the pieces are cast, blown, or pulled. It is much faster to create a cast piece than to create a piece using any other techniques, but a showpiece using all cast pieces will appear flat and less attractive. A mixture of pulled and blown elements in a showpiece will create a more three-dimensional piece, but a lot more hand skills are required and not everybody is willing to spend the time to learn and master these techniques. The beauty of sugar is that you have a lot of choices to help you represent the theme, like straw, pressed, bubble, net, cast, pulled, and blown sugar. Other pastry techniques such as chocolate, marzipan, and gum paste are more limited.

Never, ever choose to mix chocolate with sugar; there is no need for it at all. Sugar itself can be shown in so many different ways—casting alone can be done on marble, silicone paper, or aluminum foil; in silicone molds with Isomalt or granulated sugar; and can be clear, opaque, or airbrushed. Every technique will result in sugarwork with a distinct character. So there is no need to add chocolate at all, and doing so will show your lack of creativity. The same goes for accenting chocolate, which can be transformed using a huge number of different techniques with sugar. I strongly believe these two ingredients should each be showcased independently of one another.

Creating a showpiece will be a lot easier and less stressful if you take the time up front to plan out the sequence of steps and practice all the needed techniques. When working with sugar you have to work very cleanly; otherwise the sugar can easily recrystallize, and it is very time-consuming to boil the sugar again. Once you have perfected the techniques you need for your showpiece, you should work on improving the time it takes you to create each element.

Once you are confident in each of the techniques needed to create the showpiece elements and have practiced improving your time, consider the organization of your working tools. Make a plan or create a checklist of the working steps from the beginning to the end of the process, then create a timetable.

You should always start by creating any pastillage pieces first, because pastillage will take time to dry. Then create any cast pieces, such as bases, supporting elements, molds, and tubing. If you are not able to assemble the cast pieces immediately after cooling, store them in a dry place, either in a plastic bag or in an airtight container with a drying agent such as limestone, calcium carbonate, or silica gel. Then, before assembling, re-warm the pieces carefully with a hair dryer before dipping them into hot sugar or heating them over the flame of an alcohol burner. It is important to rewarm them first, as they can easily break because of a high temperature difference.

Once the cast elements are complete, you may start creating the pulled and blown pieces. This can be very time-consuming, so you will want to store the cast elements in a plastic bag or an airtight container with limestone, calcium carbonate, or silica gel before assembling the pulled and blown pieces. Then add the finer and smaller elements like bubble and net sugar.

Designing and Assembling Your Showpiece

1 Explore the theme.

2 Find elements in the same character, such as natural, modern, contemporary, or abstract.

3 Sketch the piece in the right proportion.

4 Find the right colors.

5 Create an exact drawing of the piece in a 1:1 ratio.

6 Make a cardboard piece.

7 Find all the right techniques for the different elements.

8 Start to work with sugar on the elements using different techniques.

9 Cast all the supporting pieces.

10 Assemble the whole piece.

11 Try to consolidate all similar techniques to save time.

12 Make a list outlining the order in which you plan to work and where you will store the pieces before assembly.

13 Make a list of all the working tools needed in the order in which they will be used.

14 Keep practicing, working on time and cleanliness.

While practicing, try to work in a controlled area, keeping the space small and organized. Make sure to place all your necessary tools on the table in the order in which they will be needed. Keep unnecessary tools off the table, and ensure that your work space is kept clean at all times. Be mindful of the waste you are producing at every step, and make an effort to minimize this waste.

The best way to practice the techniques and *mise en place* for creating a showpiece is to actually do mini demonstrations or timed trials, either for small groups or by yourself. Doing timed trials will help you get used to the pressure of real competition and will prepare you for what to do when something goes wrong (and it will!). During the practice session, never be tempted to throw away your mistakes and start over. By forcing yourself to learn how to fix things on the spot, you will gain the confidence needed to be a strong competitor.

Remember, being creative is only a small part of designing a successful showpiece. It is also necessary to have an understanding of the techniques needed to turn your creativity into something you can use. It can be frustrating to develop a creative idea for a showpiece without having the technical knowledge and experience to express that idea. That is why it is essential to master the fundamental sugarwork techniques before you begin the process of creating full competition pieces. With thorough preparation, a strong understanding of the principles of design, and a mastery of the fundamentals of working with sugar, you will be well on your way to defining your own personal style and creating stunning, award-winning showpieces.

Appendix

Templates

The templates on the following pages can be used to reproduce the showpieces seen throughout the book. All templates can be enlarged or reduced as needed to fit your own designs.

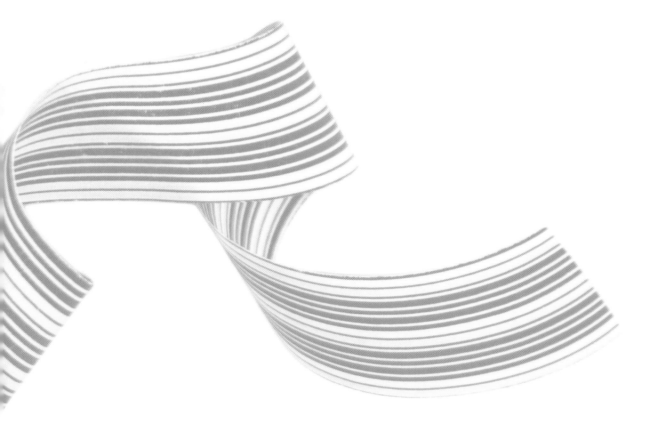

WINDFLOWER SHOWPIECE, page 6. Base (1), support (2), leaves (3), veined leaves (4), curved vine (5).

THE ART OF THE CONFECTIONER

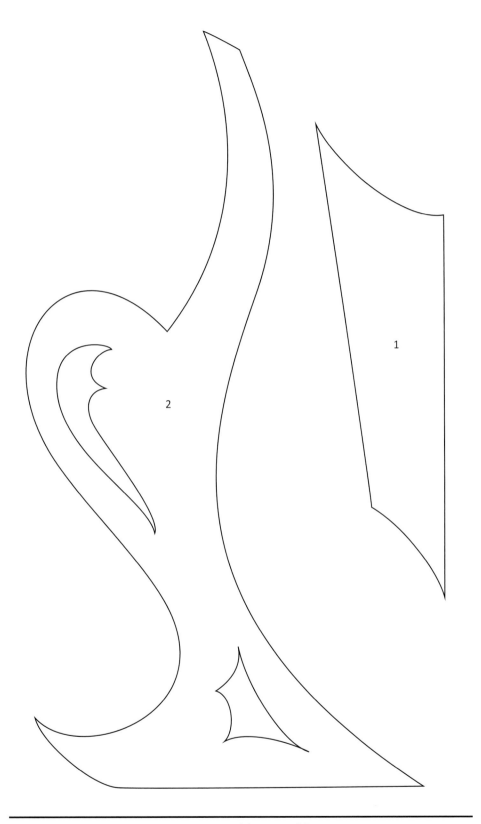

BLOOMING FLAME SHOWPIECE, page 13. Base (1), support (2).

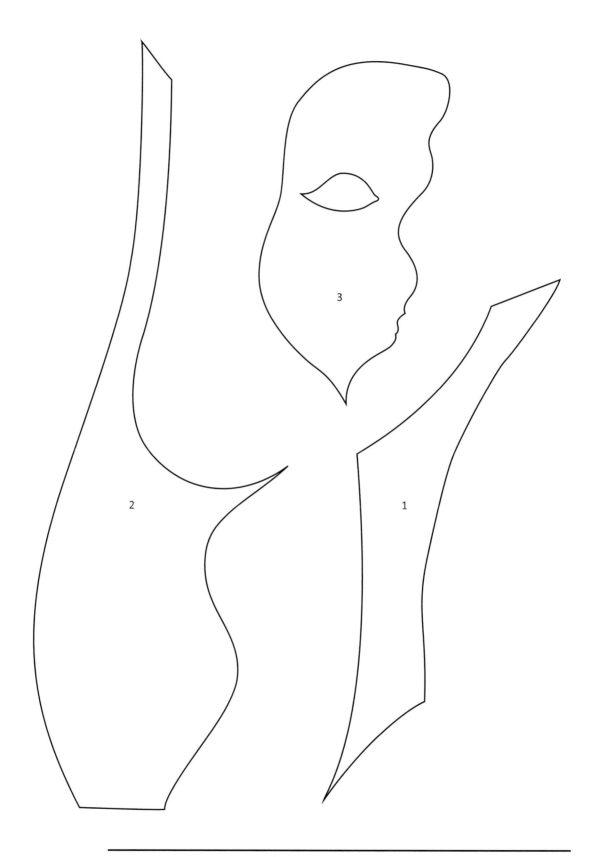

MASK SHOWPIECE, page 35. Base (1), support (2), mask (3).

THE ART OF THE CONFECTIONER

MODERN CANDY STAND SHOWPIECE, page 40. Base (1), second base (2), base support (3), ribbed décor pieces (4 and 5), circles (6), rolled curved piece (7), rectangle décor (8).

PASTILLAGE CARD SHOWPIECE, page 32. Base (1), card (2), curled décor piece (3), heart (4).

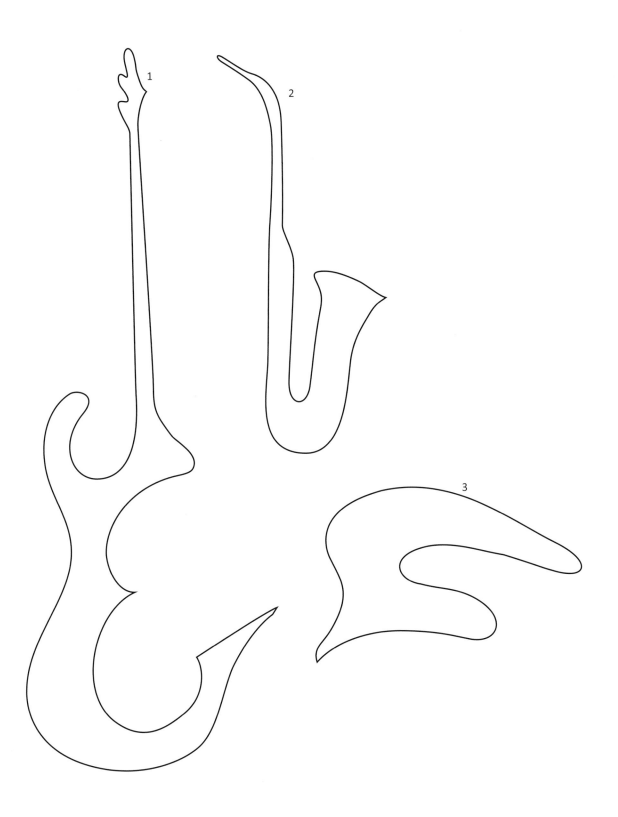

MUSIC SHOWPIECE, page 38. Guitar (1), saxophone (2), base (3).

SIMPLE FLOWER SHOWPIECE, page 59. Base (1), support (2), rolled décor pieces (3 and 4), heart (5).

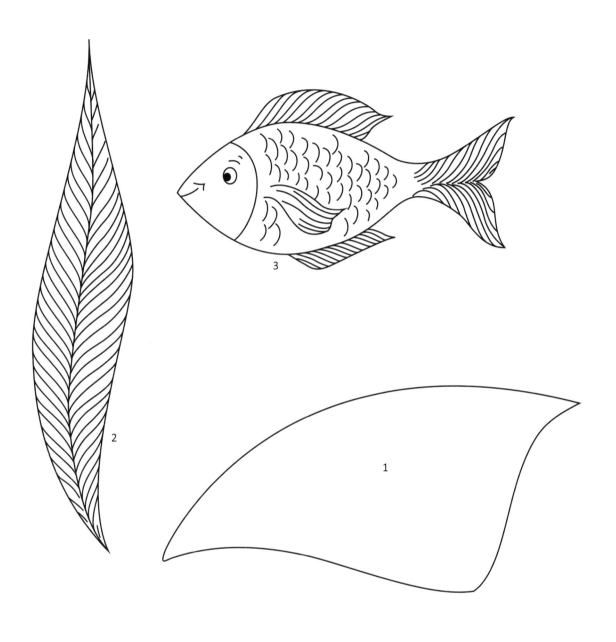

FISH SHOWPIECE, page 51. Base (1), leaf (2), fish (3).

MAGNOLIA SHOWPIECE, page 53. Base (1), flower support (2), support (3), curved décor (4), geometric elements (5).

THE ART OF THE CONFECTIONER

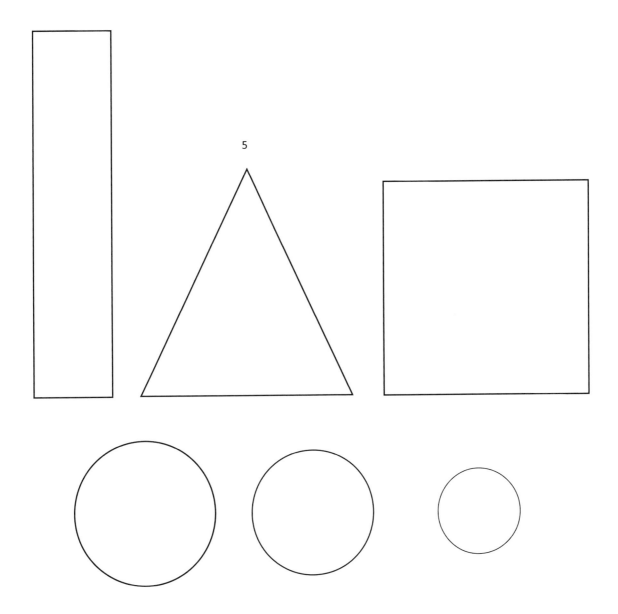

5

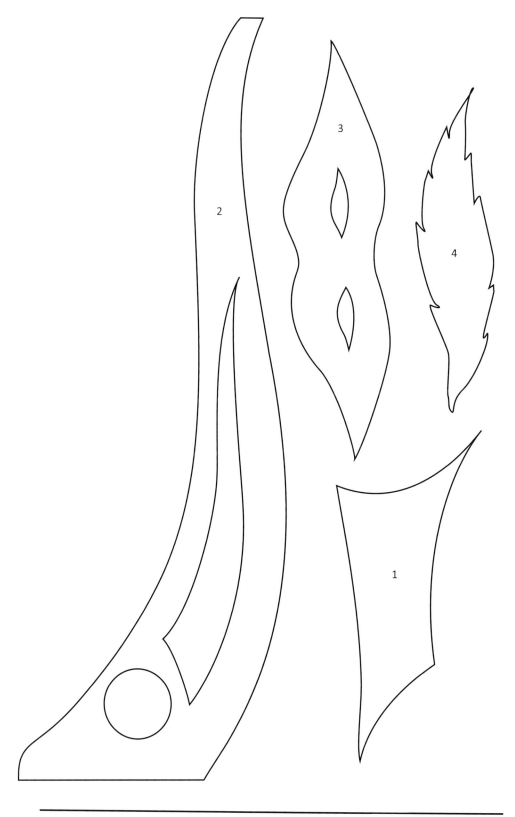

MASQUERADE MASK SHOWPIECE, page 61. Base (1), support (2), mask (3), feather (4).

THE ART OF THE CONFECTIONER

PASTILLAGE HEART SHOWPIECE, page 69. Base (1), heart (2), small heart (3), circles (4), vines (5).

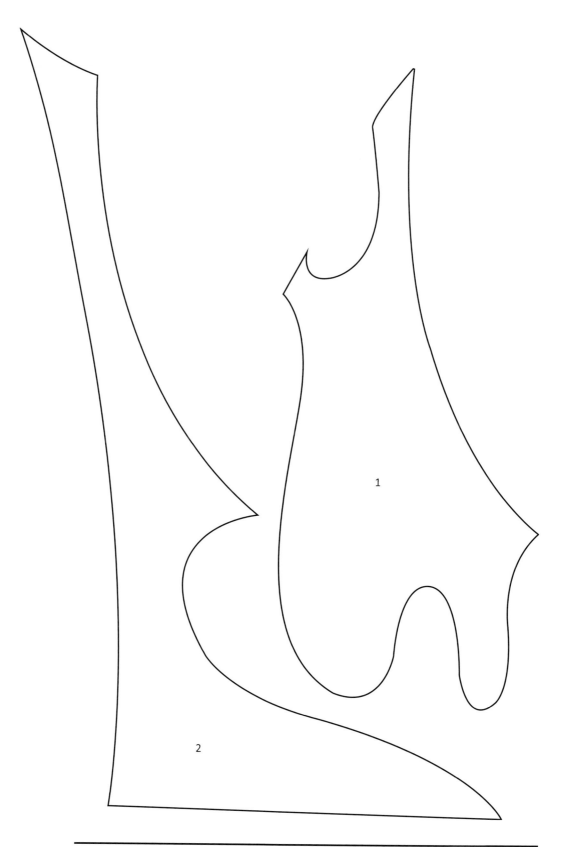

CONTEMPORARY PASTILLAGE SHOWPIECE, page 77. Base (1), support (2), curved triangle (3), geometric décor pieces (4).

THE ART OF THE CONFECTIONER

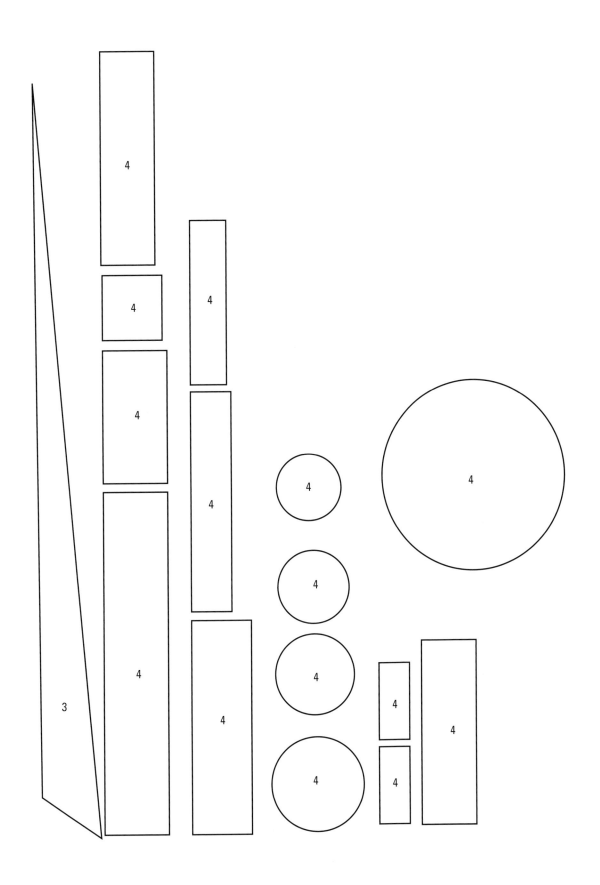

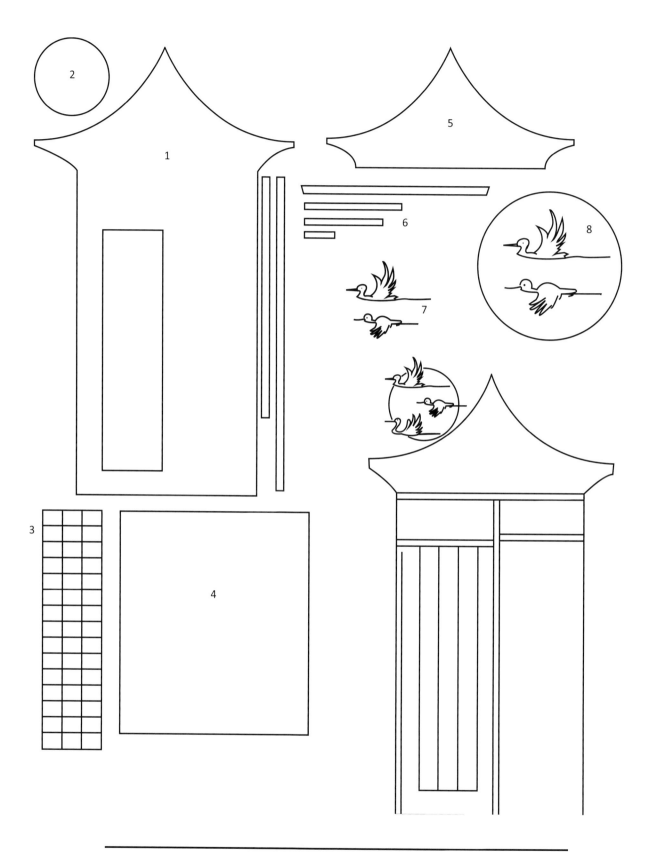

JAPANESE SHOWPIECE, page 107. House (1), umbrella (2), window (3), base (4), roof (5), beams (6), cranes (7), sun (8).

THE ART OF THE CONFECTIONER

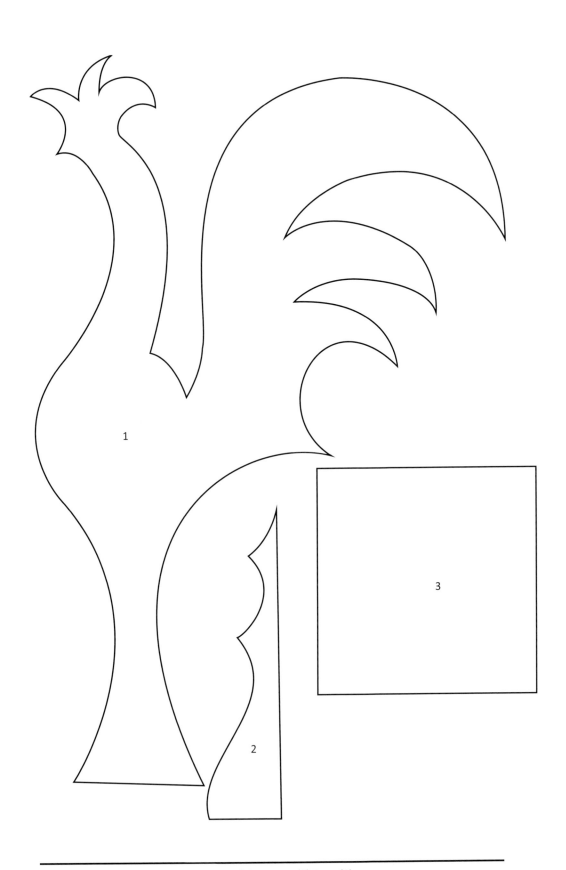

ROOSTER SHOWPIECE, page 81. Rooster (1), support (2), base (3).

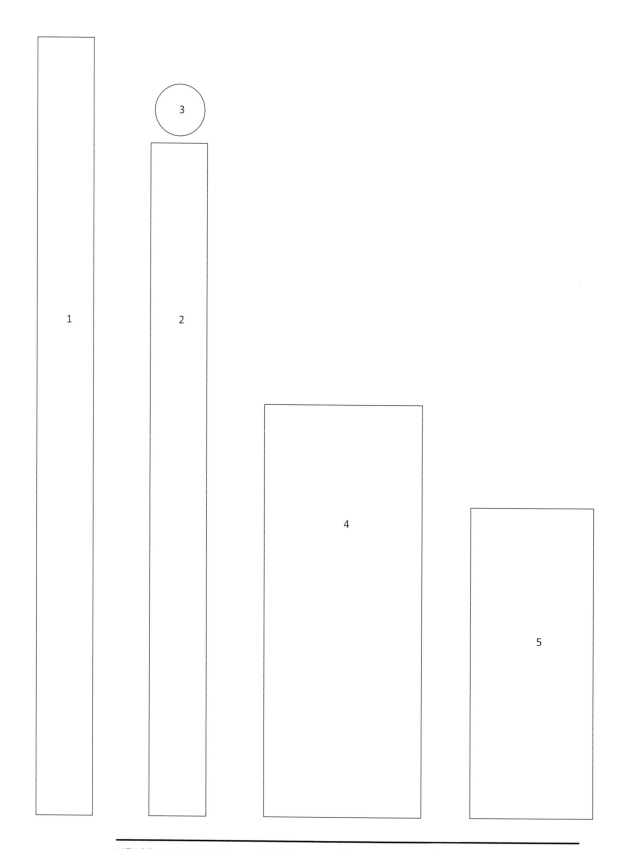

MENORAH SHOWPIECE, page 83. Side support (1), candle support (2), candles (3), lower base (4), top base (5), triangle frame (6), triangle (7), décor elements (8–12).

THE ART OF THE CONFECTIONER

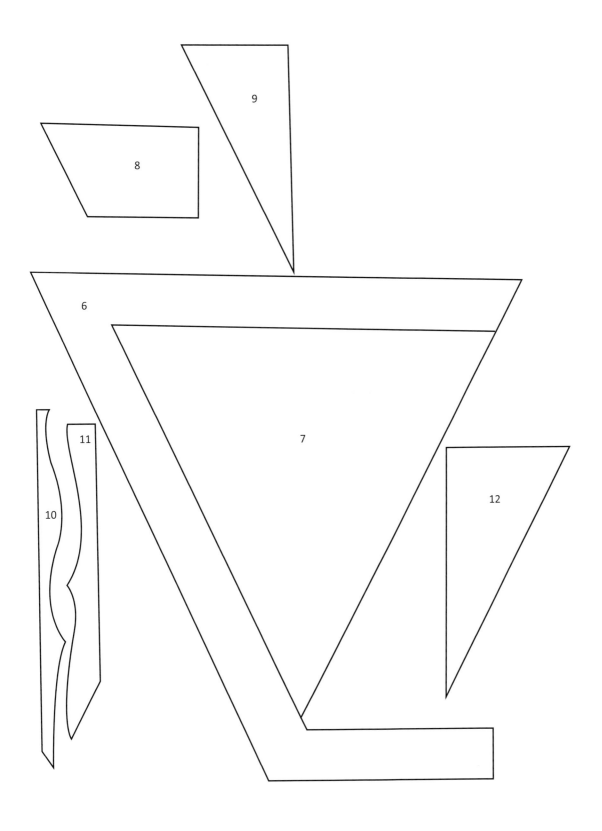

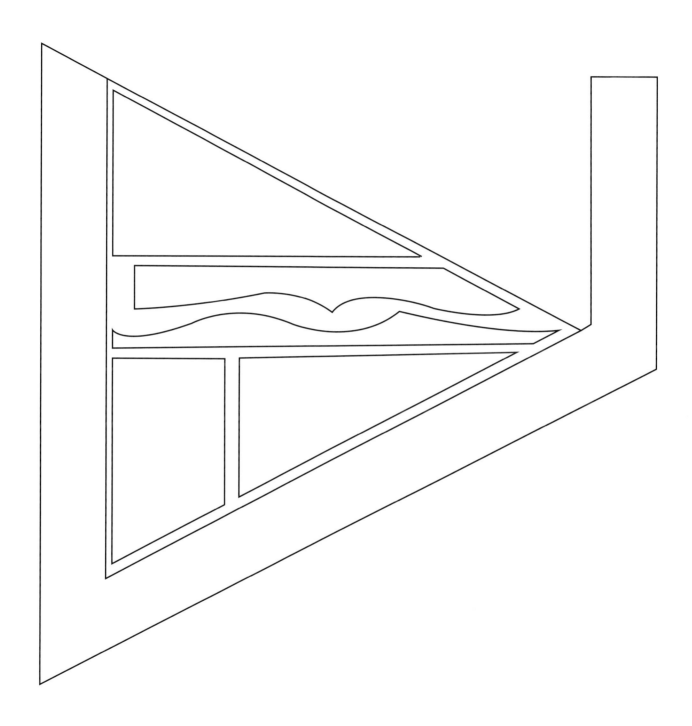

MENORAH SHOWPIECE, continued from page 333. Menorah assembly.

THE ART OF THE CONFECTIONER

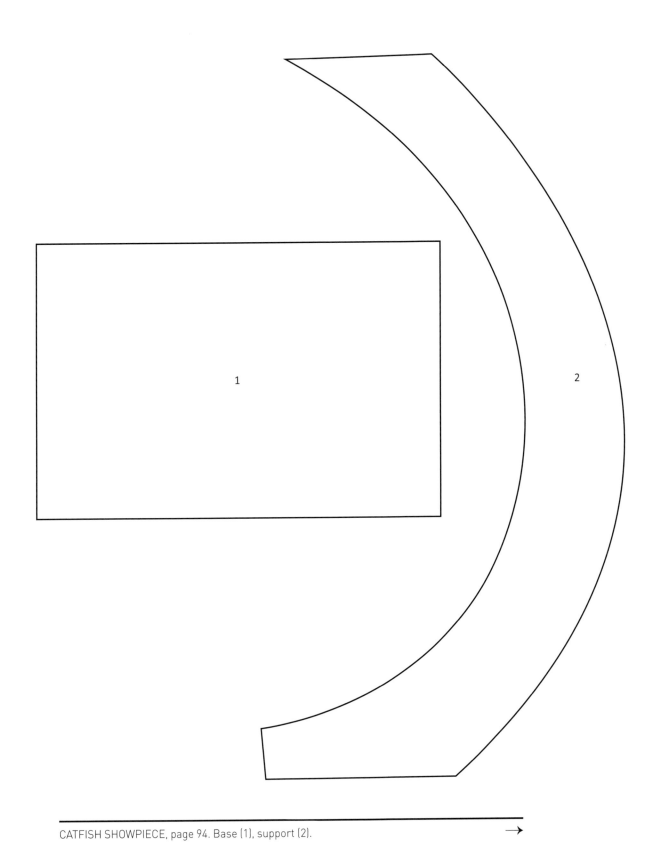

CATFISH SHOWPIECE, page 94. Base (1), support (2). $\rightarrow$

CATFISH SHOWPIECE, continued from page 335. Sea anemone (3), coral (4), stones (5).

THE ART OF THE CONFECTIONER

1 2 3

NEW YEAR'S EVE SHOWPIECE, page 103. Curved triangle (1), lower base (2), top base (3). →

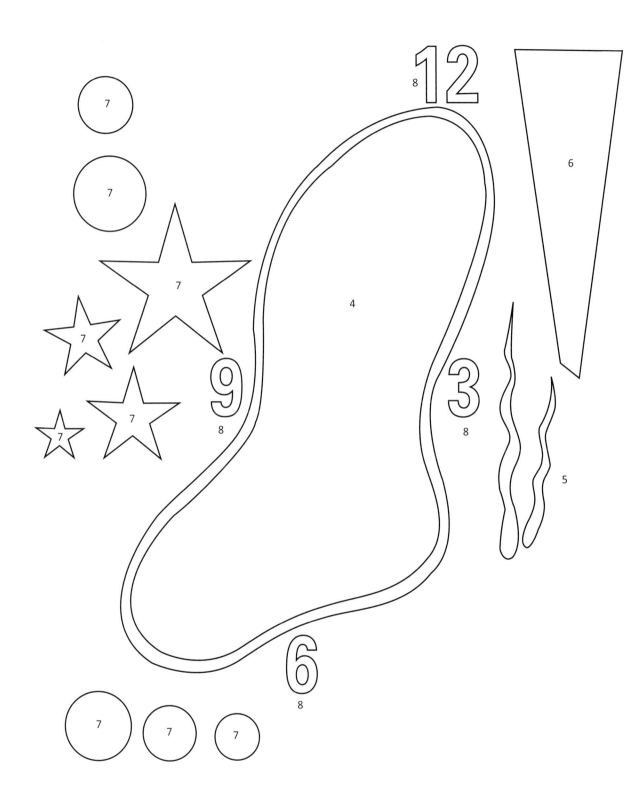

NEW YEAR'S EVE SHOWPIECE, continued from page 337. Clock (4), clock hands (5), support (6), décor pieces (7), numbers (8).

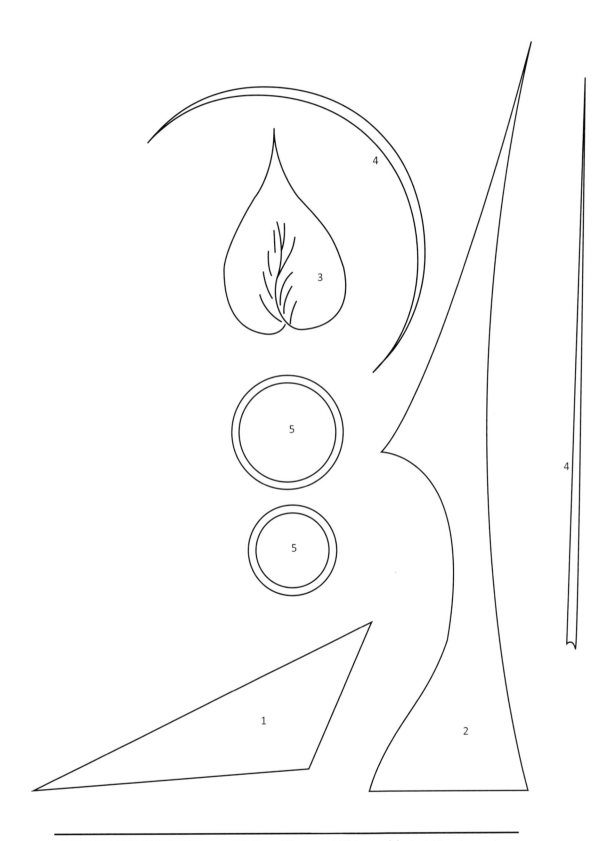

BLOWN FLOWER SHOWPIECE, page 111. Base (1), support (2), leaves (3), straight and curved sticks (4), circles (5).

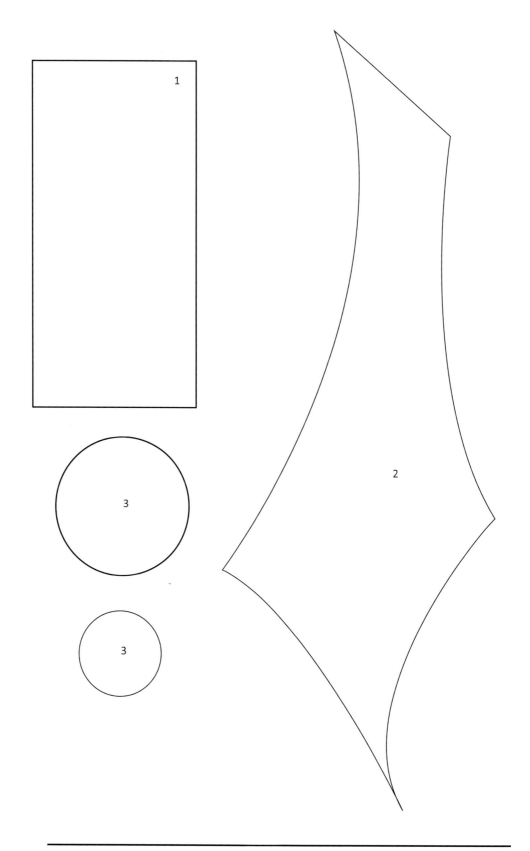

LOTUS FLOWER SHOWPIECE, page 135. Base (1), bent piece (2), spheres (3).

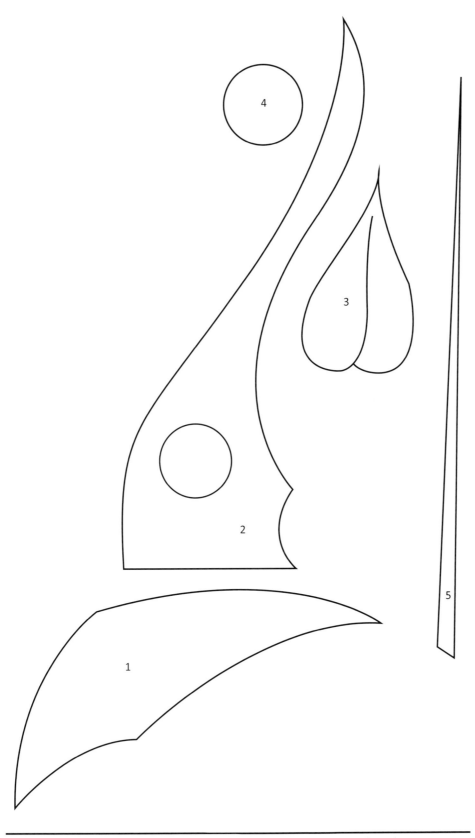

HEDGE ROSE SHOWPIECE, page 117. Base (1), support (2), leaf (3), circle (4), stick (5).

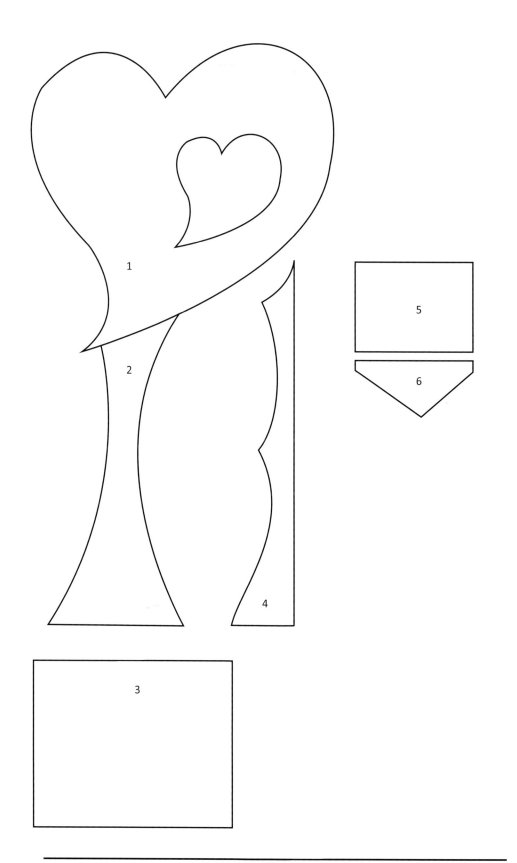

MOTHER'S DAY SHOWPIECE, page 131. Heart (1), support (2), base (3), back support (4), envelope (5 and 6).

THE ART OF THE CONFECTIONER

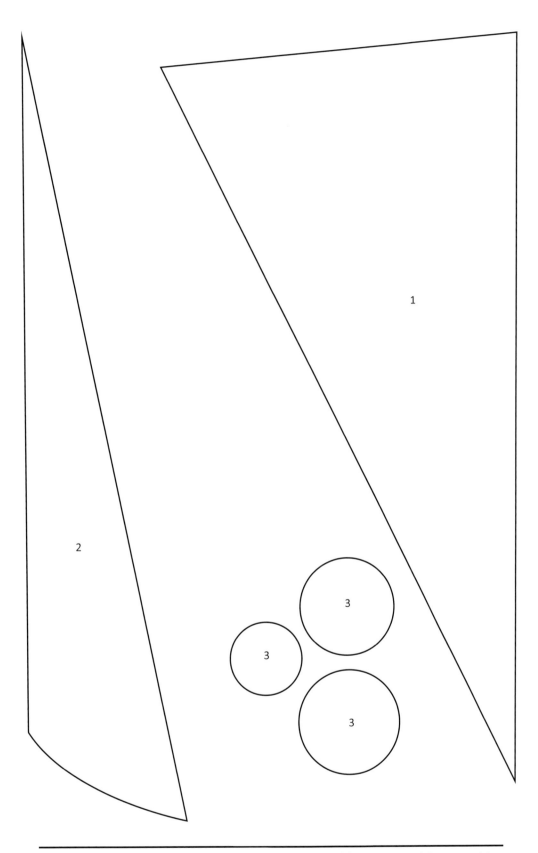

ROCK 'N' ROLL EASTER CHICKS SHOWPIECE, page 145. Base (1), bent triangle (2), spheres (3).

CHRISTMAS SHOWPIECE, page 159. Base (1 and 2), candles (3), décor pieces (4).

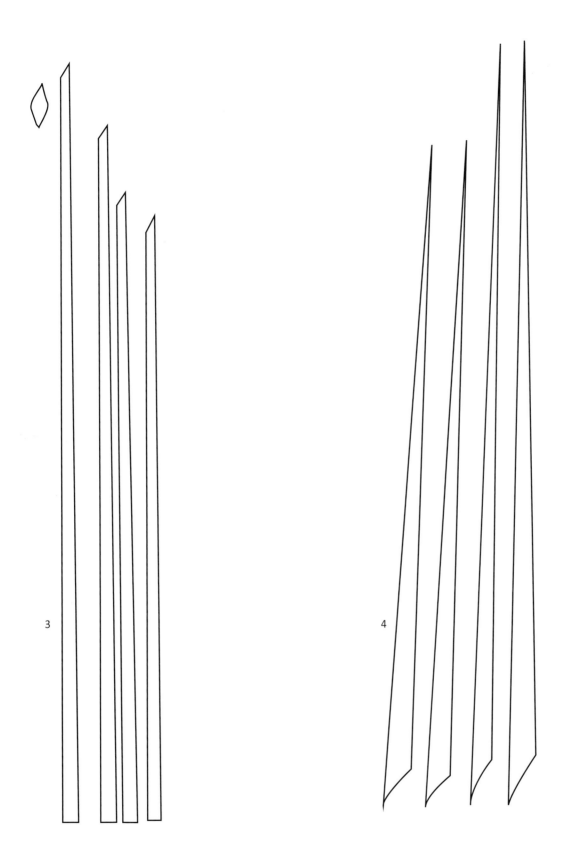

3

4

SNOWMAN SHOWPIECE, page 170. Base (1), trees (2).

BLUE MARLIN SHOWPIECE, page 202. Base (1), waves (2).

THE ART OF THE CONFECTIONER

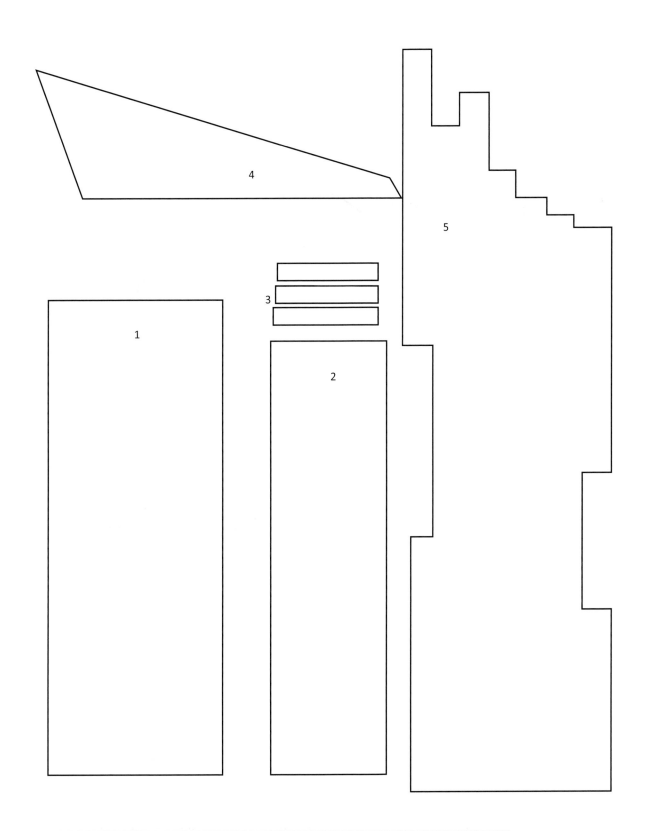

FEMALE FIGURE SHOWPIECE, page 225. Base (1 and 2), elevation pieces (3), bent piece (4), background (5).

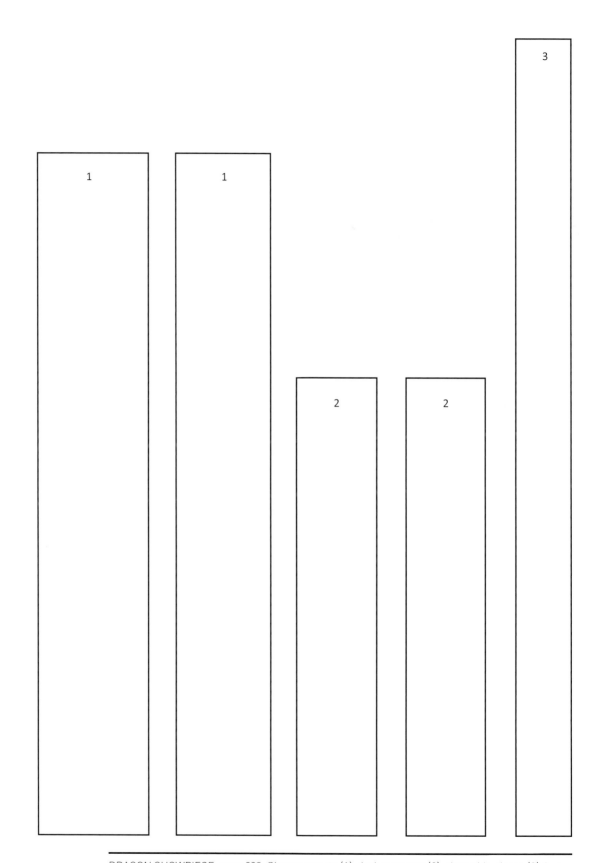

DRAGON SHOWPIECE, page 233. Clear supports (1), dark supports (2), clear side pieces (3), base (4), décor elements (5), circles (6), spheres (7).

THE ART OF THE CONFECTIONER

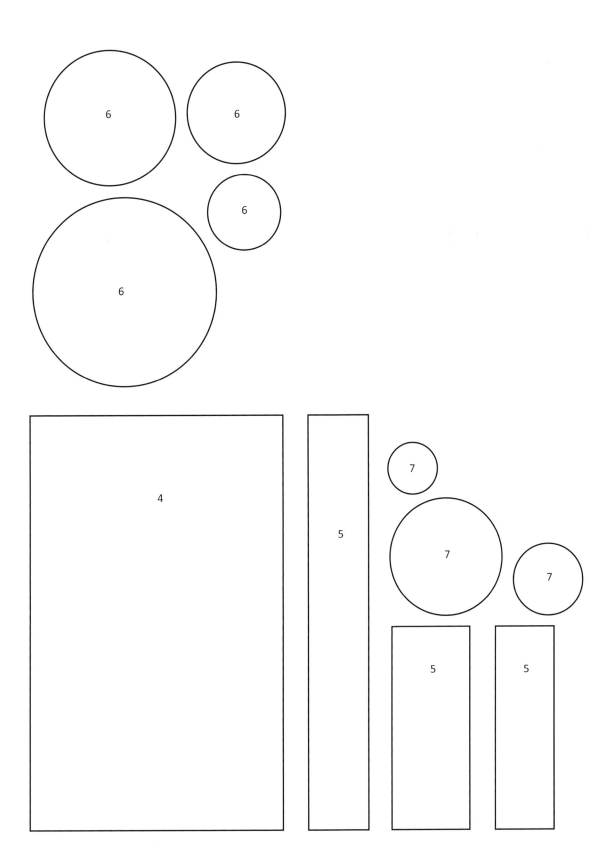

FROG SHOWPIECE, page 253. Butterfly.

THE ART OF THE CONFECTIONER

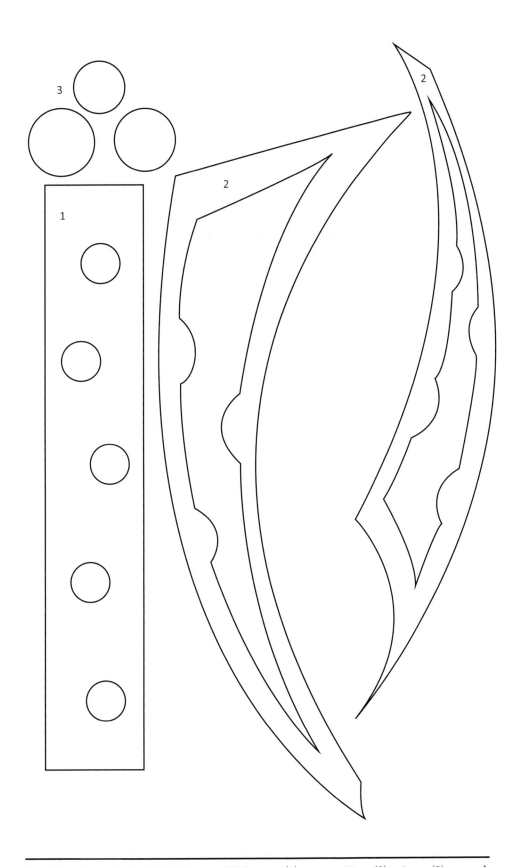

FLOWERS IN BLOOM SHOWPIECE, page 267. Support (1), cast pastillage (2), spheres (3). →

FLOWERS IN BLOOM SHOWPIECE, continued from page 353. Bases (4), pastillage leaves (5), sugar tubes (6).

THE ART OF THE CONFECTIONER

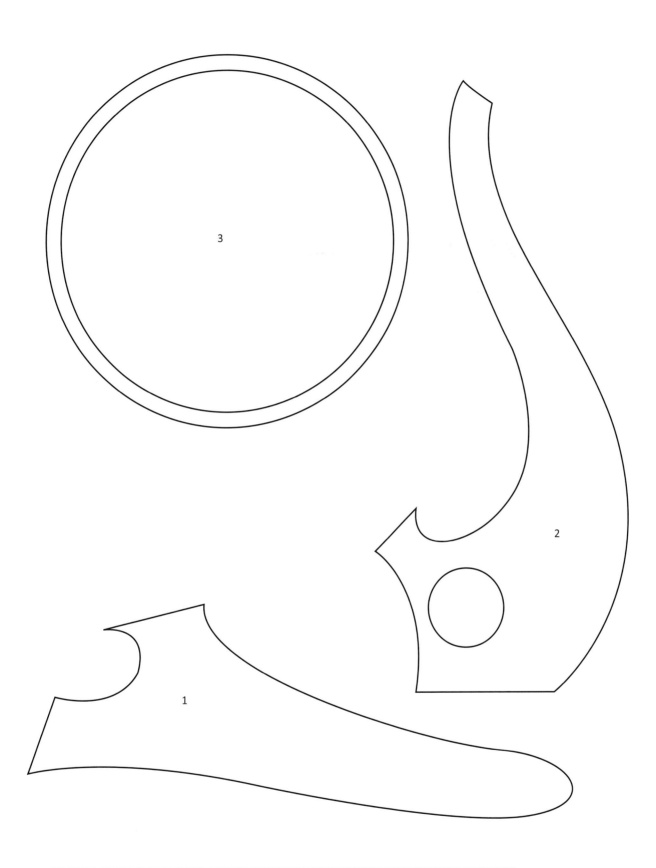

DAISY SHOWPIECE, page 287. Base (1), support (2), pastillage ring (3).

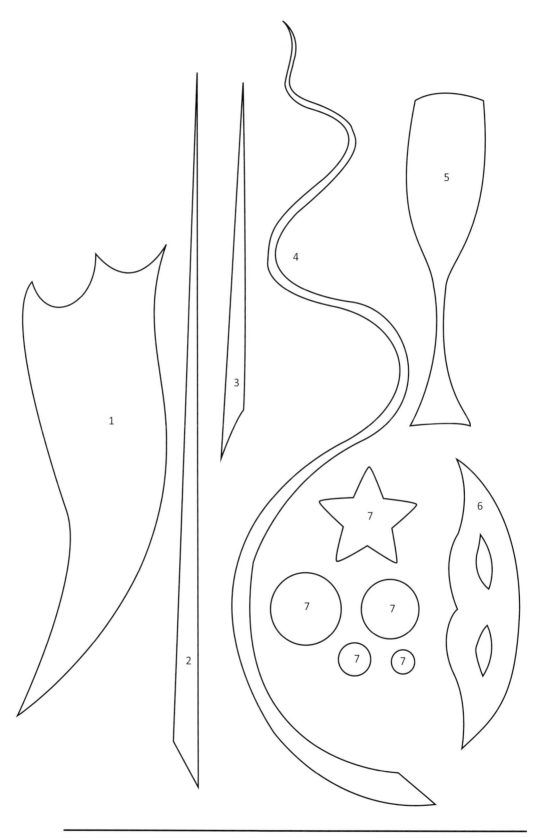

MASQUERADE SHOWPIECE, page 301. Base (1), bent pastillage support (2), bent pastillage ribbon (3), vine piece (4), glass (5), mask (6), décor pieces (7).

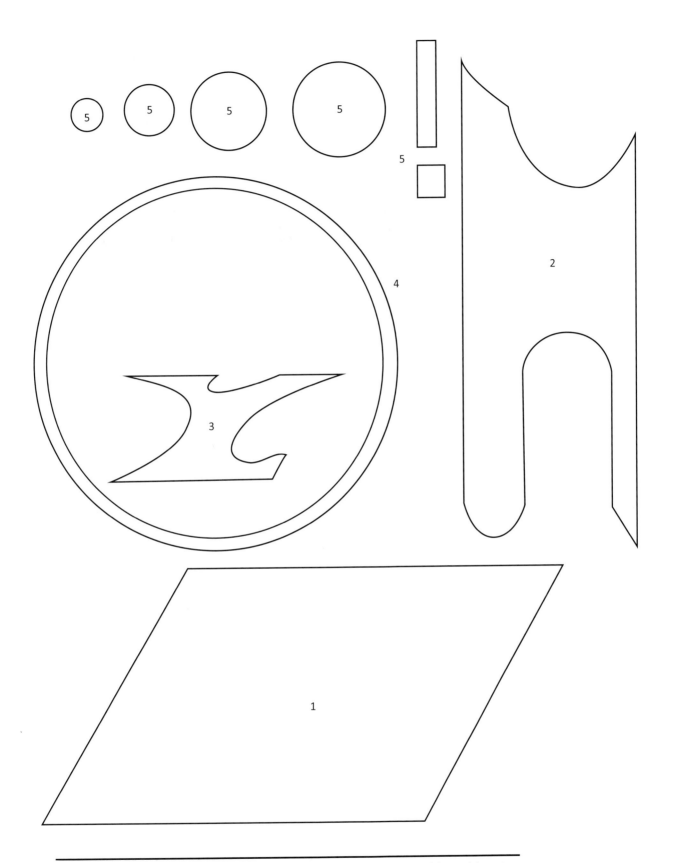

CANDY DISPLAY SHOWPIECE, page 306. Base (1), support (2), second support (3), ring (4), circle décor pieces (5).

BLACK CRANE SHOWPIECE, page 309. Support (1), spheres (2), clear bent piece (3), base (4).

THE ART OF THE CONFECTIONER

HAUNTED HOUSE SHOWPIECE, page 313. House assembly.

HAUNTED HOUSE SHOWPIECE, continued from page 359. House front (1), roofs (2), doors (3), beams (4–6), clouds (7), bat (8), witch (9), moon (10), base (11).

THE ART OF THE CONFECTIONER

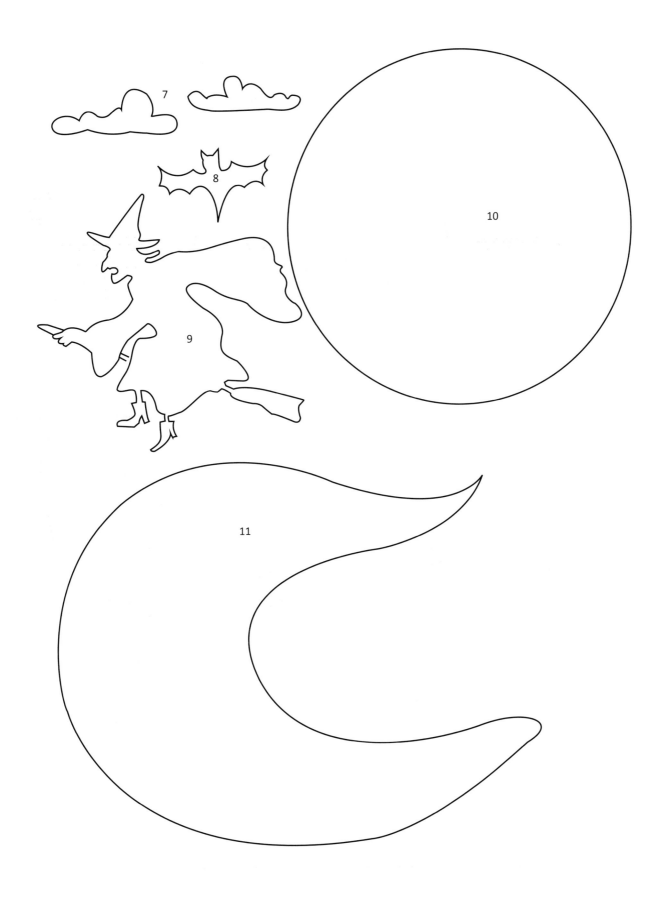

Index

Page numbers in *italics* indicate illustrations

Silpat mats, 23, 73
Size/proportion, in design, 298–300, 302
"Skipping" stones, pastillage, 44, *45*
Snowman, blown, *170*, 171–172, *172–173*
Spatula, heat-resistant, 25
Spheres
 blown, basic, 158, *159–161*
 blown, to fill basket, 148
 cast, 88, *89*, *90*
Spoons, 26
Spun sugar
 bird's nest, ladled, 261, *262*
 bird's nest, pulled, 261, *262*
 fan, *262*, 263
 sugar/isomalt recipes, 260–261
 sugar *vs* isomalt, 244
Spun sugar tool, 25
Square shape, 296, 297
Stamen, pulled flowers, 116, *119*, 128, *129*, *130*, 136
Star shape, meaning of, 297
Stencils, 22
Stones, pastillage, *44*, 44
Strainers, 25
Straw sugar, 244, 273–275, *275*
Styrofoam drying surface, 23
Sugar
 beet sugar cultivation, 15
 boiling, 15, 20, 75, 109
 cane sugar cultivation, 12
 characteristics of, 19
 consumption of, 15
 crystallization, 19, 106
 double refined, 16
 vs isomalt, 16, 19, 244
 kneading, 109
 opaque, 100
 origins of word, 12
 overworked, 106
 preparing for blowing, 157
 preparing for pulling, 115
 recipe
  for bubble sugar, 251–252
  for casting, 74–75, *75*
  for pulling/blowing, 108–110, *109*
  for rock sugar, 256
  for sand casting, 258–259
  for spun sugar, 260–261

  for straw sugar, 274
  for vinyl tubes, 264
 selecting, 28
 used, 106
"Sugar bakers", 12, 15
Sugar dough. *See* Pastillage
Sugar pump, 25
Sugarwork. *See also* Competition showpieces
 equipment and tools, 20–26, *21*
 history of, 12, 15–16
 ingredients for, 27–28
 vs pastillage, 11
 trends in, 243
Sugarwork techniques. *See also* Blowing; Casting; Pulling
 bubble sugar, 244, *250*, 251–252, *253*
 clear blowing, 244, 270, *271*, 272, *273*
 clear pulling, 244, *268*, 269, *270*
 geodes, pastillage-and-sugar, 281, *282*, *283*
 ice casting, 244, 254, *255*
 net sugar, 244, 246, *247*
 pressed sugar, 244, 248, *249*
 rock sugar, 244, 256, *257*
 sand casting, 244, 258–259, *259*
 saturated sugar
  blown sugar objects, crystallized, 280, 280
  creating/using crystals, 276, *277*
  pastillage shapes with crystals, 278, *279*
  sugar vs isomalt, 244
 spun sugar
  bird's nest, ladled, 261, *262*
  bird's nest, pulled, 261, *262*
  fan, 262, *263*
 sugar isomalt recipes, 260–261
 straw sugar, 244, 273–275, *275*
 sugar *vs* isomalt, 16, 19, 244
 vinyl tubes, 244, 266, *267*, 268, *269*
Sun shape, meaning of, 297
Swan
 blown, 174, *175*
 meaning of shape, 297

T

Tartaric acid, 27
Teardrop shape, blown, 164, *165*
Teflon sheets, 23, 73
Templates, 25
Tertiary colors, 292
Textured pastillage, *40*, 41–42
Textured rolling pin, *42*, 42
Textured work surface, 24, 42
Theme of competition showpiece, 302
Thermometers, 25
Titanium dioxide, 25, 100
Triadic colors, 294
Triangle
 meaning of shape, 296–297
 wavy, pastillage, *49*, 49

V

Vinegar, white, 27
Vines, pastillage, *47*, 47
Vinyl surface, 73
Vinyl tubes, 244, 266, *267*, 268, *269*

W

Warming case, 25
Water, in sugarwork, 28
Wavy triangles, pastillage, *49*, 49
Wedding rings, doves holding, blown, *177*, *179*, 179–180
Whisks, 26
White, meaning of color, 294
Wings, blown
 doves, *178–179*, 178
 penguin, *192*, 192
Work surface
 for casting, 73
 textured, 42
 types of, 26

Y

Yellow
 meaning of color, 294
 primary color, 290

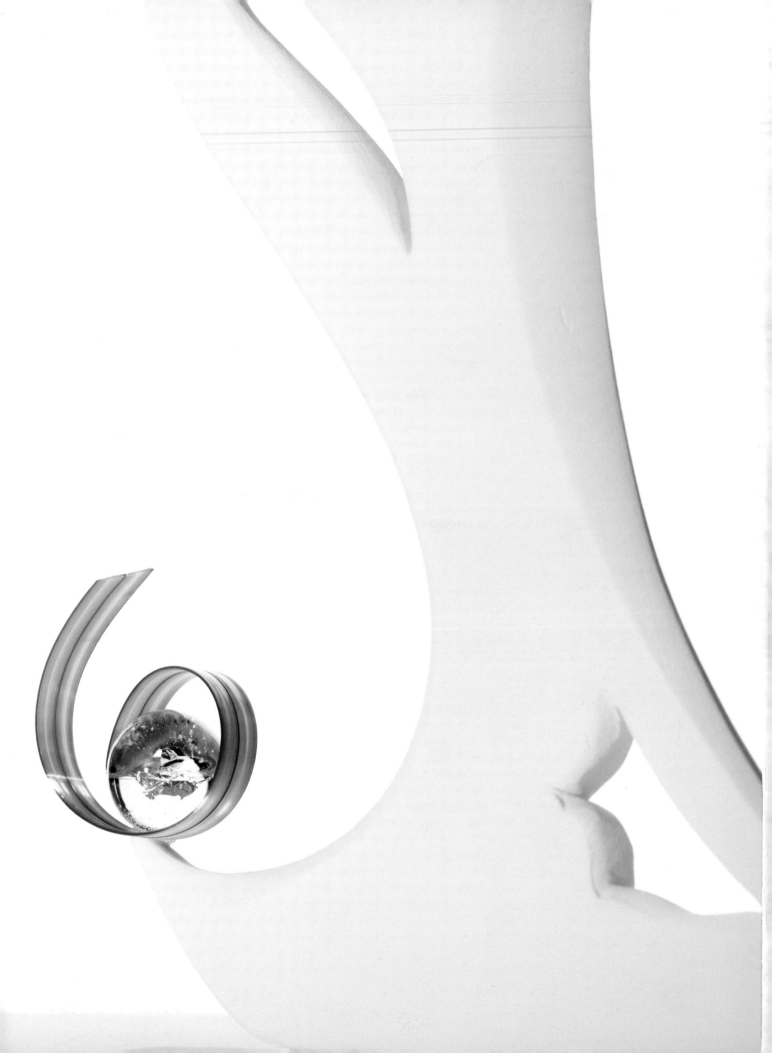